FOREVER
A
ROCK 'N' ROLL KID

FOREVER
A
ROCK 'N' ROLL KID

by

CHARLIE McGETTIGAN

A journey of music, song and stories

Scan 26 individual QR codes to listen to 26 songs

Battlebridge Press

First published in 2022 by Battlebridge Press (Ireland) Limited
www.battlebridgepress@yahoo.com

Structural & Developmental Editor: Brian Connolly
Copy Edit: Brendan O'Brien
Typeset: www.typesetting.ie
Proof-reader: Jane Rogers
Cover Design: Anú Design
Printed and bound in Ireland by Sprint Print, Dublin.

Produced & Edited by Brian Connolly, Roscommon, Ireland.

'I dedicate this memoir to my wife Goretti, my daughters Tara and Ciara and their husbands Sean and Ray. I also dedicate it to my six grandchildren and all the generations yet to come, but especially:

To our son Shane whose light always shines on us.'

A Guide to scanning the QR Code

This book contains 26 individual QR codes so that the reader can experience listening to Charlie McGettigan sing a selection of his songs for free.

    If you have an Apple phone there is a QR scanner on your phone.

1. Hold your phone camera over the QR Code as though you were going to take a photo.
2. Make sure you have all 4 corners of the QR code in your view and nothing else.
3. The link will appear.
4. Click on the link by tapping the screen.
5. The song will appear in a few seconds.
6. Click the arrow to play.
7. You can do this as many times as you want, each day/week/year.

****

If you have any other phone i.e. Samsung, Nokia, etc. you will need to download a QR Scanner to your phone. Most of them are free to download and use.

1. Go to the App store on your phone.
2. The following two sites are recommended by 'WHICH' consumer magazine as the best two options to download a free scanner.
   a. Trend Micro QR Scanner
   b. Kaspersky QR Scanner

Note: On some QR readers, you have to press a button to snap a picture, not unlike the button on your smartphone camera. If necessary, press the button.

    Your smartphone reads the code and navigates to the intended destination.

ACKNOWLEDGMENTS

I wish to express my heartfelt gratitude to Mary Gallagher who played a major role in getting my work developed and completed, and all the people who got involved in the manuscript and gave genuinely constructive feedback to help me in their own way to bring this book to publication.

Gerard Flanagan, Limerick, Deasún Lyons, Leitrim, Anne MacDonell, Leitrim, Renata Lange, Roscommon, Philomena Carty, Leitrim and Peggy Fleming, Roscommon.

FORWARD

Rock and Roll wasn't all he did

There is a certain view of people in the spotlight in many walks of life, a view that they are different, or lucky. They share snippets of their lives with the public, which makes them appear to live a more interesting existence than the rest of us, but that can often be an illusion. Somebody in the public eye is no different from his or her audience; by and large it just looks that way sometimes. We think we know these people, but in reality we don't know them at all.

I thought I knew something of Charlie McGettigan. We worked for the same company for many years, although our paths never crossed, but I was also aware of him from his music, when he played the folk circuit with his group 'Jargon'. There was a lot of long hair, beards, ballads and peace and love – just like the rest of us, but he was getting paid for it. He hit the pinnacle of his career when he won the Eurovision song contest with Paul Harrington in 1994. We were all delighted for him, a local man and a colleague doing us proud.

I didn't get to know Charlie until both of us had left our joint employer and moved on. I was looking for somebody to put music to a lyric, and a mutual friend, Sean O'Dowd introduced us. Sean reckoned that Charlie McGettigan could put a tune to the phone book, and that's a good measure of his talent. We went on to co-write a number of songs, and indeed we were given a recording contract for one of our efforts. It has been a great learning curve for me, and great fun too.

In the intervening years I have found that there is much more to Charlie than his successful musical career. Family is central to his world, as are friendships, and he is loyal and generous to a fault with his time and his talents. But now I realise I hardly knew him at all, because he had not yet laid bare his life like he does in this warm and honest autobiography.

If the past is a foreign country, then Charlie McGettigan is the best of tour guides. His book takes us back to Ballyshannon in the 1950s, avoiding the clichéd golden summers where sweetness and light prevailed. Instead he takes us around the back of the set to show us a 'warts and all' view of Irish life in what are laughingly called 'the good old days,' where poverty and deprivation were made worse by a dominant clerical presence and an often brutal schooling system that together succeeded in driving many young people away from both religion and education. Charlie pulls no punches but nevertheless manages to avoid being bitter, mixing the hard stories with heart-warming tales of childish fun from the pre-electronic days when we had to make our own.

His stories of the hard work and dedication that brought him musical success give us a snapshot of the heady days of the folk scene in Ireland in the 1970s and the 1980s, when the country seemed to be full of folk and ballad groups vying for a slice of the action. If ever the old adage of achieving overnight success after thirty years of hard graft applied to anybody, it surely applies to Charlie.

I was honoured to be asked to introduce this book for my friend Charlie McGettigan. I thoroughly enjoyed it, and I know you will too. If you are reading these words in a bookshop, just bring the book to the till and buy a copy, because once you start reading it, you won't want to stop.

John Mulligan
Author / Journalist

PREFACE

I always had it in mind to write a book of some kind. I juggled with the idea of writing a short story book. I never thought I could write anything of interest to a reader in regard to my own life. I suppose we all have that feeling of 'Sure what would I have to say?' The idea of writing something other than songs kept niggling away at me. In songs you have literally three or four minutes to get your thoughts across to an audience, and it's a magical feeling when it works. A book is a different kettle of fish.

In 2020 when the 'Lockdown' happened I suddenly found myself like most people with a lot of time to myself. I am someone who has to be doing *something* to fill the time. At first I started writing songs about how I was feeling within this whole new world we had all been plunged into, and filming them as little selfies on my iphone. I then posted these on social media platforms like Facebook and Twitter. I was surprised at how popular they were. Then one day I was hit with 'Songwriter's block' and was faced with a blank screen on my laptop. 'So…. What now?' I wondered. The book idea came into my mind again, but 'Where to start?' I wondered. Gradually I thought 'What's the first song I remember hearing?' Was it 'How much is that doggie in the window?' Then I thought 'No! It was very short piece of instrumental music called 'O Donnell Abu'. It was always played early in the morning on Radio Éireann before the day's broadcasting began.

'Where did I hear it?' I wondered, and then I remembered I heard it in my Grannie Buckley's house in Dublin. Gradually, I began to recollect memories of my very early childhood in Dublin, and bit by bit a vivid picture of urban Dublin in the 'Rare old times', as they say, began to appear in my mind's eye like an old black and white movie. I had made a start on my book! Soon, more and more memories started to flow into my head and before I knew it I had filled that blank screen with many chapters. I was reminiscing about my early days in Donegal. Then I was back in Dublin. Then I was in Leitrim, and in all these places various characters that had lain dormant in my brain for years started to appear on the page…. like ghosts.

Nearly two years later I had one hundred and fifty thousand words on my blank screen. Imagine 150,000 words! Me! I hadn't told anyone what I was doing and I was reluctant to say 'I've written a book!' But I had! Eventually, I sent it to a few friends who said that they liked it. One trusted friend, who is an author himself, told me that it would benefit from a good editor. I found one and he and I spent the bones of nine months editing what I had written and adding in other memories which came to mind as we worked. So here it is, my first book, 'Forever a Rock 'N' Roll Kid' I hope you enjoy it.

CONTENTS

1. Bottles and Jam Jars, a Penny a Time................... 1

2. Cluain Barron Days – Bonfires and Snow............... 5

3. Into the Wilderness............................... 12

4. My First Crush – Sister Rosario 15

5. Catholics and Protestants in Harmony 19

6. Childhood Heroes................................ 22

7. Scary Times with the De La Salle Brothers 26

8. A Hospital Visit – My Love Affair with Nurse Gildea 31

9. The Days Before Sliced Pans......................... 36

10. The Portable Brothel.............................. 42

11. Music to the Rescue 47

12. Formica – Your Only Man.......................... 51

13. Fun and Frolics in the Gaeltacht..................... 53

14. What's a Euphonium? 57

15. The Bargain King at the Harvest Fair 62

16. Danny Ellis and the Artane Boys Band 64

17. Bingo! Bingo! I'm in Love!......................... 68

18. The Soundstorms in a Tea Cup....................... 70

19. The Reinbous and the Assaroe Céilí Band 79

Contents

20. The Kinks Come to Town 85

21. A Garda Calls. 88

22. We All Did It 93

23. My Mother – Social Attitudes 97

24. New Horizons. 104

25. England and the Offaly Gang 112

26. Get Me to the Church on Time 116

27. Where's Arigna? 120

28. Leitrim Life and Jargon 128

29. Dapper with a Diaper. 136

30. Tara 139

31. Shane. 144

32. Ciara 152

33. Eamonn Daly Calls it a Day 158

34. Bailieboro and Me. 163

35. Jargon – Success at Last 168

36. Hey Mister Dreamer. 172

37. Songs of the Night and Other Stories 178

38. The Maura O'Connell Years 183

39. New York and Nashville 187

40. Eleanor Shanley. 193

41. Paul Gurney – A Lifetime in Music 197

42. And Then There Was Christmas. 202

43. Black Pudding for Christmas 207

44. The Songwriter – Brendan Graham 215

45. The Eurovision Final 222

46. Eurovision – The Next Day 230

47. The Homecoming – Drumshambo 234
48. The Eurovision Carousel 240
49. What's Going On in That Room? 244
50. Get Back to Drumshambo, McGettigan 246
51. Rock 'n' Roll Kids – the Album 249

CHAPTER 1

Bottles and Jam Jars, a Penny a Time

I was sitting with my granddaughter Olivia, trying to find the kids' channel on our TV, and I happened to say to her, 'Do you know, Olivia, that when I was your age we had no TV at all in our house?' I guess I was expecting a little sympathy or something, but she calmly replied, 'Could you not have watched it on your phone?' The pure innocence of children!

I found myself thinking back to my own childhood, and remembering the many wonderful moments that I've always treasured. In my memory the weather in the summer was always sunny, and in the winter there was snow and lots of fun but there was always a warm fire to come home to.

I should say I started life on 7 December 1950, in Holles Street Hospital in Dublin. It was at 22 Effra Road, Rathmines, Dublin that I spent a lot of my early childhood years. My mother – Maura Buckley, an only child – had grown up there with her mother, Julia (née Loftus). Maura's father was Charlie Buckley, after whom I was proudly named. He worked as a draper's assistant in a major Dublin clothes shop, but the family income dropped substantially when he died in 1932, when my mother was just four years old. My grandmother grew up in Swinford, Co. Mayo, and moved with her four sisters to live and work in Dublin when they were all in their teens.

A curly-headed blond boy called Dara O'Callaghan, who was around my own age, lived across the road from us. My earliest memory of Dara is when he asked me one day, 'Would you like to go treasure hunting, Charlie?' It sounded like an exciting adventure. 'What are we searching for?' I asked. 'Glass bottles and jam jars. We can get a penny each for them in Deveney's shop in Harold's Cross, and then we can buy sweets.' Soon Dara and I were spending every free minute looking for bottles and jam jars. We searched all the back yards, up and down little alleyways, and there was seldom a day when we didn't find something. It's hard to imagine little boys of that age being up to such antics now.

We also had really interesting neighbours in the Green family who lived next door. They were Jewish, and I remember spending a lot of time in and out of their house. Even in a city like Dublin, front doors were regularly left open back then, so I had the freedom of their house as well as our own place. The family consisted of siblings Becky, Louis and Himey, and they were all extraordinarily kind to me as a child. They used to go to the synagogue on Saturday evenings, and I remember not being able to understand why I couldn't go too.

Years later, when I was about fourteen, I called to see the Greens while on a trip to Dublin. I hadn't seen them for about ten years. I was greeted by what I now considered a very old lady: it was the lovely Becky. My memory of her was of a very glamorous woman, with deep red lipstick and matching heels. I was quite shocked at how nothing seemed to be the same now. Did you ever go back to the neighbourhood where you grew up? The 'adult you' will see it all so differently.

Many years after this visit, I was to go back to Effra Road again. I had just been married, and my wife and I ended up looking at an apartment in the very same house where I spent my early years: number 22, Effra Road. It was pure coincidence that a flat was being advertised for rent at the time, and I got to see around my old home again, which had been converted into four units. The whole place had become so much smaller since my last visit. In my memory Effra Road was always really long. Now, with cars parked on each side of the road, the whole streetscape seemed a lot smaller. Our house there in my memory had a very wide hallway as you walked in, and the rooms were huge. On this later visit, the whole place had diminished to an ordinary terraced house. Memory plays tricks on us all, and I suppose when you're little, everything around you seems so much bigger.

Life was carefree and easy back then, and with few cars on the roads, there was never a problem with very young children playing on the street. The only restriction we felt was being called in for tea or, worse still, bedtime. I feel very privileged to have such lovely memories of my earlier days in Effra Road.

My mother met my father in the Imperial Hotel in Bundoran in the late 1940s. She was on holiday; my father, who was from Ballyshannon, was on a night out. There must have been chemistry between them almost immediately, because when my mother went back home to Dublin, they kept in touch by letter: a sort of long-distance courtship.

While chatting to a cousin of mine recently, I learned that their relationship caused quite the uproar a few months later. Apparently, my grandmother went into my mother's room one morning only to find that my mother had left home without warning, taking all her clothes and belongings with her. My grandmother was heartbroken. She soon discovered that my mother had gone to London to be with my father, who had already moved there. Apart from the scandal that such events caused at the time ('living in sin'), my poor grandmother was badly affected by losing her daughter so unexpectedly. My father's family in Co. Donegal would also have had trouble accepting what had happened. Yet if my parents had told their respective families what they were planning to do, they would have been forcibly stopped.

The moment they met was the beginning of a sequence of circumstances that led to my birth. When you think of it, you have already won the 'lottery of life' by being born in the first place! I know that I am really only here by chance. I find myself thinking 'What if?' I know that my world, my children and my grandchildren would not exist at all if my father had not gone to Bundoran the night he met my mother, or if my mother had not decided to go to Donegal for her holidays.

People regularly claim allegiance to this county or that county, this country or that country, and talk about how great it is to be from Cavan, Leitrim or Donegal, or particularly to be Irish. In different circumstances they could be from anywhere. There are so many variables in this world. People are often surprised when I tell them I'm a Dub originally, because I've always been associated with either Donegal or Leitrim.

Eventually, my mum and dad returned to Ireland to get married and set up home. My father came and went a lot when we lived in Dublin, as he was mostly living and working in his home town of Bally-shannon at the time. He was always impeccably dressed, and looked very handsome in his double-breasted suits and shiny black shoes. He had jet-black hair, which he kept nice and shiny, held in place with dab of Brylcreem.

My mum and I moved from Dublin to Ballyshannon when I was aged about four. Ballyshannon is a town in south Donegal built on a really steep hill. There is a bridge across the Erne river at the bottom of the hill, which divides the town into two sections. It has a unique street-scape. The basic distinguishing feature one would notice on arrival is the Clock Tower right in the centre, which stands almost in the middle of the street. Then there's the Diamond, with a plinth that now hosts a statue of the legendary singer/guitarist Rory Gallagher, standing in his unique pose with his Fender Stratocaster guitar. Rory was born in the town, and these days his memory is celebrated with a highly successful festival every year.

CHAPTER 2

Cluain Barron Days – Bonfires and Snow

Cluain Barron is a large county council estate of mostly two-storey houses on the north side of Ballyshannon. Back then there were roughly seventy houses in the estate, most of which were built in the form of a crescent, around a really fine green area. Children could run wild and play on the green all day. Although my parents and I lived there for only about eighteen months, it would play a big part in my life for many years. My memory of having fun there, even after we moved into the town centre, is quite vivid.

One of the really exciting times in Cluain Barron was when the circus arrived and set up its tent on the big green area. I think seeing the whole business of the circus was the initial catalyst that sent me on my journey into the world of entertainment. The glamorous circus people would arrive early in the morning and commence erecting the Big Top. Local men would help them, and of course we kids would be in our element looking at the elephants, monkeys and ponies. The brightly coloured caravans seemed so exotic, and I often wondered what it would be like to work in the circus. It wasn't just a momentary thought: I was really interested!

Of course the performance was the cream on the cake. Trapeze artists and high-wire walkers were exciting to watch, but the clowns were our favourites. Mind you, as I got a bit older, around the tender age of nine or ten, I was fascinated watching the girls on the trapeze, mainly because you could see their knickers. It was a naughty little thrill for us innocent kids. I remember the sadness the next day, when all that was left was the grass turned yellow, and our big empty green. We longed for their return the following year.

Duffy's and Fossett's were the main circus companies at the time. Many years later I was to meet Marion Fossett, a member of the group Sheeba who represented Ireland in the 1981 Eurovision Song Contest. Who knows, maybe Marion was one of the girls on the trapeze, showing us her knickers!

I wrote this song as a tribute to all the circus people who work so hard to entertain us, throughout the country. All you need to do to hear the song is scan the QR code beside the words with your mobile phone, and you can listen for free.

'The Day the Circus Came to Town' (words and music by Charlie McGettigan)

Through a scarlet door with a yellow floor
To the Big Top four poles wide
See the usherette's silver epaulettes
As she lets us all inside
Then we grab our seats, eat our popcorn treats
Taking in most everything
Then a trumpet blares with a loud fanfare
To announce it would begin

The day the circus came to town
A magic feeling all around
Coloured caravans blaring
Big brass group painted pictures, created sound
The day the circus came to town

The ringmaster with his top hat's there and he tells us what will be
From the Pampas of South America, we'd have ponies one two three
On the high trapeze there'd be two Maltese
On the high wire an Italian
A juggler from Bulgaria and a mid-Atlantic stallion

With a roar and a cheer the clowns appear in a multicoloured car
It splutters and farts, then it falls apart and they all fall on the floor
There were tigers and that, then an acrobat who could stand on any limb
An elephant, yes an elephant, with a girl on top of him.

Then before we know, it's the end of the show, the time has really flown
And we all file out and we talk about all the wonders we have known
And the next day when we come back again it has all just disappeared
But although they're gone, it won't be long till they're back again next year

I remember the winters when the really heavy snow came, and the town was carpeted in pure white. Every kid got very excited, because we all knew this meant fun! Ballyshannon, being built on quite a steep hill, was an ideal place for sleigh rides. The really brave boys would start their journey at the top of Main Street, with the intention of reaching Paddy O Neill's shop at the bottom of the town, across the bridge. Many of us came a cropper, laughing our heads off, halfway down. It was a quarter of a mile from top to bottom, so the thrill of that descent was fantastic. People pay good money for similar thrills nowadays in amusement parks all over the country.

Some people had simple toboggan-type sleighs that would accommodate one rider only; there were also much more refined models that could accommodate up to three: the Jamaican bobsleigh team comes to mind. They had a steering mechanism at the front that made the journey to the bottom of the town much more negotiable.

There was a particularly suitable hill on the footpath in Cluain Barron where we cultivated a smaller slide, about 100 yards long. This brae was shaded from the sun for most of the day, so the ice remained solid for the duration of the cold spell. We would spend endless hours sliding down it, and when it was time to go home we would pour water on the ice so that it would be extra slippy the next day. No one ever complained, but then we always did it discreetly under the cover of darkness. Some people did mention how difficult it was to walk up that footpath on snowy winter mornings. Imagine what it would have been like for a drunk coming home after a night in the pub!

The winters were not all fun. We all suffered from the cold as well. Boys wore short trousers both summer and winter. In the winter they would be tweed or corduroy, topped with a home-knitted jumper over a vest and a cotton shirt. We always had a winter coat, which would usually be tweed. On our feet we wore rubber wellington boots with warm woolly socks inside. Socks always tended to slide down inside your wellies and had to be regularly pulled up. Garters made out of knicker elastic would help hold them up. In the winter your wellies would chafe the backs of your legs, which was really painful and uncomfortable, so you would turn the tops down. Some boys and girls wore knitted woollen gloves, but these were both a help and a hindrance in the snow. You could not make proper snowballs with gloves on, and without gloves your fingers would get numb with the cold. We knew the snow would not last, so despite the discomfort, the fun we had more than compensated.

After the fun of the day was over, there was nothing nicer than coming home to a lovely warm fire. There was no such thing as central heating, so unless you got close to the fire, houses could be chilly. Bedrooms were cold, and you never went to bed without a hot water bottle, although you could get very painful chilblains if you overused it. Usually they were rubber bottles. You could get more expensive ceramic ones, but they were not as popular, because when you hit your toes off one in the middle of the night, they hurt … a lot!

There were seasons for everything in those days: the skipping season, the hopscotch season, the glassies (marbles) season, and then the chestnut season, or, as we called it, the conkers season. The skipping and hopscotch were mostly for girls; the glassies and conkers were exclusively for boys. We bought our glassies in Pat Gaffney's shop. There were the normal glassies and bigger ones called taws. My abiding memory of the season is of little boys running around the streets with our pockets full of glassies rattling against each other.

At weekends we all went to the cinema as often as we could, to see the cowboys and Indians. When we came out of the 'picture house' we would ride home on imaginary horses, slapping our bums and shooting people with our fingers. There was another council estate in Ballyshannon called Falgarragh Park, which was quite close as the crow flies to Cluain Barron. Virtual wars broke out regularly between the kids of the two estates. The older Cluain Barron boys prepared for battle with homemade spears, bows and arrows, and I recall being very frightened by it all. I remember a boy from Back Street, Donal Hannigan, being captured and tied to a telephone pole at the back of our house. He started crying and was set free. I could say that sense prevailed, but it was fear really. Donal's mother was not a woman anyone would want to contend with if she was told of her son's capture.

Another big occasion in Cluain Barron was bonfire night. It was just one of four big bonfires in Ballyshannon. The Fair Green, a stone's throw from Cluain Barron, had its own bonfire. The bonfire in Falgarragh Park was so hot that many of the windows in the neighbouring houses cracked. There was also a bonfire on the Rock, across the river on the southern side of the town. We kids collected materials for the bonfires in the weeks before, and often there were raids on another gang's stash to steal materials: old tyres, wood and anything flammable that could be found. Often people would use the bonfire to get rid of furniture that had seen better days. Everyone would gather around the bonfire to watch the spectacle. Health and safety was ignored. That we survived as the huge flames shot up into the sky is a miracle.

Cluain Barron was a huge part of my early childhood, and I remember it as a magical place where everyone knew everyone. Large and small families lived there, and everybody seemed to pull together really well. They say that kids have it a lot better today, and I guess they do in many ways, but when it comes to having simple fun and just being a kid, sometimes I wonder!

Many years later I wrote this song as a tribute to the Cluain Barron estate and all the genuine people who lived there. It will always have a special place in my heart. To hear the song for free, just scan the QR code with your mobile phone.

'Cluain Barron Days' (words and music by Charlie McGettigan)

Back in the Cluain Barron days
The world was such a different place
We had joy, we had fun

In the heat of the sun
Back in the Cluain Barron days

I remember every number,
Who lived in every one
I love to sit and remember
The people who have come and gone
There were bankers and there were plumbers
There were farmers and there were sparks
Guitar players and drummers
There were good guys and there were sharks

Summer days in Rossnowlagh
Everybody on the narrow gauge
Mothers with babies howling
People of every age
Autumn time was for conkers
From the chestnut trees on the Mall
Back to the school with the Brothers
Some things I don't like to recall
Winter brought ice to the footpaths
And slides on the side of the hill
Toys in Stephens's windows
Santa Claus footing the bill

Suddenly it's forty years later
Where did all the good times go?
Time is a tough regulator
And memories are all I know

Back in the Cluain Barron days
The world was such a different place
We had joy, we had fun
In the heat of the sun
Back in the Cluain Barron days

Back in the Cluain Barron days
Life was at a different pace
We had fun in the snow
Then the fire would glow
Back in the Cluain Barron Days

CHAPTER 3

Into the Wilderness

Granny Buckley's rheumatoid arthritis deteriorated very badly in the early 1950s: she was more or less bed-ridden now, and needed full-time care. This meant my mother was spending a lot of her time in Dublin. Sometime in 1954 it was decided to bring my grandmother to Ballyshannon and look after her there. The house in Cluain Barron was too small to accommodate a wheelchair and other equipment, so we moved to a rented house on the Mall, in the town centre.

The house we rented was called 'The Wilderness': I don't know why or what it meant, but the name must have been important to someone. It was a dark, gloomy place with the kitchen and dining room in the basement and the sitting room at ground level. There was a bedroom on the ground floor that was ideal for my grandmother, and two more bedrooms upstairs, one for me and one for my parents. The house was on the sheltered side of the street, which meant it was almost permanently dark, no matter which room we were in.

The house next door was famous: William Allingham, the renowned poet, was born there in 1824. He is probably best known for his poems 'Adieu to Ballyshannon' and 'The Fairies' ('Up the Airy Mountain'). There is now a plaque on the side of the house stating its provenance. Of course Allingham meant nothing to me at the time. An elderly couple, the Hills (no relation to the poet) lived in the house when we were next door. They were always very kind to me.

We were there only a couple of months when something very strange began to happen. I remember vividly a man appeared at the foot of my bed. This happened on several occasions, and to this day I am convinced it was the ghost of a man who had hanged himself two or three doors away. I kid you not! It was the one and only supernatural experience of my life, so ever since then I don't easily discount things that I don't understand.

'The Fairies' (a poem by William Allingham)

Up the airy mountain,
Down the rushy glen,
We daren't go a-hunting
For fear of little men;
Wee folk, good folk,
Trooping all together;
Green jacket, red cap
And white owl's feather!

Down along the rocky shore
Some make their home,
They live on crispy pancakes,
Of yellow tide foam;
Some in the reeds
Of the black mountain lake,
With frogs for their watchdogs,
All night awake.

High on the hill-top
The old King sits;
He is now so old and grey
He's nigh lost his wits.
With a bridge of white mist
Columbkill he crosses,
On his stately journeys
From Slieveleague to Rosses;

Or going up with the music
On cold starry nights,
To sup with the Queen
Of the gay Northern Lights.

They stole little Bridget
For seven years long;
When she came down again
Her friends were all gone.
They took her lightly back,
Between the night and morrow,
They thought she was fast asleep,
But she was dead with sorrow.
They have kept her ever since
Deep within the lake,
On a bed of fig-leaves,
Watching till she wake.

By the craggy hillside,
Through the mosses bare,
They have planted thorn-trees
For pleasure, here and there.
Is any man so daring
As dig them up in spite,
He shall find their sharpest thorns
In his bed at night.

CHAPTER 4

My First Crush – Sister Rosario

Growing up in Ballyshannon gave me many happy memories, and I have always treasured them. But there is one exception, which I have come to learn was not confined to Ballyshannon. School was a time of fear for kids, from 9.30am to 3.30pm every weekday.

I remember going to school for the first time from The Wilderness. My memory of that first day is seeing this giant penguin speaking to me in a very deep voice. The penguin's name was Sister Lazarian: she was the headmistress, and I was very frightened of her. By the time the 11 o'clock break came I had had enough of school, and I walked off the premises and somehow made my way to Cluain Barron and Mrs Kerrigan's house. It must have been the lure of the sugar sandwiches I always got there. Of course there was a major panic at the school and search parties were sent out. Eventually I was traced and the panic was over. The next day I was back at school and could feel the penguin's eye determinedly fixed on me, especially during the breaks.

I soon settled in, and in First Class (following a year each in 'Low Babies' and 'High Babies') I got to know and love an ever-smiling nun called Sister Rosario. She always looked like she was blushing, perhaps because her wimple was too tight. She would occasionally slap us gently with her little ruler if we were being bold, but my memory of Sister Rosario is always of a lovely bright and positive person who was full of fondness.

In First Class we were getting to know the ropes, as it were. Later in my life a friend told me a funny story about an incident in Sister

Rosario's class. It seems that two little boys were beginning to 'know the ropes' too well. One boy, Peter, would put his hand up to draw the attention of the teacher, and then say 'Bhfuil cead agam dul amach don leithreas?' ('Am I allowed to go out to the toilet?'). Sister Rosario, delighted at his use of the Irish language, permitted him to leave the class. The next day it was the same, except that a little boy called John asked if he could go out too. Sister Rosario permitted John also to leave the class. This carried on for a few days.

One day she decided to go out after them, to see what they were up to. She found the two boys competing to see who could pee the highest on the wall of the school yard! She instantly brought them to Sister Lazarian.

'Do you know what these two boys were doing, Sister Lazarian?'

'No. Tell me.'

'Well, they were urinating up against the side wall of the school, to see who could get their urine up the highest on the wall.'

'And what did you do?'

'Well – I hit the roof!'

'That wasn't bad, sister … for a nun.'

I don't know how true the story is, but anyway …

As the months went on, Sister Rosario started to prepare us for our First Holy Communion. This involved learning a lot of stuff in our catechism. She would have little quizzes based on what we had learned. There would be a prize of something like a holy picture or a miraculous medal. A girl in our class, Goretti Gallagher, was a regular winner, and that really annoyed me at the time. We would also practise taking communion by sticking our tongues out for Sister Rosario to stroke with a lollipop stick. Imagine!

We were also given instruction in confession, with a list of possible sins we could confess in the dark recess of the confessional box. The one item on the list that still resonates with me was 'having bad thoughts'. None of us knew what that was, but I thought this meant that you were thinking of things like hitting someone or not liking someone. I remember I said I had had bad thoughts three times. I could almost feel the priest flinch. 'Tell me about these thoughts, my son,' he said. I said that I had thought of pulling Esther Grimes's hair, stealing Arthur

Greene's colouring pencils and, worst of all, stealing Goretti Gallagher's holy pictures. I could sense him calming down. Enough said!

When the big day arrived, I was dressed in a brand-new tweed suit with short trousers, and a white ribbon was draped on my right arm. The ensemble was rounded off with a brand-new white prayer book. I looked the bee's knees, I was told at the time, but looking back on the photos now, they were lying! On arrival at the church, I noticed that all the boys were in similar suits, and the girls in lovely white lacy dresses. Anyway, it came time for crabby old Dean McGinley to serve communion. We were all lined up at the altar rails and I could hear the Dean shouting at some of the other children, 'Open your mouth, child!' I awaited my turn with trepidation.

Eventually the Dean placed the host on my anxious tongue, and then moved on to the next child. Well, my first instinct was to spit it out. I managed to make my way back to my seat, at which point I passed out. My mum raced up the church and carried me outside. To even think of spitting out the host was considered a sacrilege. My mum, who was a practical person, placed it in her hankie and brought me back to my seat. Nothing was ever said about it, and I enjoyed the rest of the day with everyone else.

Today, kids are treated to high dining in a restaurant, a bouncy castle perhaps, and hundreds of euro in donations. We were treated to jelly and ice cream in the school's 'cocoa room', and I think I received almost a pound in shillings and pennies. That was a lot for a kid back then!

Oh … when I was a kid!

'When I Was a Kid' (words and music by Charlie McGettigan)

When I was a kid we could wander away
Never be seen for the rest of the day
Swam in the river, played on the road
Brushes and brooms were the horses we rode
So many wondrous things we did when I was a kid

When I was a kid we had so much more
We ran in and out of everyone's door

Rode on our boxcars, climbed in the trees
Ran to our mothers when we grazed our knees
All those wondrous things we did
When I was a kid

These days our kids have no freedom
It's all been taken away
Maybe I'm wrong, but where's the wisdom
When little children can't play?

When I was a kid the world was a place
Where we seemed to live in sanctified grace
Church on a Sunday, that was the rule
We didn't know we were all being fooled
The innocence of things that we did
When I was a kid

These days our kids have no freedom
It's all been taken away
Maybe I'm wrong, but where's the wisdom
When little children can't play?

When I was a kid there were no paedophiles
We just believed in everyone's smiles
Trusted our neighbours, trusted our friends
It's such a shame it all had to end
We never lifted the lid when I was a kid

When I was a kid: I know, a cliché
Don't think we'll ever go back to those days
We lock up our children, lock up our doors
They can't just wander away anymore
Not like all the times we did
When I was a kid

Happy days!

CHAPTER 5

Catholics and Protestants in Harmony

Religion was a major part of life when I was growing up in Bally-shannon: I guess it was for most Irish people in the 1950s and 1960s. The town boasted two Catholic churches, one Methodist, one Presbyterian and one Church of Ireland. We had four primary schools – two for boys and two for girls – and two secondary schools. We also had what was known as a technical school. The Sisters of Mercy ran the girls' primary school and a secondary school on College Street. The De La Salle Brothers ran the boys' primary and the secondary school on the Rock. The technical school didn't have any religious connection that I know of: it was run by the Department of Education. A wonderful man called Louis Emerson was the principal of the technical school at that time. There were also two private schools.

As Catholics we were brainwashed into thinking that ours was the only true religion, and that all others had gone down a completely wrong road. As the years went by I heard many comedians making jokes about that. One of the best – I can't remember who told it first – tells of a man who dies and is being shown around heaven by St Peter. They are walking down a long hallway with many doors, which St Peter explains are doors to the heavenly kingdoms of Jews, Hindus, Muslims, and so forth. Then he tells the man to stay absolutely quiet as they pass another door. The man asks, 'Who is in there, then?' St Peter whispers, 'That is the Catholics' door and we have to be quiet, because they think they are the only ones here.'

It was considered a mortal sin for any Catholic to enter a non-Catholic church. For the non-Catholics reading this, a mortal sin was the worst stain you could have on your soul, and if you died with such a stain you were going straight down to the fires of hell. Therefore these forbidden churches had a certain mystique about them. We never saw inside them. Even so, Catholics and non-Catholics lived peacefully side by side in Ballyshannon, and members of all religions cooperated well with each other. The brainwashing of those days has all gone now, thankfully.

Just a few years ago the mystique I felt as a kid was lifted when I played a concert in St Anne's Church of Ireland, Ballyshannon. It sports a huge square bell tower with four clock faces, one on each side. Seeing the interior of the church for the first time, I was highly impressed with how bright and beautiful it was. It had a fully surrounding gallery, which was something I had never seen before.

I had grown up listening to the bells of St Anne's striking every quarter of an hour and playing carols at Christmas. Ivan Diver, a very nice man, allowed me to climb the ladder into the spire where the bells were, and showed me how they were played. This was a really special moment for me. I knew that the Church of Ireland parishioners were few at the time, and I asked who looked after the building, which to my mind was in pristine condition. It turned out that the Catholic community contributes to the upkeep of the place, and it seems that the Protestant community contributed to the building of St Patrick's Catholic Church in the nineteenth century.

Recently, I was asked to speak at a North/South cooperation event in an Orange Hall near Cootehill, Co. Cavan. My childhood friend John Hannigan came with me. He had lived in Co. Cavan for most of his life, and knew the geography of the place really well. Believe it or not, we found two Orange Halls before we found the right one, and we were still in the Republic of Ireland.

It was kind of surreal to see all the banners and Orange Order regalia in the hall. There were a number of guest speakers. Peter Quinn, former President of the GAA, was one; a drummer called Quincey Dougan from a Belfast Orange Band was another. My piece was about growing up in Ballyshannon and my memories of how well Protestants and Catholics got on together, in both business and in recreational activities.

I spoke about how we mixed easily in the musical society, the drama society and the badminton club as well as in business activities. For example, Protestant businesses employed largely Catholic workers.

When we had all spoken, there was a discussion about everyone's presentations. Quincey insisted that I was making it up about how well Catholics and Protestants got on. I was wondering what I could do to prove my point when a brainwave hit me.

'I'm going to sing a song,' I said to Quincey, 'and I'll bet you that you'll sing along.'

He gave me a sceptical look. I started to sing:

> It is old but it is beautiful, and its colours they are fine,
> It was worn at Derry, Aughrim, Enniskillen and the Boyne,
> My father wore it as a youth in bygone days of yore,
> And on the Twelfth I love to wear the sash my father wore.

It was of course 'The Sash', which we used to sing in Bundoran all through the sixties. Game, set and match! It's a funny old world.

These days my own children very rarely attend church, and religion plays quite an insignificant part in their lives.

CHAPTER 6

Childhood Heroes

We had all kinds of pastimes back in the 1950s, but the nights could be long with nothing but the radio for entertainment. For that reason we read a lot. As well as the official local library there was an independent library, run by newsagent Patsy Croal, where you could borrow books for a small fee. It specialised in romance, western and crime novels. Patsy was a lovely affable man with a slightly camp style. His shop was on Main Street, across the road from our grocery shop. Most families had membership of both libraries.

Patsy was a magnet for the women of the town, including my mother. I think it was because he was always interested in women. He'd always say things like 'That's a lovely new coat, Maura' or 'Who did your hair?' He had all the latest news of the town, so little titbits of scandal were shared in his shop.

Our official library was run by a woman called Birdy Higgins, who wore fancy spectacles and was very strict on us youngsters. She was a lovely woman and made the process of borrowing a book easy for us all.

For some of us children, though, books seemed too intimidating. I much preferred comics: picture books with speech and thought bubbles and no mesmerising pages full of endless words. Most Saturday nights when I got my pocket money, which wasn't a lot in those days, I'd head for Patsy Croal's to purchase the latest issues. There were American comics with full-colour illustrated stories of my many heroes: characters like Roy Rogers and his horse, Trigger, or the Lone Ranger with his faithful Indian scout, Tonto. I also loved the Lawman series and Laramie.

British comics like *The Beano* and *The Dandy* were much cheaper: around 3d (about 1.5 cents today). I often purchased a *Beezer* or *Topper* as well, depending on how much money I had. Comics like *The Victor* and *The Hotspur* were specifically for boys, and *Bunty* and *Judy* were for the girls. We also had our heroes in the British comics, like 'Alf Tupper – the tough of the track' in the *Victor* and of course Roy of the Rovers, who appeared in *Tiger and Hurricane*. Of course a good deal of swapping went on, which meant that you could read a wide variety of comics.

I think my introduction to Westerns would have been when my father brought me to the cinema to see *Davy Crockett: King of the Wild Frontier*, starring Fess Parker as Davy. After that I became obsessed with Western heroes and I even got a Davy Crockett suit for Christmas, minus the most important part: the coonskin hat with the tail at the back. Someone made me up a fur hat with a tail, but it was black and nothing like the real thing. My house opened directly onto the street, so the Tennessee mountaintops were hard for a six-year-old to conjure up.

Shortly afterwards we moved to a bungalow on the Donegal Road, opposite the County Donegal Railways (CDR) narrow-gauge station, which became a huge part of my life. The trains were mostly driven by Joe Thompson, who had a dark-blue uniform and a peaked cap. As far as we were concerned, Joe had the best job in the world. He always had a cigarette dangling from his lips, as did a lot of adults in those days.

The stationmaster was a Mr McMahon, who had a station house assigned to him and his family. He was a lovely quiet man: we'd mostly see him as he sold us our tickets to go to Rossnowlagh (four pence) or Creevy (three pence). A previous stationmaster was a Mr Patterson. His family went on to become the enormously successful Pattersons folk group, who appeared regularly on BBC Television's *Morecambe and Wise Show*.

The station opened up a whole new world of adventure for me, as most days I could play there when Mr McMahon wasn't looking. The train came and went through what we called the Station Rocks, a rocky 'gulch' just like the ones in the Western comics. We could stand as the train sped by beneath us and imagine ourselves as train robbers like Butch Cassidy and the Sundance Kid. There might also be a 'Red Injun' hiding behind every boulder, waiting to attack us.

The land through which the train passed was owned by Packie McGarrigle, whose sons P.J. and Sean regularly joined in the cowboy games. They had relations in America who regularly sent them presents for birthdays and Christmas: really good replicas of 'six guns', with imitation bullets. I was so envious of these toy guns. The only ones you could buy in Ballyshannon were British-made and looked nothing like the revolvers my heroes used.

The cinema opened up a whole new world for us Western fans. James Stewart was a really good Western hero, as were John Wayne and Gary Cooper. We weren't so keen on Randolph Scott, who seemed too old. *Shane*, starring Alan Ladd, was my absolute favourite, with *Broken Arrow*, starring James Stewart, a close second.

Of course we had favourite 'baddies' as well. Chief among these was Lee Van Cleef in films like *High Noon*. We also liked to hate Ernest Borgnine, who seemed to be cast as a baddie quite a lot in those days.

After a Western movie, all of us kids would race home slapping our backsides as if we were chasing baddies on our horses. We played cowboy games endlessly in the Station Rocks, splitting up into teams of 'baddies' and 'goodies' on the toss of a coin. Occasionally we made bows and arrows from tree branches, which allowed us to be 'Injuns' as well ('Injuns' were always baddies in those days).

We sometimes veered into alien territory with our bows and arrows and became Robin Hood and his Merry Men. All in all, though, it was 'cowboys and Injuns' that dominated our imaginations in the 1950s.

So, here's a little song about them all.

'Childhood Heroes' (words and music by Charlie McGettigan)

Where are my childhood heroes?
Where have they gone?
Those simple childhood heroes
They still live on
I think of old Roy Rogers

All of those six-gun dodgers
Where have my childhood heroes gone?

I dream of Davy Crockett
On the wild frontier
He wore a buckskin jacket
He killed himself a bear
Kit Carson and old Gene Autry
Their memory still haunts me
I hold my childhood heroes dear

I followed them along the trail to happiness
I still recall each small detail of how they dressed

Where is the old Lone Ranger?
Never outrun
He rode his white horse, Silver
Silver bullets in his gun
His faithful Injun, Tonto
Always helped him to pull through
Where have my childhood heroes gone?

In our imagination we were like them
We played around that railway station
Way back when
We were just little laddies
Playing goodies and baddies
They were our childhood heroes then
They were our childhood heroes then

CHAPTER 7

Scary Times with the De La Salle Brothers

J ust a few weeks after our First Communion, Sister Rosario told all the boys in First Class – about twenty of us – to line up in the schoolyard. In my innocence, I wondered what this was all about. It wasn't a break time: what was it?

Soon we were marching down Castle Street, two abreast. We went over the temporary wooden bridge that was in use while a new bridge was under construction. A lot of boys wore hobnail boots in those days, so you can imagine the clatter and the click-clacking. Next we were climbing the steep steps behind Sweeney's Hotel in the West Port area of town; we emerged onto the Rock. There stood the very imposing Brothers' School, a dark and dreary edifice from the nineteenth century. This day turned out to be the start of eleven of the mostly terrifying years for us all, at the hands of the De La Salle Brothers: first in primary school and later in secondary school.

We were led into Second Class and told to grab seats. Standing in front of us was the rather nervous and jittery Brother John. I remember him as a frail man with a red face and a strange smile. We were hardly sitting down when he started taking names. 'Cad is ainm duitse?' (What is your name?) he asked each of us, and we answered *as Gaeilge*: in my case, 'Cathal Mac Eiteagáin is ainm dom' (Charlie McGettigan is my name). Some of the lads started giggling down the back, but Brother John spotted them and, gritting his teeth, said 'Stop grinning, boy!' We knew instantly that this was an order not to be disobeyed.

No one had told me that this was going to happen. I was not prepared for all this change. The desks were old and brown compared to the lovely bright desks in the Convent School. The room was bright but very old-fashioned, with a slightly frayed map of Ireland on the wall at the front, beside the blackboard.

Brother John was a shy and inoffensive man: he did his best even if he was, in my opinion, a square peg in a round hole. When I told my dad about our sudden evacuation from the Convent School and our arrival in Brother John's class, he laughed. I asked 'What's so funny?' He said 'Brother John', and told me about a day when he had won an award for catching a 33.5 lb pike in the local Dam Lake. Apparently, Brother John was fishing nearby when my dad caught the pike, and so he asked him to be ready with the gaff (a large hook with a three-foot handle) to pull the fish ashore. When Brother John saw the size of the pike, he dropped the gaff and ran away in fright. That might give you some idea of what he was like. My father laughed again, and I laughed with him. I said no more about my discomfort at being moved so suddenly, without a hint of notice. Apparently it was no big deal to my dad.

I remember that Brother John would ask a different boy every day to recite a short story in Irish in front of the class. We had to do all the actions, like smoking a pretend pipe, wielding a walking stick and wearing a pretend cap. It was his way of introducing us to the world of 'drama'. He also took us in on Saturdays to learn the Latin mass, as part of our training to become altar boys. I still remember a lot of it: 'Pater noster qui es in caelis' and more. Who says that learning things you don't understand off by heart doesn't work?

Not all teachers were as gentle as Brother John. Some were a different kettle of fish altogether. One fellow – let's call him Brother X – used the cane at every opportunity and was merciless in his use. He had two pets in the class, who were considered a 'cut above' the rest of us and rarely got the cane. They had attended a private school before arriving at the Brothers'. These were ESB boys: their fathers worked in the electricity generating station on the Belleek Road. They had also advanced further in their reading skills, and were allowed to read library books. Those two boys were not very popular with the rest of us, as you can imagine!

I have a frightening memory of Brother X standing at the blackboard, beating a lad severely because he couldn't pronounce a word written on it. The boy in question had a severe speech impediment, but he was still beaten mercilessly as he tried to pronounce the word. It was as if Brother X thought he could beat the speech impediment out of him. The rest of us sat and watched in sheer terror.

On another occasion, when a boy hadn't his homework done, Brother X smiled. 'Here's sixpence,' he said. 'I want you to go up the town to Stephens's shop. You know where the toys are?' The boy smiled nervously. 'Just inside the door you will see a box of bamboo canes on display. Buy the longest one you can and bring it back to me – good lad.' It was about a fifteen-minute walk to the shop, and fifteen minutes back. You can imagine what must have been going through that boy's mind. He knew he was buying the instrument that Brother X was going to use on him first. That's only a fraction of the terror that this brother brought to our little lives.

Now imagine this: he was one of the most popular brothers with the ladies in the town! He looked like a film star with his shiny slicked-back hair. He was a smooth-talking charmer, even to my own mother, and he flashed his film-star smile at all the women on his way between the Brothers' house in College Street and school. But inside the classroom, he was the reincarnation of the devil to us.

Our next year was with Brother Fideles, of whom my dad often talked fondly: Brother Fideles used to bring him and his friends hunting rabbits and fishing, so I was looking forward to being in Fourth Class. I was not disappointed. Brother Fideles loved teaching us songs, and I for one am forever grateful to him for that. I'm sure he took out the cane on occasion too, but I have no memory of it. Every day after the 11 o'clock break, he would produce his tuning fork and commence teaching us to sing. We learned all about tonic sol-fa (do-re-mi), but I was never great at reading it. What I did learn was the joy of singing great songs like 'Báidín Fheilimí' and 'Dilín ó Deamhas'.

My friend John Hannigan, who has a great memory of those days in the 1950s, recalls there was no Fifth Class as such: we went directly into Sixth Class from Brother Fideles' class. I don't know if that makes sense, but anyway here we were in the frightening Sixth Class and under another Brother who shall be nameless. This Brother – let's call him Brother Y – was a large, rotund man in his late fifties or early sixties who came from Kerry. I know because he told us that every single day. He was sadistic with the cane, and would actually hit us across the back as well as on the hands. He was an out-and-out republican, and all the history he taught us was from that perspective. We learned rebel songs like 'Roddy McCorley' and 'Boulavogue', and were taught to believe that there were no green fields in England, only brown ones.

Brother Y had a drink problem and Mondays were the worst, because he invariably had a hangover and would lose his temper easily. We used to pray that Kerry had won a match on the previous day, because then he would be unable to get up and come into school after his celebrations. We could see the Brothers' house from the school: if Kerry had won or he was sick, a certain window would have the blinds closed. We prayed for the blinds to be closed; it meant the difference between a day of terror and a day of relative calm. Imagine a kid today having those thoughts every single day as they went to school!

In those days the County Council gave a scholarship to cover the fees for secondary education, which I think amounted to £39 per year, to those who could pass what was known as the County Council Examination. Free secondary education hadn't yet arrived in the early 1960s. There was huge competition for this exam, and only the cream of students would even enter. With this in mind, Brother Y ran what was known as Seventh Class, a post-primary class held in the primary school. Nine boys from Sixth Class were picked to do Seventh Class. I was one of them. I knew I would never pass this scholarship exam, but my parents would have to pay for my second-level education if I failed, so I had to try.

Brother Y taught us to the level of Third Year secondary school standard in subjects like Irish, geography and history. It meant that I had to go through another year of fear and violent days from the cane of that Brother. I went to school afraid every day. We were beaten black and blue, not just in the school week but also on Saturdays, and even Sundays when the exam was close.

They were the most traumatic and terrifying years of my life. The fear and terror of those days has always stayed with me, and I know

now what a negative experience it was for any kid at that time. I guess the fun we had outside school hours was what saved our sanity. That's the important thing. I didn't get the scholarship, but my parents scraped together enough to send me to secondary school.

Corporal punishment continued right up until Leaving Cert, when it became more embarrassing than painful. I remember in Leaving Cert getting six of the best in front of the class because I refused to shave off a moustache that I had lovingly created over a period of weeks. I was a good six inches taller than the Brother, who administered the punishment, and I could have knocked him sideways with one punch, but still I stood and took it. I often wonder why I did, at that age.

Nothing like this would happen in today's schools, thankfully! In fact, during my entire education, fear is what I mostly recall. I look at my grandchildren these days, looking forward to going to school, without a worry or a care. It is tremendous that they can.

CHAPTER 8

A Hospital Visit – My Love Affair with Nurse Gildea

We were living on the Donegal Road at this stage. My father's brother-in-law Joe Gallagher was an architect and he designed the house, which was really just like something out of *Bungalow Bliss* (a book that was first published in 1971). The whole project cost well under £500 (imagine that!). I don't remember the moving process; I just remember being in the new house for the first time. It had a dining/living room with what was known as a scullery off it, a sitting room, a bathroom and three bedrooms.

A scullery was what we might call a utility room these days, and it was always very tiny. This is where housewives had to cook and wash clothes – no such things as washing machines or dryers – and if you had told them that in the future all this work would be done by machines, and that there would even be a machine called a dishwasher to do the dishes, you might have got a bucket or dish of the soapy water thrown over you for being so stupid. There was no insulation and no central heating, so I remember our house on the Donegal Road as a cold place, most of the time.

I shared a bedroom with Granny Buckley; my much younger brother, Declan, who had arrived in November 1955, was allocated a room of his own. My parents had the back bedroom.

Sleeping with Granny Buckley was a unique experience, and I was fascinated by all the underwear she had to wear: big pink knickers and corsets with metal stays. This paraphernalia was draped across a chair in the room. Granny had me all to herself to poison me against my father, and to frighten me with her stories of the Black and Tans. In fairness, the poor woman had a dreadful existence in that she went from the bed to the fireside and back, and that was the extent of her mobility. She was obsessed with the idea that I should get a job in the bank or the civil service, where I would have a pensionable income and regular hours. It's remarkable how her brainwashing worked on me, and dictated my ambition completely. Eventually Granny became totally bedridden, and in the end had to go into a nursing home when my mother just wasn't capable of giving her the full-time nursing care she needed any more.

When we first moved to live in Donegal Road I struck up a close friendship with a bespectacled boy from around the corner, Arthur Greene. I am still in touch with him to this day. Arthur would be the best man at my wedding many years later. He was the first really close friend I ever had, and we spent many happy childhood days together. He was a big reader of books, and I was a reader of comics. He loved all the Enid Blyton books, whereas I loved the picture-filled comic books. I always thought of him as much more 'intelligent' than me, and he was.

The Greene family lived in one of the bungalows of the Cluain Barron estate that overlooked the Fair Green. They were a lovely family. Niall was the eldest; next were Sheelagh, Patricia and then Arthur and Deirdre, the youngest, who had a shock of ginger hair. Their mum was a really nice lady called Alice; she came from Castlecomer in Co. Kilkenny. We used to joke with her and recite the rhyme 'Alice Kelly broke her belly sliding on a lump of jelly.' Their dad, Robin, who hailed from Holywood, Co. Down, worked as a mechanic in Miller's garage. He had a very 'British' moustache, and he always seemed to me to be a very 'British officer' type of man. Every Saturday, Arthur and I would bring his lunch to him in Miller's, and he always gave Arthur a thrupenny-bit reward. One particular Saturday he said, 'I'm sorry, Arthur; I have no change this week.' Arthur replied 'Well fuck you anyway,' which was followed by a right wallop across the ear from his dad. Even I was shocked by Arthur's reply, because he never ordinarily used bad language, but it shows how much that thrupenny bit meant to us.

Arthur and I went through all the usual scrapes and bruises that childhood brings. It was mostly fun, but we did have occasional disagreements. Arthur was normally a very mannerly lad but could lose his temper occasionally, and when he did – look out! I remember him throwing a compendium of games that I had lent him right out of the door of his house, scattering all the contents across the yard. I can't remember the reason, but I certainly felt the force of his anger that day.

Arthur was very fond of gardening and had green fingers. Army Sergeant Sean Doherty, who lived a few doors down, was a keen gardener too; he took Arthur under his wing and became his gardening mentor. One hot Saturday afternoon Arthur and I were helping Mr Doherty (every man over twenty was called 'Mr' in those days) in his garden: or, more than likely, Arthur was helping and I was just getting in the way. Anyway, I was in something of a dilemma. After being out in the garden most of the day, I found that I couldn't pee. As the day went on I urgently needed to pee, but I just couldn't. The pain was getting worse, so eventually I had to go home and tell my mother.

I was only twelve at the time, so having to talk to anyone about strange pains near my 'private parts' was a major embarrassment and made me blush. My mother was just mildly alarmed but as the evening progressed and the pain got much worse, she thought she'd better call Dr Quinn, our local GP. He was a nice man but of course he had to check me out, which involved a lot of prodding and poking around my sensitive region. I was embarrassed by this and slightly alarmed when he decided that I should be admitted to the Sheil Hospital for further investigations, as soon as a bed was available the following day.

The Sheil Hospital was one of two hospitals in Ballyshannon at the time, both of which were run by nuns. The Sheil's resident surgeon, Mr Sunderland, had big black bushy eyebrows. He looked fierce when you first met him, but he was a friendly man. It always amazes me how lucky we were to have such facilities in a small town: surgery, maternity, accident & emergency, etc. all on our doorstep. There were never patients on trolleys or on waiting lists back then, and Sligo General, where we all have to go to now, was never mentioned. My brother Declan joined the world in the other hospital, known as the Rock Hospital, which was across the Erne on the south side of the town.

Indeed, Rory Gallagher was born in the Rock Hospital. (Wasn't it well named?)

I arrived in the Sheil Hospital on the Sunday evening. I was slightly nervous, but my mum and dad stayed with me until I was settled in. I had fresh pyjamas and a toilet bag, which was left in the locker beside my bed. A big bottle of Lucozade was also left for me, which was a real treat. The pain I had been experiencing was gone at this stage, so I wondered why I was there.

Lights went out around 10pm. There were five or six other patients in the ward, mostly old men. I remember the sound of snoring, belching and farting all through the night. In the bed opposite me was an old priest called Father Gallagher who chain-smoked through the night, lighting each fresh cigarette from the one he was finishing and throwing the cigarette butt on the floor. The smell of smoke became more intense at one point, and I soon realised that a lit cigarette had landed on his bedclothes. The bed was actually on fire. I screamed for help, and a nurse quickly arrived on the scene, followed by the orderly, John Quinn. The fire was extinguished by throwing a jug of water over it. Thankfully, Father Gallagher survived unscathed.

The next morning I was awakened by the lovely Nurse Gildea. She asked me how I felt, and if my bowels had moved. 'My bowels' I asked. 'Your number two's,' she replied. 'My number two's … my poo, you mean?' We had different names for this, but I had never heard of 'bowels' before. Then she told me that I would be going down to the theatre at 10 o'clock. I asked 'Is there a show on?' I didn't know what a theatre was in medical terms. She assured me that everything would be fine, and gave me a pre-surgery injection to calm me down. I was kind of looking forward to going to the theatre, and eventually found myself looking up at a blinding light and seeing the large frame of Mr Sunderland hovering over me. I was given another injection and told to count down from ten to one. I think I got as far as eight and suddenly I was asleep.

The next thing I know, I'm waking up back in the ward and Nurse Gildea is asking me if I'm OK. I was very drowsy, but bit by bit I became more aware of my surroundings and a very severe pain in my nether regions. I tentatively pulled back the bed clothes: I was horrified to see the bandages around my sensitive organ, and I wondered what they had done to me. I screamed in my mind. I was too embarrassed to ask Nurse Gildea as she changed the dressing, but she assured me that having this procedure was quite normal and that all would be well soon. I never knew until then that there was a certain part of my anatomy that I apparently didn't need. OUCH!!!!!!!!

After about a week I was discharged from hospital. During that week I had fallen completely in love with Nurse Gildea. She was very kind to me, as were all the staff, but in my mind Nurse Gildea was special. I remember that I was not happy to be leaving the Sheil. I had been pampered by all and sundry in there, and facing the real world did not appeal to me. I had got to know a lot of the other patients, and even Father Gallagher had become a friend. He had had a stroke and couldn't talk to me, but I knew by looking into his eyes that he liked me.

For months after that, Arthur and I used to visit the patients in the Sheil after school. I was always looking for a glimpse of Nurse Gildea – the real reason for my visits – but sadly I never saw her again. I guess she was my second crush, although I didn't know about such things at the time.

CHAPTER 9

The Days Before Sliced Pans

In Ballyshannon in the 1950s and 1960s there were those who were very well off, and then there were the rest of us. Although most people thought we were a better-off family because we had a business, nothing could be further from the truth. It was a town where most of the population could find jobs and earn a good living, but it also had its poor and needy. The St Vincent de Paul Society discreetly looked after them. Bread and jam with cocoa was supplied, and it was free of charge in all the schools for whoever wanted it. My dad's shop was one of the suppliers. I used to carry the bread, buttered and jammed, to school every morning. It made me very aware that there were less well-off people in the town.

There was no such thing as sliced pans back then, so my dad would have to slice the bread by hand with a knife, and put butter and jam on it before I left for school. He would wrap it all up in a brown paper parcel, held together with string. Occasionally it would fall apart on my way to school; I would have to pick up the mess and head nervously back to our shop. Of course it was never my fault: it never is when you're a kid! If my dad had tied it securely enough the package wouldn't have burst in the first place. I can still see my father throwing his eyes up to heaven when he saw me returning so soon. It meant he would have to do the whole operation again.

There were those better off than us as well. People considered anyone who had a well-paid pensionable job, such as ESB workers, gardaí, teachers and bank officials, as being well off. All in all, though, we were happy with our lot. These days, I always try to 'live in the now' and enjoy every moment as it happens. Of course as a child growing up I was not the least bit conscious of 'living in the now', yet I can recall so much, and in great detail, about those years: more, in fact, than from more recent years.

There was a certain amount of snobbishness in our family. We were a 'business' family, which subconsciously made us feel a little superior to some other members of the Ballyshannon community. In my early years the business was McGettigan and McGowan, a grocery on Main Street, right in the heart of the town. The name was emblazoned on the front of the building in gold paint, and the shopfront was painted in a lovely wine colour. Items of stock like buckets, brushes and some vegetables were displayed in the front, on the street. The windows would be filled with eye-catching displays, usually of chocolate and sweets as well as tobacco products.

Inside the shop it was quite dark. There was a counter on each side, with space for customers to stand and browse what was displayed behind them. The only items available outside the counter were biscuits, contained in glass-top tins. There was no such thing as packets of biscuits. You bought a pound of Rich Tea or fig rolls, or, if times were tough, a half pound or even a quarter pound of Marietta. Phil McGowan, my grandfather's partner, stood behind one counter and my grandfather, Joe, stood behind the other. Phil was Fianna Fáil and Joe was Fine Gael, which might have explained the sometimes quiet distance between the two men.

On my grandfather's side the stock consisted of bread, butter, jam, biscuits, etc., while on the other side Phil sold cigarettes, tobacco, snuff and farm products such as calf nuts and Clarendo (also for calves). Bread would have to be sold on the day – otherwise it would go stale. I remember two types of bread, both white but with different textures: the batch loaf and the pan loaf. They were delivered daily by 'bread men', and there was nothing as pleasurable as the smell of hot bread as it was delivered to the shop. Often a sliver would hang off the end of a batch loaf: when no one was looking I would grab it, and it tasted only delicious.

One bread man who springs to mind is John James Lawn of the Ballyshannon Bakery, which was just around the corner in the Mall. He drove a red van, never over fifteen miles an hour, and was a well-loved character in the town. His family was mostly involved in cattle dealing and they lived in a big house at the top of Main Street. John James was a daily visitor to the shop and he would shout out what he had delivered to my grandfather. It would go something like 'Three dozen of batch at five pence three farthings, three dozen pans at four pence three farthings,' and my grandfather would write all this down in a big book. John James was legendary in that he never got a mental calculation wrong, even though he could not read or write. He would often talk to my grandfather about a whist drive or card drive the night before, and could remember every game in the entire drive and who played what cards. He could do all this while calculating the bread quantities. Mental arithmetic was very important in those days as there were no calculators.

Other visitors to the shop would be people like Tom McEniff, who delivered Castlebar sausages twice a week, and Cathal McGinty, who delivered fruit and vegetables. I remember a big scandal in the town when a family in College Street all contracted food poisoning and rumour had it that Castlebar sausages were to blame. I don't think it was ever proved, but after that I was always reluctant to buy Castlebar sausages, which were easily the most delicious sausages of all. Thankfully I have got over that, and love Castlebar sausages these days.

A very popular visitor to the shop was John Joe Stephens. He owned a pub at the end of East Port and was a really jolly man, with the walk of Charlie Chaplin and the figure of Oliver Hardy. He was always good for a laugh and a story, and was often a victim of laughter himself.

John Joe's pub was the first you would see as you entered Ballyshannon from the east. Some of the workers in the ESB power station were his best customers, as his was the first pub they would meet after leaving work. One particular Friday evening the pub filled up with about ten men from the power station. They had just got back money from some wage agreement or other and so they were all flush with cash. The first fella decided to buy a drink for the house, and produced a twenty-pound note (a rare thing in the 1950s). John Joe hadn't change, so he said the man could pay him later. This happened with each of the men, and then everybody left and poor John Joe was never paid for any of the drink. (I'm sure they all paid him eventually.)

People were always playing tricks on John Joe. Another evening when the craic was good, somebody showed him a new trick. One fella stood on a chair, lifted a pint of Guinness and held it flush with the ceiling. John Joe was asked to get a brush and to hold it tight to the bottom of the pint. He thought he was doing great holding the pint to the ceiling, then everybody left. I don't know how he got out of that one, but I can guarantee he never got caught again.

There was no such thing as a fridge in those days, so I can only imagine the state products like butter and bacon must have been in. I remember the cooked ham and corned beef being sliced on the same slicer as the uncooked bacon. How we didn't die of salmonella poisoning I'll never know. The shop was also known as the Tea House, which I think was because it had the distribution licence for tea during the Emergency rationing. As the tea came in big tea chests, it had to be bagged in-house in one-pound and half-pound bags. Sugar had to be bagged too, as well as potatoes (always with the clay still clinging to them), as did Clarendo and calf nuts. A day was assigned each week for bagging the various items.

As I got older, I had to help with the bagging after school and on Saturdays. There was a specific skill in this. The bags were sealed with string that hung from the ceiling, and you had to learn how to tie the bag and cut the string to the correct length. If you didn't do it right you would quite literally cut the top of your finger off.

In those days customers were served individually and most of them had credit. If the customer wasn't sure what she wanted (they were almost exclusively women), you had to rhyme off a list of the things she might want: tea, sugar, butter, jam, etc. Some people came in with a shopping list; it would be read out and the goods would be parcelled up (another special skill). The items would be entered in the customer's handbook and priced. They would usually be delivered later to the customer's house on the messenger bike.

The messenger bike was a dangerous piece of machinery. It was basically a 'high Nelly' with a large box at the front into which the parcels for each customer would be loaded. We were a little like the postman in that we had to know where everyone lived, and the parcels would have to be placed in the box in the order of the addresses. Main Street was a very steep hill. If the delivery was to a customer at the top of the hill, the bike would have to be pushed up there fully loaded. If it was at the bottom of the hill it was easier. You could freewheel down the hill.

The shop employed a young boy known as the messenger boy: he was the main user of the messenger bike. I remember cycling the messenger bike myself, and it was a very special skill. The weight at the front created a strange imbalance in the steering. If you weren't used to it, you could come a cropper with a basketful of groceries in paper parcels tied with string. Imagine the horror of having to sort out a mess like that. It happened to me once: it's a credit to the parceller that not one of the parcels broke open.

Eventually Phil McGowan decided to retire and my grandfather bought out his share. My father was then brought in as a partner, and the business became known as McGettigan and Son. Being a young man, my father was a like a new broom sweeping clean. I remember he bought the first calculator: a large machine with a handle. You entered the figure and had to pull a handle to engage the calculator section. This was seen as the height of modernity. Mind you, we had two old-fashioned cash registers in the shop as well, which were quite sophisticated: a bit like the one Arkwright used in *Open All Hours*. The next thing that was installed was a telephone, which really broadened the business' horizons.

My father worked from eight in the morning until six in the evening on weekdays, and until 10pm on Saturdays. The shop became a meeting place for people as they waited to be served, and lots of juicy gossip would be picked up there.

I spent a lot of time working in the shop, and learned all the tricks of the trade. I remember Christmas being a very busy time. The customers expected that they would receive a free Christmas box. There were always problems with this, in that the better customers would receive better presents. For example, a good present would be 100 cigarettes (which came in special packages of 100 at Christmas); a lesser present would be a box of Afternoon Tea biscuits, and an even lesser one a box of Rich Tea biscuits. Housewives would obviously discuss what Christmas boxes they received, and war would break out if a customer felt hard done by. Diplomacy was required in these situations.

Most customers were on the 'book' system. They might miss a week's payment, and this might run into two or three weeks. Then they might pay a 'little bit off the bill', or even go to another shop and not return at all.

Eventually so much money was owed to my father that it became a problem. If he sent out a bill he might be spoken of, behind his back, as being mean, and a lot of bills were left unpaid for months. Going through some of the account books in later years, I found that the worst defaulters were the people with the most money.

This financial situation, coupled with mental health challenges that my mother experienced, culminated in my parents and my younger brother, Declan, leaving Ballyshannon to start a new life in London.

CHAPTER 10

The Portable Brothel

The big exam at primary school was the Primary Certificate, which we all completed. It doesn't exist these days. I think it would have been the equivalent of the British Eleven Plus. Your results would informally determine which second-level school you went to: the secondary school if you were academically minded or the technical school if you were more inclined to practical subjects. In September 1963 I started secondary school in Ballyshannon. It was in the same campus as the primary school, and was also run by the De La Salle Brothers.

The secondary school was an all-boys school, and a whole different ball game to primary school. However, they had one thing in common: the violence continued. We had a new set of teachers, a mix of brothers and lay teachers. Some were great, some not so great and some down-right bastards. Sorry, but that's what some of them really were. We were mostly taught through the fear of getting caned. I got into a few scrapes with both teachers and other pupils, but that was all part of the learning curve at that time.

On our first day we started to get to know our new teachers. Brother Canice was the principal and he was a gentleman. He had taught my father in primary school. He became the musical director of the De La Salle Boys' Brass Band, and I was quick to join. We also had some great lay teachers who stick out in my mind to this very day. One was a shy kind of man called Brendan Hayden, who taught us science and physics. He was known as 'Taw'. Ernest Dillon taught us maths and religious knowledge. He was known simply as 'Ernie'. There were others, but more about them later.

On our very first day we had a religious knowledge class with Ernie. Under discussion was a prayer called the Magnificat. Ernie instructed us to learn all twenty lines of it that very night. 'This has to be a joke,' we thought. 'We're not going to have all of it learned by tomorrow.' The next day he asked the class, 'Have you all learned the twenty lines of the Magnificat, as I told you?' A silence descended. I forget who was asked first to start reciting, but none of those asked, including me, could get any further than the first line, so we were told to stand by the wall. Out of nowhere a long cane was produced, and we all got three strokes on each hand.

Ernie had his own special technique. If your hand wasn't stretched out straight enough, he would clip the back of it to raise it to a position where he could get a good wallop out of each stroke. He was a keen golfer, so his aim was straight and sore. I often wondered if teachers were taught how to use the cane in training college. The process was over in a few minutes due to his efficiency, but the pain lasted much longer. We learned that when Ernie asked us to do something, we had better do it.

Ernie also assigned us little duties, one of which was called 'window'. When he said 'window', the assignee would open the window of the classroom. Ernie would then produce his packet of Churchman's cigarettes and light up. Smoking was obviously not approved by school management, and Ernie hoped that the open window would dispel the smell of his smoke.

Taw's teaching style consisted of reading out notes in a very loud bass voice, which we copied into our notebooks. Occasionally he would draw a diagram on the blackboard, which we would also copy. We didn't understand a lot of what we wrote, so my knowledge of physics and science generally is sadly lacking.

Taw had no great passion for his job; he was just going through the motions. He surprised us all one Sunday night, though, when he took part in a boxing match in the Abbey Cinema. We were shocked by this side of his character, because we considered him a very gentle man.

He fought well enough, but at the end of the fight he was badly beaten. This gained him a whole new respect from us all for his courage in getting into the ring in the first place, and then taking the beating like a man.

One of my favourite teachers in secondary school was Sean Daly. I don't remember him having a nickname. He had a really good teaching style, so my favourite subjects were now the ones he taught – history, English and geography. We would have to study a Shakespeare play as well as prescribed poets such as Chaucer and Yeats. Mr Daly made them all really interesting, as he taught us how to appreciate the beauty of the English language. A good teacher can make such a big difference to a kid's learning. I have no memory of him using a cane, but I do remember receiving 'lines' as punishment. If you didn't know a poem, you'd have to write out a verse twenty times. You would certainly remember it after that!

We were in our very early teens at this stage, and puberty was planting new thoughts in our heads: 'SEX!' I think the nearest any of us had been to sex was a quick kiss behind the wall if we got lucky, or furtive perusals of the underwear adverts in our mothers' magazines.

In the first week of secondary school I got my first experience of sex. It was a colour picture of a naked woman, which one of the Bundoran boys had brought in. They didn't have a secondary school in Bundoran, so quite a few lads who lived there were bussed into Ballyshannon every day. I was quite startled by this picture, as I had never seen a naked woman before. I don't know what I was expecting!

I cannot recall any official class dealing with the subject of sex, other than being warned about bad or impure thoughts, and not really under-standing what was meant. 'Company keeping' was a term for having relations with girls, and the expression 'entertaining bad thoughts' was mentioned a lot. On reflection, I think I had a lot of 'bad thoughts' at the time, but didn't feel that I was 'entertaining' them – in fact they were entertaining me!

I remember reading one of the early James Bond books by Ian Fleming, which was banned at the time. It was called *Dr. No*. I don't know where I got hold of it, but I kept it under my mattress and read and reread the 'dirty' bits endlessly. 'Dirty' was the word that described anything sexual. Of course we talked endlessly among ourselves about sex in secondary school, and it was rarely far from our minds.

One lad, who shall remain nameless, had a great business sense, and told us that when he grew up he would set up a 'portable brothel'. We all encouraged him and asked questions. His plan was to drive to out-of-the-way places in a van specially designed for the ladies, and provide a sexual service for lost and lonely men in rural areas. It was like he was doing a pitch on today's *Dragons' Den*. I don't think his idea ever came to fruition, but who knows? It was great helping him in the planning stages, and we all laughed uncontrollably at some of the ideas suggested!

As time went on, we gained some knowledge, albeit warped, of what sex was about. There would be an annual religious retreat, and although sex was never mentioned per se, we knew what they were really talking about. The Bundoran boys knew a lot more than us for sure. One particular boy from there would develop an erection during the 'impure thoughts' sermon of the retreat. He would point out the bulge in his trousers to all and sundry in his vicinity. This resulted in giggling fits as we all tried to suppress our amusement, and slight embarrassment. Imagine what you would say if you were asked 'What are you laughing about?'

When we were in our second and third years, word began to spread about a certain brother who was known to fondle the boys' testicles if he got them on their own. The stationery store at school where we bought our copies, pens, etc. was a very small space, and the story was that it was not a good idea to get caught in there with this brother, because he would want to 'feel your balls'. In my innocence I thought that this was some kind of medical examination he would carry out, and I certainly did not want to have my balls touched at all, thank you very much, brother.

Nothing was said about all this outside school. To relate such details to our parents would have resulted in a quick slap on the ear for spreading false rumours. However, this brother eventually tried it on with the wrong pupil, who incidentally was another lad from Bundoran. This lad reported the incident to his father, who thankfully took his son's word. Well, soon 'the shit hit the fan', as they say, and almost overnight the brother disappeared from the scene.

Many years later I met a former school friend when I was playing a gig in Mullingar. We got chatting about our schooldays, and inevitably the discussion turned to the big 'sex scandal'. He told me that he had been on holidays in West Cork, and wandered into a bar where there happened to be a photograph of a local football team on the wall. Who was included in the picture but the very brother who had been touching up the students in Ballyshannon back in the day!

He called the barman over and asked him about the brother in the photograph. The barman replied, 'Oh, you mean the paedophile?'

CHAPTER 11

Music to the Rescue

My great escape mentally from the daily terrors of school was my growing interest in popular music. I first felt the lure of the guitar when I saw a picture of the Everly Brothers holding two identical black Gibson guitars, on the back of a card from a deck of playing cards. I would have been about eleven years old at that stage. There was a big craze in Ballyshannon of collecting picture cards that came with various products, mostly cigarettes and chewing gum.

There was one product called LM bubble gum. With each packet, which cost about 3d (three old pence – about 1.5 cents today), you received a free playing card, on the back of which was a picture of an American rock 'n' roll star. The idea was that you would eventually accumulate a full deck of 52 cards. This took on a life of its own, and every youngster in the town was trading the cards. If you got a full deck, you could send away for an album to display all your cards in.

My mum and dad used to listen to Radio Luxembourg. Horace Batchelor, who advertised on one of the shows, was famous for a special formula that was claimed to give you an extra chance of winning the pools. My dad was a big fan. Horace had a unique voice and used to talk about his infra-draw method, which was 'almost guaranteed' to win. His spelling out of 'K-e-y-n-s-h-a-m', the town in western England he operated from, was his trademark quote. Radio Luxembourg was essentially a pop music station, so I began hearing the pop songs of the day. Radio Éireann and the BBC Light Programme rarely played pop music in those days. 'Venus in Blue Jeans', sung by Mark Wynter, is the first song I remember hearing on Radio Luxembourg.

Then one night a piece of music was played by a guy called Duane Eddy. There were no words, just the huge sound of his guitar. I think it was a tune called 'Because They're Young'. I was smitten, or, as they used to say in those days, 'sent'! After hearing that, I listened out for anything featuring the great sound of an electric guitar.

The next guitar I heard was played by Hank Marvin of The Shadows, who were Cliff Richard's backing group: we began to see them on TV quite a bit. Hank, Bruce Welch and Jet Harris were playing Fender guitars and basses, but later they began to play Burns guitars, which were English-made. They were shaped like a more aggressive version of the famous American Fender Stratocaster, with a whammy bar that bent the strings to make bluesy notes, and lots of knobs and switches. The sound they made was just amazing. I couldn't get enough of them.

Around this time a man called Cecil King, who owned and ran the *Donegal Democrat* newspaper, decided to get into selling guitars. The first one I saw was in the shop window of the *Democrat* office. It was a green acoustic guitar with a palm-tree motif painted on the front. Most days on my way to school I would stand and gaze at this wonderful guitar in the window, and imagine myself holding it, and making the sound that Hank Marvin made.

Then one day it disappeared from the shop window. I was devastated, but a few months later I discovered that a guy called Roy Doherty, who lived in Cluain Barron, had bought it. I called to his house and asked him if I could see it. He let me hold it. I strummed the strings, and of course it sounded nothing like Hank Marvin. This was when I discovered that you had to learn how to play it.

I was determined to get a guitar for myself by hook or by crook. I was banking on winning the County Council scholarship scheme, to the value of £39, to cover the annual fees for my secondary school education. If I could win that, perhaps my parents would buy me a guitar to celebrate. I didn't win the scholarship, as I've already mentioned, but my best friend, Arthur Greene, got a very high mark in this exam and was awarded the scholarship. As a treat, his mother told him he could buy something of his own choice.

By this time – September 1962 – Cecil King's son Cecil Junior had opened a fully fledged music shop called The Music Box. I somehow persuaded Arthur that he should get a guitar as his treat. There were several guitars in the shop, and Arthur bought an acoustic one for £3. However, he very quickly lost interest in the guitar. It just wasn't for him, thankfully. I asked him if I could borrow it, and he very kindly consented.

I bought Bert Weedon's *Play in a Day* book in The Music Box, but I couldn't make head nor tail of it. Somewhere along the way I acquired a book of the songs and music of Josh White. It contained the lyrics and the chord tablature (an alternative music notation system). I had heard my mum singing a song called 'I Know Where I'm Going', and this song was in the book. I struggled, but I managed to learn it. After that it was 'The Blue Tailed Fly' and a Leadbelly song called 'Where Did You Sleep Last Night?'. My mother was terribly impressed with my skills, so it was not difficult to persuade her to buy me a guitar. My father had an account with a wholesale company in Dublin called Walker's, and we had a catalogue of their products. I spotted an Egmond guitar in the catalogue and my dad agreed to buy it for me at Christmas. I think it was about £10, which was a lot of money in those days.

On Christmas morning the guitar arrived. It was a 'lamb skitter'-green solid-body guitar with a white plastic pickup, and it looked exactly like the picture in the catalogue. However, I didn't realise I would need an amplifier to make it heard. I thought you just plugged it into the wall and by some miracle it would sound like an electric guitar. That tells you about my knowledge of technology in those days.

I was disappointed, but I soon discovered an ingenious method of making it sound better. I slept in a wooden-framed bed, which sat on a wooden floor. If I pressed the back of the guitar against the bed the sound became much bigger. In other words, the bed and the floor became my soundboard.

The Beatles were starting to make inroads in the music world, and I remember having a book of Beatles songs. The first song I learned from it was 'Misery', and I created a lot of misery practising it. Michael Travers, who was also a guitar player, lived just up the road, and he taught me my first few chords. I remember singing 'Misery' for his dad,

Henry John. I don't think he was very impressed. That old Egmond was a dreadful instrument. It was basically a piece of wood with strings attached, and almost impossible to play as the action was so high. Despite this I managed to get by with it for the next three years, and I learned a lot about guitars on it. For the record, George Harrison and Paul McCartney of Beatles fame, Queen's Brian May and many others started out with Egmond guitars.

CHAPTER 12

Formica – Your Only Man

As I have mentioned, my father became a partner in the grocery business of McGettigan and Son. He bought a motorcycle to deliver groceries, but quickly realised that this wasn't enough, so he invested in a car. His fishing pal Peter Garland gave him some driving lessons.

Our first car was an Austin Seven (Mini). It was tiny, but to us it opened up a whole new world: we could go anywhere we wanted. Every Sunday we went for a spin to some exotic place like Donegal Town or Rossnowlagh. On Wednesdays we would regularly go to Enniskillen, where they had Mars Bars and Milky Ways. Crossing the border was a big deal back then, and my father would have to get a bond from the Customs and be back at a certain time. We were scared stiff of the Customs officers, who seemed very officious when they asked us if we had anything to declare.

In Belleek, just across the border, certain items were cheaper. Butter must have been much cheaper, because if anyone was going to Belleek they were always asked to 'Bring us back a few pounds of butter.' I remember one winter every child in Ballyshannon was wearing a duffel coat. Doherty's drapers in Belleek were stocking these wonderful cosy garments: it seems most people bought their duffel coat in Belleek and wore it crossing the border so the Customs didn't notice. Innocent times!

Around this time, supermarkets were beginning to appear, and our poky but delightful little shop seemed inadequate to the needs of a modern business. Dad took the bull by the horns and borrowed £5,000 for renovations. This was a huge investment, and the shop was transformed into what might these days be called a minimart. The old shop had beautiful artefacts that were just thrown out to make room: wooden shelving units with cubby holes for snuff, tobacco, etc.; big enamel signs for 'Player's Please' and Woodbine cigarettes. The old wooden counters were replaced with Formica worktops. Formica was seen as the height of style, but in retrospect it was just ugly plastic.

We also got our first phone then. I think the number was something like Ballyshannon 25, so there were only twenty-five phones in the town at the time. My father would ring his brother Sean – a vet who worked the horse-racing tracks in England – every week to get some tips for possible winners. I remember one horse called Cullen that was a huge betting coup for my father and David Vaughan across the street. Telephone operators who had been listening in on calls would often call my dad and thank him for the tips. Is that mad or what?

On the same subject, a few years later I answered an advert in the *Evening Press* for a Gibson guitar. It turned out to be too expensive, but a few minutes after the call the phone rang. The voice on the other end said 'I hear you're looking for a Gibson guitar. I have one for sale.' It was the operator, who had been listening in to the phone call. As it turned out, he was a guy called Bobby Kelly, who had been a member of the Sands Showband and was someone I really admired. I didn't buy the guitar, but many years later I became friendly with Bobby, who sadly passed away a few years ago. It's a small world.

CHAPTER 13

What's a Euphonium?

I was never interested in sport when I was going to school: I was totally preoccupied with music and becoming a 'pop star'. I was regularly picked for the school GAA team because I was tall and strong, but my passion was music. I had no idea how to read a game and really couldn't care less whether we won or not.

The team played games in places like Irvinestown and Enniskillen in Northern Ireland, and that was my only attraction to football. I liked the travelling, and of course you could buy 'girlie' magazines up there. We would cast lots to decide who would negotiate the purchase of such literature. These magazines were quite innocent by today's standards, but boys will be boys, and we never missed an opportunity!

The lure of music took me in a different direction when I joined the De La Salle Brass Band with my friend Arthur Greene, to see what we could learn. Brother Robert was in charge at the time; he handed each of us a cornet and gave some brief instructions. He told us to spit into the mouthpiece rather than blow. Arthur and I couldn't stop laughing at the squeaky sounds we were making. I kept breaking down and giggling until eventually I felt a thump to the back of my head, administered by Brother Robert. The mouthpiece smashed into my upper lip and gums. Blood spewed out, and I thought to myself 'More violence! This is not for me.' That ended my first attempt at a brass instrument.

A year or so later Brother Canice took over the band, and I was asked to join again. This time I was handed an E flat bass euphonium, a large brass instrument with a strap, which you put over your shoulder to hold it across your chest. There were three valves to create all the notes, which mystified me, but I liked the big bass sound it made and I warmed to it immediately.

There were two euphoniums; the other one was played by a lad called Danny McGrory. Danny could read music, so I just found the notes that he was playing and copied him. I was bluffing my way along, but somehow it worked. All the other boys seemed to find it very easy to learn to read music notation, but to this day I have never learned.

It was great being in this large assembly of musicians. We travelled near and far to play at street parades, football matches, Christmas carol services and more. My best friend Arthur ended up playing the cymbals. Jimmy Melly was the snare drummer, and we had mighty fun in Jackie White's van on our way to gigs, singing all the pop songs of the day, accompanied by Jimmy's snare and Arthur's cymbals. Brother Canice didn't know a lot about music, but his heart was in the right place and we all enjoyed the experience. We had uniforms that consisted of a white shirt, a blue tie, blue trousers and a little cap we wore slanted to the right of our heads, like the one American GIs wore.

I remember playing at the Corpus Christi procession one very hot day. The procession wound its way around the streets of Ballyshannon, and benediction was celebrated at various points. We eventually reached the grounds of the Sheil Hospital. The heat was terrible and the strap of my instrument was cutting into my shoulder, making me wince with the pain. The next thing I remember is someone waking me up. I was lying on the ground with the euphonium on top of me: I had fainted. Maybe I was hoping Nurse Gildea would come to my aid!

David Murphy was the coolest member of the band. He was also a member of a rock group called the Erratics. David considered himself a cut above the rest of us musically, and he probably was. Being a musician, he always wore very trendy suits and shoes. We were playing at a football match in Donegal Town one day. Everyone was admiring David's great new fashion purchase, a pair of brown suede Beatle boots. All the other boys were envious. I'll never forget getting out of the van on to a muddy pitch and seeing David's beautiful Beatle boots sinking ankle deep into the mud. They were ruined, and I must confess we all laughed. We thought David needed a little bringing down to earth.

Playing in the Ballyshannon Brass Band was a great experience. We were supplied with instruments and music (even if I couldn't read it), and I think Brother Canice did his best for us, in all fairness. It was a great feeling as the big bass drum led us off before every tune, and getting in step with all the other boys. I have very happy recollections of my brass-band days.

I also joined the Ballyshannon Musical Society when I was about fifteen, and persuaded some of my friends to join with me. It was another of the organisations that brought Catholics and Protestants together. Sadly, in my time the society never produced any of the great Gilbert and Sullivan operettas that I had seen them perform down the years. Gilbert's lyrics were amazing, and to this day I love the music in shows like *The Mikado*, *HMS Pinafore* and *The Pirates of Penzance*. We had some mighty fun doing revues over those years, and I particularly remember singing 'We're a Couple of Swells' with Benny Dorrian. Brian Stephens was the musical director in my time, and he was also a wonderful tenor.

These shows took place in the Abbey Cinema (although it wasn't a cinema at the time), accompanied by a fine orchestra made up of local musicians: people like Tom 'Tae' Gallagher on drums, Cecil Stephens on the 'bull fiddle' (double bass) and my wife's aunt Mary Rose Gallagher on violin. The dressing rooms were under the stage, and if you were over five foot ten you would have to move around with your head bowed.

My grandfather Joe McGettigan and a few others built the Abbey Cinema during the construction of the ESB power station, when upwards of 2,000 extra workers were living in the town. My father often talked about working as an usher in the cinema. He recalled one occasion when a prominent member of the community was tragically found dead in his house. Dad had the unenviable job of informing the deceased's wife, who was in the cinema at the time. He located the woman and quietly whispered what had happened. 'I'll be down when the film is over,' she said.

When the construction work was over, the town reverted to its normal population: this wasn't enough to sustain the cinema, which closed its doors. These days the building houses the wonderful Abbey Arts Centre.

There were some really beautiful older women in the society and all us boys developed crushes on them, even though they were happily married. To us we were Dustin Hoffman in the film *The Graduate*, and they were Mrs Robinson. However, none of our fantasies were ever realised.

I learned a lot about harmony while singing in the musical society, and this knowledge served me well in my musical endeavours in later years. The discipline of singing only the harmony parts of a song could be difficult, but I fell into it very easily. I sang the bass line, and still do to this day with the Drumshanbo Adult Church Choir. I was so lucky back then, and I never fail to remember and appreciate those early experiences.

The local drama society ran a fantastic festival every year with groups from all over the country, and adjudicators such as Micheál MacLiammóir and RTÉ newsreader Charles Mitchel. I remember that when Mitchel's familiar face appeared in person in the town, we couldn't believe he was in colour, as we only had black-and-white television in those days!

CHAPTER 14

Fun and Frolics in the Gaeltacht

My life was about to change when I was about thirteen years old, and going through all the usual teenage angst. You could say I was going from being a kid to being a young man. To give me a chance to engage with others in Irish, my parents decided to send me to Falcarragh in North-West Donegal, to have the Gaeltacht experience with a bunch of other kids my age and older. Although I had spent holidays away from home with my relations at different times, this was my first experience of being outside the family context. I loved Irish, I suppose because I could always hear the music in it.

I can't remember how we got there, but in those days it would have been a two-and-a-half-hour journey from Ballyshannon. I do remember being greeted by the bainisteoir, Mr O'Neill, who drove a VW Beetle and spoke a language that bore no resemblance to my 'school Irish'. The main rule was that we were to speak in Irish only at all times for the next three weeks. If you were caught speaking any other language, you would be sent home straight away. We had been told all this before we started, and even though Mr O'Neill was speaking to us *as Gaeilge*, we fully understood his every word. I immediately vowed that not one word of English would pass my lips while I was there: a vow I kept for almost two hours! I soon learned the trick was not to get *caught* speaking English.

We were assigned our digs for the next three weeks. I shared a room with three other boys: two from Belleek and a lad from Dublin. We were lodged with a lovely 'Bean on Ti' (woman of the house) and her family about three miles from Falcarragh. The boys from Belleek were Ray and Donal Sweeney. They attended the De La Salle Secondary School where I was a pupil, so I knew them, especially Ray because we both played on the school football team. Ray was a hell of a good footballer at the time.

The first thing I noticed about the house we were staying in was that there was no bathroom or toilet. The toilet was at the end of the yard: a simple plank of wood with a hole in it, and a bucket underneath. I was horrified! In Ballyshannon we had all the basic mod cons like hot water and a bathroom with a proper toilet. For the next three weeks we were expected to evacuate the contents of our bladders and bowels in this primitive piece of apparatus. As you can imagine, we used these facilities as little as possible, reserving our bowel movements for the town of Falcarragh, which had proper public facilities.

When we went to bed that night, I heard for the first time the music of Roy Orbison. Donal Sweeney, who was a couple of years older than me, had Roy's full repertoire, and he was fearless when reproducing Roy's soprano voice. He sang songs like 'It's Over', 'Blue Bayou' and even 'In Dreams'. These unaccompanied renditions sounded wonderful, and it was a lovely way to drift off to sleep. As for speaking in Irish, he wasn't speaking ... he was singing. Nobody told us we had to sing as Gaeilge as well.

In the morning we scrambled to wash and brush our teeth, all at the outdoors tap, before heading off to Falcarragh, where there were classes in Irish until lunchtime. We had a lovely múinteoir (teacher) there called Joe McGeady, who had a healthy disregard for rules, so he taught us Irish in a bilingual fashion. The afternoons were given over to games and walks around the town. We could see the beautiful Muckish Mountain and Sliabh Eireagil in the distance, with the famous Tory Island out off the coast. It was truly a beautiful place on a nice day. We played games like netball and rounders until 4pm then walked the three miles back to our digs, where we had dinner.

I have been plagued by being a very picky eater all my life, and it is a dreadful source of embarrassment to me right up to the present day. For example, I cannot abide potatoes, and still get physically sick at even the thought of eating a spud. At that time I wouldn't touch vegetables of any kind either. I seem to have passed this trait on to my children and grandchildren, who had similar feelings about vegetables at a tender age! I have since softened on the vegetables.

The first time the Bean an Tí placed a big plate of spuds in front of me, I nearly puked. She just couldn't understand, and thought I must be some kind of alien or else mentally deranged. An Irish boy who doesn't eat spuds? What? I can't remember how we compromised, but I don't remember it being a problem after that.

After dinner we would go to the *céilí* in a big hall just outside Falcarragh. The music was supplied by a lovely man playing an accordion. I had never been to such a session before, but I was aware of *céilí* music: Ballyshannon had its own Assaroe Céilí Band. I have to confess that at that time, it was all 'diddley-eye' to me. Each of us was paired off with a girl for the first dance, which would have been the Siege of Ennis or the Walls of Limerick. The feeling of holding a girl's hand in this way for the first time sent a lovely mild shot of electricity through me. It was my first really close encounter with the opposite sex. It was a magical feeling!

I learned all the movements for the *céilí* dances, and over the next three weeks I fell in love many times. I remember taking two or three girls on 'holding hands' walks, and gently serenading them with songs like the Beatles' 'Do You Want to Know a Secret?'… They all said 'No!' When I think about it now, I must have been in a real romantic frame of mind that summer!

After a few days in Falcarragh, we found a cafe with a jukebox and a television, where we could watch *Top of the Pops*. Had we been caught, this would definitely have been breaking the rules. First of all we were all talking English, and secondly we were watching pagan music on TV. Those in charge would not have appreciated the Rolling Stones, with Brian Jones strumming the big chords of 'It's All Over Now' on his white Vox teardrop guitar.

I made many good memories in the Gaeltacht, which I will never forget. Some of them are funny when I look back, like the outside toilet with the wooden plank and bucket. Another event that feels funny now, but wasn't so funny at the time, happened on our second-last day there. We decided to have a little party that night in our digs, and we all bought large bottles of Taylor Keith lemonade.

We chatted and joked for hours in our bedroom while drinking all the lemonade. Eventually we dozed off to sleep, only to wake up a couple of hours later with our bladders full to bursting. It was bucketing rain outside, and the 'toilet' was thirty yards away at the bottom of the muddy yard. Donal Sweeney, who was the tallest of us, succeeded in urinating out the sash window. However, the rest of us couldn't quite get our willies up to the window. Then I came up with the bright idea of urinating into one of the empty TK bottles. I left the bottle of urine in the wardrobe, and the next day after school when I came back to the digs to get rid of the bottle, it had disappeared. It had looked half full of lemonade, so to this day I still wonder what happened to it. The mind boggles!

On our last night there was to be a dance in the hall after the *céilí*. When we arrived for the *céilí*, the band that was due on later that night for the dance was checking their sound equipment. They were a fully professional band called the Playboys, from Derry. I couldn't believe what a huge sound they were making as they rehearsed a few current pop songs as part of their sound check. This was the first 'real' band I had ever seen, and I was smitten. I was so excited by the sound they made. They had electric lead guitar, bass guitar, drums and keyboards, augmented by sax, trumpet and trombone, with a lead singer completing the line-up.

Bhí na laethanta saoire go hálainn. My time in Falcarragh was one of the best holidays I ever had. We had very little chance to engage in any real conversation *as Gaeilge* when we were there, but I would highly recommend the Gaeltacht experience to any young person. I left the Gaeltacht not just with a better knowledge of Irish, but with a determination that one day I would be part of a 'real' music group. My destiny was taking its shape and I was completely unaware of it.

We all had lots of stories when we returned to school, for the other lads who did not go to the Gaeltacht that year. No one asked how much Irish we learned. All they wanted to know was what we got up to with the girls we met. We were preoccupied with girls by now, and I'm not aware of any who were preoccupied with boys, but obviously statistically there must have been one or two. The term 'getting off with' a girl was how we described having some kind of a relationship. In my own case it was never more than cuddles and kisses, but if you were to believe some of the stories boys told, there were fellows having full-blown sexual intercourse with every girl they 'got off with'.

These stories of sexual conquests, which were mostly untrue or grossly exaggerated, made most of us feel somehow inferior, because we had got no further than a kiss or a love bite. We always felt obliged to try it on with a girl, because we thought that that was what we *had* to do. It led to major embarrassment for both the boys and the girls. In most cases we didn't really desire sex. In fact, if any of the girls had said 'Yes', we wouldn't have known what to do anyway.

CHAPTER 15

The Bargain King at the Harvest Fair

W e were blessed with great recreational organisations. Bally-shannon Boxing Club thrived, and we had our own boxing heroes like Seamus Gallagher and Paddy Doherty, who had gained national recognition.

The GAA was hugely important, and many members of the Aodh Rua club represented the town on the county football teams down the years: Martin Carney, Mickey McLoone, Brian McEniff, Gary Walsh, Alan Kane and Brian Murray spring to mind. There was a snooker club that I was never allowed to attend (which didn't mean I didn't) because my mother used to say that being a good snooker player was the sign of a wasted youth.

Once a month a livestock fair was held in the Fair Green at the top of the town, where bargains were secured following loud negotiation, spurred on by whoever happened to be standing by, with a spit in the hand followed by a hearty handshake. Inevitably the fair overflowed onto Main Street, as did the cowshit and piss. The stench would remain for a few days afterwards, but the business for the local shops more than compensated. One fair day a cow somehow got into our small grocery shop and wrecked all around it. There was a smell of dung in the shop for months afterwards.

Many people from surrounding country areas came to town on fair day. They would barter goods like eggs and butter for things they couldn't make or grow themselves. I used to love the salty taste of what we called 'country butter' on a slice of warm batch bread with a sprinkling of sugar on top – delicious!

A really big event every year – in September, as far as I remember – was the Harvest Fair. Then the town was thronged with people, and we children would get the day off school. As well as the normal livestock fair, stalls would be set up selling all kinds of exotic goods.

I remember particularly the 'spud guns', which shot small pieces of potato a distance of two or three metres. Every child in the town would buy one of these for a few pence. To get hit by one of the missiles was painful enough.

The 'Bargain King' – a precursor of Del Boy – always came to roar his spiel over the noisy crowd assembled in front of him. He had some great one-liners. I remember an ESB (Electricity Supply Board) van struggling through the masses on Main Street and the Bargain King shouting out 'The charge of the Light Brigade!' On another occasion a plane flew low overhead and he yelled 'Another consignment of goods for the Bargain King!'

A carnival would be set up in the Market Yard, with swing boats, dodgems (or bumpin' cars, as we called them), a shooting gallery, etc. The Harvest Fair day was one of the highlights of the year in Ballyshannon.

CHAPTER 16

Danny Ellis and the Artane Boys' Band

Down the years I have had many ambitions and obsessions. As a youngster, one of the musical icons I admired a lot was the famous Artane Boys' Band. I would watch them proudly march around Croke Park on All-Ireland day and wonder what it was like to be a member of that band. Their uniforms were so smart, and the precision of their marching was so clever, not to mention the fabulous sound they made playing the popular marching music of the day. It was my fantasy to be a member of the Artane Boys' Band, like a lot of other kids back in the 1950s and 1960s, but I didn't know how I could join. I thought you had to live in Artane in Dublin.

Later in life I was to meet a man who had been a member of the Artane band when he was a boy: probably someone I watched on numerous occasions, both live and on television, even though I didn't know him personally at the time. It's strange how paths in life can cross at some point. I have been privileged to present radio programmes on Shannonside/Northern Sound radio for about twelve years now. I have guests every week, many of them from the world of music. It has been a joy to chat to well-known people such as John Sheehan of Dubliners fame, Paul Brady, and internationally renowned artists like Steve Earle and Guy Clark. The programme is a sort of potpourri of people from the world of arts and entertainment, including visual artists, playwrights and authors, peppered with lots of live music and song.

One of the guests I will never forget is Danny Ellis, who had just released his new book and CD. The book is called *The Boy at the Gate* and the album is called *800 Voices*. The 'boy at the gate' is a reference to the time when his mother left him, aged only eight years, at the gate of Artane Industrial School, promising that she would return and collect him at Christmas. He never saw her again. The '800 voices' is the sound he heard immediately after his mother left him: the 800 children confined, for one reason or another, in the industrial school. They were having a moment's fun playing in the playground when he arrived.

I read the book in advance of Danny's spot on my show. It is a riveting read and the companion CD is full of amazing songs, written by Danny and inspired by the events he describes. The book and CD changed my opinion of the Artane Boys' Band completely. I learned that the industrial school was a violent and horrific place – the children were regularly beaten and treated inhumanely – but Danny took us through his time there with a light and humorous style of storytelling. Quite amazing!

While my own memories of school are mostly of beatings and fear, that fear ended at 3.30pm each day for me. Danny's fear went on for twenty-four hours of every day of the eight years he spent in Artane. His book is mostly full of the funny things that happened between the boys there, but the truth of the situation is unavoidable: it was a hell on earth.

Danny will tell you that his success in the music business came from the eight long years he spent in Artane. After he left that hellhole he became a professional musician, playing trombone in many of the top Irish showbands of the 1960s and 1970s. He has become a wonderful singer and an even better songwriter, as you can hear on his albums. His songs reflect all that is bad and all that is good in the human psyche.

As I got to know him, I wondered how any kid who went through eight terrifying and painful years in any institution of that time could turn out to be such a lovely human being. The answer came to me as I listened to one of his songs: I feel it was the love of a good woman that saved Danny. The song I am talking about is called 'Give Us Our Innocence Back'. I am including its lyrics here.

'Give Us Our Innocence Back' (words and music by Danny Ellis)

How often I've wondered what people would do
But now I know better, now I know they all knew
And the whole damn country looked the other way
As the bold Christian Brothers battered our childhoods away

Yeah they shattered our bodies and they scattered our minds
And they broke us and bent us till we were twisted as twine
Then they cut us all loose, like rats from a sack
Now there's no amount of money gonna buy us our innocence back

And we ran from the sunshine and we ran from the rain
And we ran into trouble tryna run from the pain
'Hey I need to feel something, so come on do your worst'
But I never felt nothing but the feeling that life was a curse

Took me ten years to notice that sign on my back
Saying 'Come on big world why don't ya give me a smack'
But the harder they hit it, the harder it packed
And there's no sledgehammer gonna buy me my innocence back

It took the kindness of others to stop me in my tracks
Made me cry like a baby for the love that I lacked
It was tougher than the beatings much harder to face
That stark recognition that a part of my soul's been erased

Now I wish the lads justice and I wish the lads luck
But whatever they give ya it won't be what they took
May you always find shelter from the dreams of the black
And may the grace that creates you grant you your innocence back

Danny says about the song above: 'Here, I permit myself some expression of the anger I held as a child towards society, for allowing the abuses of the Christian Brothers. Since writing this song, I've come to know that most people, while they knew the "Brothers" were a tough lot, had no idea of the horrors some inflicted. Here also are my hopes for the healing that's graced me to touch others.'

Danny has remained a valued friend since he spoke and sang on my radio show. He now lives in Asheville, North Carolina with his wife, Liz. He gives singing lessons there, and performs at concerts all over the United States. His books and CDs, including the song above (from *800 Voices*) are available from his website (www.dannyellismusic.com). There's a lot of material there that is well worth your attention.

I feel that Danny's story is inspiring: overcoming the worst possible start, being released at sixteen years of age (as he says in his song, they 'set us all loose like rats from a sack'), and then achieving all that he has achieved in life. I don't know how I would have coped had I been put in the same boat at only eight years of age.

CHAPTER 17

Bingo! Bingo! I'm in Love!

The seaside town of Bundoran in Co. Donegal is a favourite holiday destination for many people from all over Ireland. I got my first summer job there in 1964 when my dad secured a position for me at the Olympia Amusements Arcade on the main street. The Olympia, the biggest arcade in Bundoran, was run by a couple of very shrewd individuals, Ken Page and Denis Porter. I started working there in the bingo room. I had no idea at fourteen years of age what bingo was, but I learned fast.

I was put in charge of a machine that held individually numbered ping-pong balls. When you switched it on, a continuous blast of air would send the balls flying around the drum, and a random ball would shoot up through a tube; I would grasp it and place it in a number-specific recess. Simultaneously I would press a switch that lit up that number on a giant display, which all the players could see. They would check to see if they had the number.

The players would purchase a card with numbers on it. These were totally different from what we now know as bingo books. There were little slide devices that they could cover a number with if they had it. Prizes were given for a continuous line across, a line down, four corners or a full house. It was thrupence a game (about 1.5 cents in today's money), which was collected before each game, and the prizes went from as low as half a crown (about sixteen cents) to £5 in the final game of the evening, plus, as the boss used to say, a 'gold-*coloured* cup' ... in reality the cup was a cheap plastic trophy.

I spent most of that summer working there, and it really was a joyful time. The bingo every evening attracted some very colourful characters and really devoted players. I remember that Mrs McGee from Ballyshannon could play four cards at a time, and would get quite animated if I made a mistake.

At around 10.30pm, Harry McFadden and his wife, Eileen, would arrive in. They were very entertaining people from the world of show business, which always attracted me. They ran what they used to call the Portable Theatre – one of the last 'fit-up' theatre companies – and put on a different play every night. Harry and Eileen would be fully made up from the latest play. Many years later, when I moved to Drumshanbo, I met Harry's brother Marcus, who ran a fish-and-chip van in the town.

I remember buying 20 Marlboro cigarettes and a pair of Beatle boots with my first wage packet. I thought I was the coolest dude in town, in my new Cuban heels and with a cigarette between my lips as I strolled about. I made many friends that summer, and I enjoyed every minute of it. I worked long hours, but it was so good that I went back and worked there the following summer as well. Bundoran then was a magical place for a young teenager, and I felt so lucky to be there. It would become even more important in the following years, and I'll get to talk about that later.

CHAPTER 18

The Soundstorms in a Tea Cup

Recently my grandson Cathal attended his first disco: he was just coming up on fourteen years old. He was really looking forward to it, and I was looking forward to hearing about his new experience.

A few days later he showed me some videos he had recorded at the disco, and it was so different from my first experience of such a night out. Everybody was dancing, but not necessarily in a boy/girl couple. They were all out on the floor at the same time, and all jumping up and down to the music, which was completely new to me. As far as I was concerned it was like high-energy bedlam, but it looked like they were all having lots of fun.

I wish I could show Cathal a video of my first 'hop' (as teenage dances were called back then) when I was fourteen. Most young Catholic girls who lived in Ballyshannon at that time were members of a religious organisation within the Catholic Church called the Children of Mary. It organised a teenage hop in the Rock Hall on a Sunday afternoon, with a live group, and everyone was welcome.

Playing at the hop was a talented young man called Liam Travers, who was from Bundoran. Liam played a very flashy electric guitar, and he owned a beautiful gleaming WEM amplifier which gave him a great sound. I have to say that at the beginning of the dance I was giving Liam only peripheral attention, as I was mostly concentrating on the girls, who were all lined up on one side of the hall. I had recently turned fourteen years old, and after spending the previous summer in the Gaeltacht I was seriously into exploring female company further, and re-evaluating the idea that 'boys hated girls'.

I walked around the hall looking for a girl to dance with. I was quite intimidated by the girls, especially when it came to asking them to dance. My mother had told me that the correct way to approach this situation was to go up to a girl and say 'May I have the pleasure of this dance?' I tried it a few times and was greeted by giggles and polite refusals. The more I got refused, the more apprehensive I became, and my confidence was waning. In the Gaeltacht in Falcarragh I had had very few refusals at the *céilís*. This was all more formal, and not what I expected.

Somewhere towards the middle of the dance I heard my name being called over the public address system: someone had found out that I played guitar and suggested I might like to get up to sing a song. Not knowing any better, I wasn't the least bit nervous going up on stage, so I readily agreed. Liam's guitar felt strange in my hands compared to my own awful Egmond, but after I strummed a few chords it felt much better.

What to sing? I had just been working on a lovely song by Pete Seeger called 'Where Have All the Flowers Gone?', so I decided to sing that one. I felt the hall go quiet as the strange new voice drew people's attention. Gradually a small crowd gathered at the front of the stage. They seemed to be enjoying my singing, and that gave me my first experience of the chemistry that's possible between an audience and a performer.

I finished the song and wanted to stay up there all afternoon. Liam, however, had other ideas. This was his gig and his guitar, so he quickly took it from me and started singing his next song. My first brief moment in the limelight had ended.

As I was coming down from the stage, people were telling me how much they had enjoyed my singing. I think it was the most enjoyable few minutes of my life thus far. The next girl I asked to dance agreed immediately, much to my surprise. Also, I had not used my mother's suggested approach. That girl was Margaret White, who lived in the West Port area of Ballyshannon. I had never seen her before, but when she flattered me by telling me she thought my song was very good, my self-confidence soared from the low I felt earlier, and I fell instantly in love with this beautiful human being. It happened like that in those days. I now began to realise that there was a bonus to this music lark, other than the joy I got playing the guitar and singing. It actually opened up doors to girls' hearts.

Until now I had just been playing songs for my own enjoyment at home. However, singing on the stage in the Rock Hall gave me a desire to sing and perform in public again. It became my dream, and I knew deep inside that if I worked hard enough, it could come true.

As it happened, one day I was walking home from school and fell into step with a guy called John Hannigan. John lived in what was known as the Back Street, and we had encountered one another many times as kids in the Fair Green and other places where we had played down the years. John told me he played guitar, and asked if I'd like to call around sometime to play a few tunes with him. I didn't have to be asked twice.

John Hannigan's mother was everyone's mother in those days. The first day I arrived at his house, we adjourned to the front room. Every house had a front room back then. It was where the priest and other important figures would have been brought when they visited. The Hannigans' front door was always open, and everyone was welcome to call in if they were passing. I remember one day walking into the kitchen and finding John's granny washing her feet in a basin of water while chatting with two or three other callers who had dropped in for a cuppa and a chat. You never knew who or what you would meet in his house.

John brought me into his good room so that we could get a little peace to strum a few songs together. He owned a Connoisseur guitar, which I had previously seen displayed in the window of The Music Box priced at £12. This guitar was so much better that my old Egmond, but very quickly we found a few songs that we had in common.

John Hannigan and I continued our little sessions for a few weeks, and soon began to discuss the idea of putting a 'beat group' together. In those days a beat group was seen as progressive. It was very different from the conventional band. As far as we were concerned, beat groups were much cooler. The Beatles, the Kinks and the Rolling Stones were all beat groups.

John knew this guy called Johnny Ferguson who lived down the street. Johnny got a set of drums for Christmas, so we invited him to join our group. We decided we would call ourselves the Soundstorms. Can you imagine the three of us at that age, having a very serious debate about what we should call ourselves? Several suggestions were rejected before we unanimously agreed on the Soundstorms, and it was also time for bed.

I knew a guy called Michael Dalton who played the piano, so he was invited to play in the group as well. However, we soon discovered that Johnny was not the best drummer in the world. In fact, he had no idea at all, really, of how to play the drums. Like many aspiring beat groups of the time, we put together a music set we could perform if we got a booking. It included songs like 'If I Had a Hammer', 'Wipe Out', 'Misery', 'I Saw Her Standing There' and 'Do You Want to Know a Secret?': a song I sang many times to impress girls. I was obsessed with the Beatles and in particular George Harrison, so in my mind it was essential that I be the lead guitarist. Whenever we did play, John would very graciously let me play his guitar. Mind you, we didn't have any amplifiers, so we were quite limited in the beginning.

'John and Charlie's Good Time Garage Band' (words and music by Charlie McGettigan)

We grew up together, we shared every dream
We thought we held the future in our hands
We were birds of a feather, we had guitars that shone and
*   gleamed*
In John and Charlie's good time garage band

We played at any dancehall where they would let us play
We dreamed that one day we'd play one night stands
We thought that we knew it all, that rock 'n' roll was the only way
In John and Charlie's good time garage band

John and Charlie's good time garage band would one day be
The number one sensation in the land
We lived out our fantasy, but no one waved a wand
For John and Charlie's good time garage band

I often think of how we were before we went our separate ways
Before we picked up new emotions, new demands
I still strum this old guitar and I guess I will always
Like in John and Charlie's good time garage band

Life is made of hopes and dreams, and I'm glad that I've had mine
Though things did not turn out the way we planned
I wouldn't change a single dream or change a single line
Of John and Charlie's good time garage band

John and Charlie's good time garage band have never been
The number one sensation in the land
And although we've lived out our fantasies, no one waved a wand
For John and Charlie's good time garage band

During the first half of the twentieth century, things did not change much between one decade and another. Basically you had kids (anyone under eighteen years old) and adults. 'Teenager' was not a word you'd hear then. In the 1950s there were small signs of change. For example, the adult men would go to the barber's at least once a month, to get a short back and sides and a fresh application of Brylcreem. As they used to say back then, some men didn't go to the barbers for a haircut, they went for an oil change. Mainly influenced by the new breed of American music stars like Elvis Presley, a few of the younger men sported side-burns and what was called a DA, a duck's arse hairstyle. They always carried a comb somewhere on their person to keep the duck's arse in place. While stars like Rock Hudson or Cary Grant would have been the style template for those over 21, Elvis Presley and people like Gene Vincent and Cliff Richard became the template for the younger kids.

That all changed in the 1960s when, out of nowhere, four young musicians from Liverpool changed how all young people saw the world. They wore funny collarless suits, they combed their hair forward instead of back, and their music was uniquely 'English' even though they sang American-style rock and roll songs. The Beatles had arrived, and would inspire a whole new fashion outlook as well as the lifestyles of young people.

I was a big Elvis fan up until this time, and I also liked British artists like Cliff Richard and Adam Faith. However, as soon as the Beatles appeared on my radar, my life definitely changed. It's difficult to describe in words the effect the Beatles had on me as I approached my teens. There was a new freshness in their early songs like 'Love Me Do', 'Please Please Me' and 'She Loves You' that lit up my life. They were four cheeky chaps who had really thick Scouse accents, and as far as I was concerned they could do no wrong. I know many kids felt the same.

During my first year in secondary school I became a regular visitor to Coyle's Cafe, on the corner of Main Street and the Mall in Ballyshannon. It had a big shiny jukebox and we went in mostly to play our favourite songs. We didn't have record players at home, so, apart from the radio and television, Coyle's jukebox was the only way to enjoy our favourite music, and at the proper volume. (And I had another reason for going to that cafe, which I will come to shortly.)

There were two schools of thought among the Coyle's clientele: Beatles fans and Rolling Stones fans. The former bought *New Musical Express* while the latter bought *Melody Maker*. Every evening on our way home from school we'd spend half an hour in Coyle's. If any older boys like David Murphy or Eddie McBride got there before us, the menu would be the Stones, Them or the Yardbirds, but if we got there first it would be the Beatles, the Hollies or the Searchers. It was really cool to play the B sides of the singles rather than the A sides all the time. It showed how 'sophisticated' our tastes were.

Sometime in 1965 my dad bought our first record player: a red Dansette with a built-in speaker. You could load several records on it; after one finished playing, the next one dropped down onto the turntable. Dad was a big Jim Reeves fan at the time, and I think he thought the record player would be reserved for Jim's songs. I was never a fan and I never played Jim Reeves songs on that player. I did almost wear it out playing the Beatles, however.

Before we got the record player my listening was confined to whatever was being played on Coyle's jukebox or on radio and television. I listened a lot to Radio Luxembourg at home, but the signal was often bad. Radio Éireann didn't play a lot of pop music at the time, but we could pick up the BBC Light Programme. I would listen to shows like Brian Matthew's *Saturday Club*. It never crossed my mind that one day I would have my own radio programme, as I have now, twice each week with Shannonside/Northern Sound.

The first record I bought was 'Keep on Running' by the Spencer Davis Group. The Music Box, right across the street from our shop, kept well up to date with the new releases. It sold the sheet music as well. However, the Beatles topped my chart. We were so lucky to grow up with their music and develop our own music in parallel with theirs. The early albums included quite a few cover versions, but as time progressed the vast majority of the songs on their albums were their own compositions. For me their 'coming of age' album was *Rubber Soul*, which came out in 1965. They released 'Day Tripper' and 'We Can Work It Out' as a double-A-side single at the same time.

It was remarkable that in two really busy years of touring the world, they developed from innocent beginnings to creating these amazingly inventive songs. George Harrison's unique guitar introductions and solos lit up my life. Ringo's drumming was perfect for each song, and of course the songs were just so complete. There was a huge diversity of songs on *Rubber Soul,* and indeed all their albums. The plaintive 'Michelle', the quirky 'Norwegian Wood', with the introduction of the sitar, and the rocking 'Drive My Car' … I don't think there's a bad song on this album, and that's rare.

This period was a great time to be involved in music. We learned the chords and sang the Beatles songs with real enthusiasm. We followed their progress and we developed under the influence of albums like *Revolver* and the legendary *Sgt. Pepper's Lonely Hearts Club Band*. Each album brought us further and further on our musical journey. To this day, although a lot of groups came close, none, in my humble opinion, has ever surpassed the Beatles.

There were some other great groups along the way. To me, the Kinks were the nearest thing to the Beatles you could find, because of their

'Englishness'. I also liked the Hollies for their harmonies, but my main musical soundscape throughout my teenage years was the Beatles. I still love them!

Many years later, Maxi and I wrote this song after Maxi visited 20 Forthlin Road, Liverpool, the childhood home of Paul McCartney. My wife and I visited the house on a different occasion. Between the three of us and our memories of the place, we came up with 'The Man from 20'. It is based on the thoughts of the caretaker of Paul's old house, which is now a National Trust property.

'The Man from 20' (words and music by Charlie McGettigan)

I'm the man from 20; kindly form a queue
Those who do remember, let me look at you
Yes, I'm the man from 20, and I've yet to see his face
A burger from the takeaway, and it's back to his place

They've got his old piano here, and someone played a tune
And someone sang along with them, and we danced around the room

Yes I'm the man from twenty, and I've been me for a year
Teary eyes and silence and I deaden it with beer
Once he came a-knocking; he didn't have a key
And I was busy shopping when he needed me

Oh I hate dancing sober 'cause I feel like such a fool
I'm the Liverpool Loafer and they say I must be cool

Mary calls at midnight, there's flour on her hands
She talks of tiny babies, angels in the sand

Michael's on his bicycle; he says he saw Our Kid
And Jim he trims the hedges as she watches from the bed
Minis at the Inny, letters for the Queen
Collars shaped like roundabouts, ah the things I've seen

And early in the morning ladies come to stare
Ginny puts her pinny on and she says 'He isn't here'

Yes I'm the man from 20; kindly form a queue
Those who do remember, let me look at you

CHAPTER 19

The Reinbous and the Assaroe Céilí Band

My first group, the Soundstorms, was a major progression in my life, but we didn't have the equipment we needed. Necessity being the mother of invention, John decided that it might be possible, with a bit of ingenuity, to use the family radio as an amplifier. A radio in those days was a large brown wooden affair with a big built-in speaker. John took the jack plug off his guitar lead and attached the two wires directly to the amplifier / speaker of the radio. Eureka! We had sound.

All the top beat groups of the time were writing their own songs, so John and I decided to try our hands at writing. Every Saturday night we would plug in our guitars and write songs. They were awful! I remember one was called 'Summertime Love', about a girl I met in Bundoran the previous summer. Another, called 'I Don't Know Why I Love You', was even worse than the first. Of course we thought they were the best songs ever written. More recently, John told me that around that time I announced that I would win the Eurovision Song Contest some day, and he said to himself, 'Yes, and I am going to win the pools and become a millionaire.' Little did we know?

We used to do spots at concerts in the town. There had to be a piano or we couldn't play. Michael was a really good piano player, and the only officially trained musician in the group. As I have mentioned, Ballyshannon had the Assaroe Céilí Band at that time: a fully professional band led by Cyril Curran. His piano accordion player was his niece Breege Curran. She played a new instrument called a Cordovox: an electronic accordion that caused quite a stir around the place. I think the Assaroe was the first *céilí* band to have a Cordovox. We did a few concerts where they were featured. Michael discovered that if you laid the Cordovox on its back, it could be played like an electric organ. We played a few gigs with Breege's Cordovox like this: buying an electric organ or piano was not an option, as money was scarce. Unfortunately, Michael began to withdraw from the Soundstorms.

Just up the street from John's house lived another talented fellow called Jimmy Rafferty. Jimmy had been taught how to play the drums by his uncle, Tom Gallagher, who was an accomplished drummer. We invited Jimmy to join the Soundstorms and he readily agreed. He borrowed £110 from the local credit union to purchase a brand-new set of drums. That was an enormous investment at the time.

At this point we decided to change the name of the group. We became the Rainbows, but spelt it 'Reinbous' just to be extra cool. We thought the spelling was so clever that we even had John's brother Donal paint the name on the front of the bass drum. It was still two guitarists and a drummer, so a bass player was what we needed next. The only bass player we knew in the town was Eamonn Travers, and he was already part of a great R&B group, the Erratics. We knew that there was no way he was going to join our little ensemble, but we had to find someone.

At the technical school in Ballyshannon, John became friendly with a guy called Jimmy Gallagher, whose brother Sean was a full-time guitarist with the Richie Fitzgerald Céilí Band. It turned out that Jimmy was a bass player with a group called Federal Aviation (what a great name!). The only problem was that he lived in Bundoran, four miles from Ballyshannon: a long distance in those days. He was very keen to join our group while still playing with Federal Aviation, and so he offered to thumb a lift to Ballyshannon from Bundoran whenever needed, to practise. Imagine asking a fifteen-year-old today to go to that kind of trouble to follow his dream. Jimmy was a fantastic bass player, and just what we needed. He was also very good-looking and all the girls around Ballyshannon and Bundoran were mad about him, which was a bonus.

We also added a lead singer so that I could concentrate on being George Harrison. Danny Kerrigan lived in Ballyshannon and was always hanging around Hannigans' when John and I were practising. I don't know how we found out that he could sing, but he was a fine singer. Danny was the real thing. He always wore black clothes and had many rings on his fingers. Some years later I wrote a song called 'Ringo Ray' based largely on his character.

We were now a five-piece group with very few gigs. We mostly got 'relief' group spots at dances around the area. It was the next step up for small groups to play before the big group came on stage. The joke was that we called ourselves a relief group because people said it was a relief when we finished playing. Mostly they were right. We just wanted to play music and eventually we saved up enough to get our own amplifiers for our guitars. This created a new problem: everybody wanted to be the loudest musician, so they were always at maximum volume and we created a dreadfully loud wall of noise.

We found all kinds of places to play as the feature act. The Abbey Ballroom, now the Abbey Arts Centre, held concerts regularly. We were the new thing. Our claim to fame was that we were Ballyshannon's only 'beat group'. Mind you, we weren't the only music group in the town. I mentioned the Erratics earlier. They specialised in rhythm and blues, playing the music of Howlin' Wolf, Jimmy Witherspoon, Muddy Waters, etc. I have often wondered where they found their material in the early 1960s, especially in a small place like Ballyshannon. Imagine if these great blues legends knew their music was being played so enthusiastically in a small town in Co. Donegal, Ireland. I'd say they would have been chuffed.

We played our own dance events in places like the Rock Hall, just down the road from the Rock Hospital. One night we actually paid to get into the annual Danby Horse Show Dance, which was in a marquee there, so that we might get a chance to do a spot. The main band was Paddy McCafferty's, from Ballybofey, whose members wore lovely green tartan jackets. They were a fully professional, polished outfit. Paddy agreed to let us play while his band went for a cup of tea. We had played three songs when Paddy came rushing back to the stage to rescue the audience from the dreadful noise we were making with the amplifiers so loud. Nobody seemed to appreciate that we put hours of practice into creating this noisy racket!

We used to practise in a cold, draughty shed called the Market House, right in the centre of the town. John Hannigan's brother Donal (known as Dodo) had become our road manager. He was a dab hand at overcoming technical problems, even if he was regularly putting us in danger of electrocution. Dodo was full of ideas and was a great help to us back then, because he really believed we were going to be the next Beatles.

With our amplifiers turned up to full volume, the people in the area around the Market House began to complain, so we were quickly stopped from practising there. I remember one Saturday night we decided to practise in Jimmy Rafferty's house, but were swiftly stopped when Jimmy's dad came roaring into the room, complaining that the electricity meter was spinning around at 100 miles an hour. Everyone was against us!

However, we were very determined, no matter how many knock-downs we got. We were asked to play at a dance in the Abbey Ballroom, but we didn't have a public address system. Jimmy's parents were the sacristans in the local church, St Patrick's, so he got the bright idea of borrowing the PA system from the church. Of course he didn't tell anyone in charge. It was only a short walk from the church to the Abbey, so we all helped carry it to the venue. Everything was going well until during one song we blew the speakers, which were totally unsuitable for a rock 'n' roll group. The sound was completely distorted, but we persevered and played right through to the end of the dance, oblivious to how awful we sounded.

We dismantled the PA system, and Jimmy brought it back to the church the following morning just before Sunday mass. As soon as the priest began his opening prayers, the congregation, including us, started covering their ears. Everyone, including my parents, thought the system had developed a fault. I started looking for a hole to crawl into. No one ever knew that it was actually us who had destroyed the church PA system, until now I suppose. Sorry! Sadly, a few years later our lead singer Danny lost his life in a drowning accident off the coast of Bundoran.

We were constantly on the lookout for opportunities. Out of the blue on Christmas night in 1965 someone knocked on our door in Donegal Road. It was a cold, blustery night and when I answered the door a windswept Cyril Curran, leader of the Assaroe Céilí Band, was standing there.

'Our guitar player is sick,' said Cyril, 'and I was wondering if you would be available to play with us.'

'When would you want me?' I asked

'Tonight,' said Cyril. 'We have a dance in Rossinver Parish Hall.'

Even though I had never played with Cyril's band and I had no idea where Rossinver was, my first instinct was to say 'yes'. My parents weren't too happy about it, but they reluctantly agreed to let me go. I don't remember much about the dance, but I felt like a real pro to be playing with the internationally famous Assaroe Céilí Band. I do remember Cyril being a lovely gentleman with a friendly way of looking at you. I think that particular night Geoffrey Power from Bundoran was playing the Cordovox and the wonderful Micilín Gillespie was on drums, with Cyril on fiddle. At the time *céilí* bands were having a tough time surviving, as the showband scene began to take over. So I was, I guess, the 'pop' music element in the group.

A few months later, on St Patrick's Night, I was at a dance in the Abbey Ballroom. I felt someone sidle up behind me. It was Cyril, who slipped a piece of paper into my hand. 'That's for Christmas Night,' and then he walked away. I opened my hand to find it was a ten shilling note (a lot at the time). It was the first time I received money for doing what I loved to do, and that ten shilling note meant so much to me. I have never forgotten it, or the man who gave it to me. When I think of it, the Abbey Cinema, the Abbey Ballroom and the Abbey Arts Centre are now basically the same venue with different names.

I was lucky to play with the Assaroe Céilí Band many times after that, and it was always a joy. They were all great musicians at the top of their game, but sadly the band's days were numbered. A few years later Cyril moved to England, where he taught the fiddle and played the odd gig. He sadly passed away a couple of years ago, but I am always thankful to him for giving me my first big break.

'Ringo Ray' (words and music by Charlie McGettigan)

I got a fellow in my memory
When I think of him it tickles me
'Cos he was the guy that I wanted to be
I just loved that Ringo Ray

He was the leader of a back street band
Knew all the moves, he knew all the slang
But he never came when the school bell rang
I just loved that Ringo Ray

Ringo Ray, oh Ringo Ray
I wonder is he around today
At that crazy old cafe we used to go to.
Ringo Ray oh Ringo Ray
I believed everything he'd say
All the fantasies he made I used to cling to

Back in 61 or 62
Just a bunch of kids with nothing to do
Ray was the skipper and we were the crew
It just seemed the natural way
We were listening' to rock 'n' roll
Sweet sixteen and breakin' all the rules
I t didn't matter that the kid was a fool
We just loved that Ringo Ray

Now he's nothing but a memory
I wonder why he meant so much to me
He showed us a world that we needed to see
In those free an' easy days
I tried to find only yesterday
But he was buried underneath the clay
Just a few words that I wanted to say
About my hero Ringo Ray

CHAPTER 20

The Kinks Come to Town

In the summer of 1966 I got a phone call from a man called Sean O'Brien. He had leased the Palace Bar in Bundoran for the summer season, and was expecting a bus-load of visitors from Northern Ireland to descend on his venue that night. The group he had booked had let him down at the last minute. The 'singing pub' phenomenon had arrived, and every pub in Bundoran had live entertainment nightly. Sean needed some musical entertainment fast; he had heard of our group and asked if we could help him out.

This was an opportunity not to be missed, so I got a message to Jimmy Gallagher and a great musician friend, Neil McBride, who played piano and guitar. They both agreed to come with me to chance our arm, and that's what we were doing, really. My dad agreed to drive us to Bundoran, and I bought the *Guinness Book of Irish Ballads* in Paddy O Neill's shop on the way. Yes, we were a lofty beat group in our own minds, but when money was on the table we would play anything.

We got all this together in a matter of hours, and arrived in the Palace Bar full of enthusiasm. The bar had a 30-watt Elpico PA system with one microphone, and we had a small green 15-watt Watkins guitar amp. Jimmy had made his own bass amp and cab as a school project. I can't imagine any group, no matter how amateur, starting out to do a gig like that these days!

We struggled through the evening, which lasted three hours, but the punters seemed to like us. We must have been doing something right because at the end of the gig, Sean offered us the chance to play nightly for the rest of the summer. We would receive £8 each per week, and would be expected to play seven nights for three hours each night. That was a lot to us at the time, and a summer residency anywhere was a big vote of confidence. When you're that young and that ambitious, it all helps. As the summer progressed we got better and better, spurred on by the warm feedback from our audiences.

We were very confident and comfortable when we were performing our own sets, but when we had to back singers from the audience, trying to keep their singing in the right key was a valuable learning curve. These could be Sinatra-like crooners, Ronnie Drew-type ballad-eers or even Larry Cunningham-style country and western singers. There were some great singers but some dreadful ones as well: those who would drift into several different keys in the course of a song. We had to keep changing the backing once we figured out which key they were now in. It's a nightmare for any musician, because we know that if they sound dreadful, we will get the blame.

Jimmy, Neil and I learned so much that summer. It was tough going, but it was also so much fun. It was easily the best learning experience of my life, and I still sing songs from that period today.

We played in the Palace Bar for two whole months, and by the end of our stint we probably knew every guitar chord that ever existed. We had become 'professional' musicians. After that we had as many gigs as we could handle. We even got to play as a 'relief group' in Bundoran's most popular ballroom, the Astoria. It was easy for us to put a five-piece group together with all the talent in Ballyshannon and Bundoran, so that opened up our options enormously. I remember negotiating a fee of £15 with Jimmy Smyth, leader of Larry Cunningham and the Mighty Avons, to warm up the audience before the main attraction came on (in those days we were called relief groups; nowadays we would be called support acts, which I think is much better). That was the going rate back then. They would have been on about £500 themselves, but we were happy with what we got.

Bundoran was a lively spot in those days, and the entire street would be lined with cars on both sides. Nobody seemed to be short of money. I suppose you could say they were the 'Celtic Tiger' summers of the 1960s and 1970s! The Astoria Ballroom had dancing seven nights a week, with all the top groups like Brendan Bowyer and the Royal Showband, Butch Moore and the Capital, not to mention Dickie Rock and the Miami, to name but a few.

One of the most exciting nights I remember there was when the Kinks came to play. Imagine today getting someone like Ed Sheeran to play in a small ballroom in Bundoran! The Kinks had 'Sunny Afternoon' in the charts. We all had been anticipating this event for weeks, and I couldn't believe my eyes when brothers Ray and Dave Davies arrived on stage with drummer Mick Avory. Pete Quaife was replaced that night by another bass player, John Dalton.

They opened with 'You Really Got Me', and as soon as they started a girl who was standing in front of our drummer, Jimmy Rafferty, got so excited that she fainted and landed in his arms. Jimmy luckily caught her and, being the gentleman he is, proceeded to carry her outside to get some fresh air into her lungs. The Kinks played for an hour and were leaving the stage just as Jimmy and the girl, now fully recovered, returned inside. What a disappointment for poor Jimmy. I don't even think he 'got off' with the girl.

The Kinks were fantastic that night: raw and unpolished. They just plugged into the amplifiers on stage, and off they went. To this day they are one of my favourite groups. Ray Davies was, and still is, a fantastic songwriter. Songs like 'Waterloo Sunset' and 'Dedicated Follower of Fashion' sound just as good today as they did in the 1960s.

CHAPTER 21

A Garda Calls

By the time I was fifteen years old I had become a very busy teenager with a full diary. I don't mean only music bookings. I was still at secondary school, helping my dad in the shop, practising with the brass band, trying my hand out with the local musical society, and most of all writing songs and practising playing my guitar. Days were generally exciting in a good way, but there were exceptions. The fear we felt during our school days was always with us, but I had another distraction in my life: my little brother, Declan. He was, as they used to say, a 'holy terror'.

One day at lunchtime, there was a knock at our door. On opening it, I saw Garda Aidan Murray standing there in full uniform.

'Does Declan McGettigan live here?' Silly question, I thought, because he knew damn well he did.

A hesitant 'Yes' was my puzzled reply.

'I have a warrant here for his arrest, and I have to take him to the Garda Station for questioning.'

I shouted at him, 'You can go and fuck yourself, you're not getting our Declan!' and slammed the door in his face.

I raced to tell Declan to vamoose as fast as possible. My mother and father didn't seem to be as alarmed as I was.

'Garda Murray wants to take Declan to the barracks!' I screamed. My father went to the door and came back with the garda behind him.

Looking directly at Declan, my father said, 'I am afraid you'll have to go with the garda.'

'Dad' I pleaded. 'You can't let him take our Declan away!'

'Well, he has been warned,' said my father. 'He was caught stealing from the collection box in the church.'

I pleaded with Garda Murray, saying that Declan would never do anything like that again.

'I'm sorry,' he said, 'I'll still have to take him away.'

I asked my mother to intervene, and saw the garda's face soften. I knew my mother's charm could melt a stone.

'Well,' he said, 'normally I have to exercise a warrant, but I might make an exception if Declan puts ten shillings in the collection box in the church as restitution.'

Declan agreed, even though ten shillings was a lot of money in those days.

As I learned later, dad had asked Garda Murray, who was a drinking buddy of his, to give Declan a scare. It worked … for a while!

When I thought about what had happened, I began to have serious worries about Declan. He was always getting into some kind of trouble. I remember going into his room one morning when he was almost two years old, to find that he had managed to smear the entire cot, the walls and the floor with his excrement.

From the very start Declan was what one might call 'different'. He was born in the Rock Hospital in November 1955, as I have mentioned. I don't remember a lot about his first year, but when we moved to Donegal Road in 1956 his presence began to be a big part of all our lives. He had the little box room all to himself, which meant I had to sleep in Granny's room.

When he was about four years old he was allowed to play out in the garden, but you couldn't take your eye off him for a second. A lot of people of all ages passed our front garden, and we began to notice that people were going to the other side of the road to pass our house. It seems that our Declan took great delight in throwing stones at every passerby. He thought it was funny and I guess so did we, but my mum always scolded him for it.

As he grew older the offences got bigger. At Halloween he would put lighted fireworks into people's letterboxes, which even then was a bit too much. He would steal the money out of the church candle box every time he got a chance. There was a well-maintained grotto beside the church in Rossnowlagh, with a beautiful fountain. It had a pond where people used to throw in their coins and make a wish. Declan and a friend his own age was caught pilfering the coins. If there was any devilment to be done in Ballyshannon, you could be sure that Declan would be in the middle of it.

At the time I had my own friends, and little brothers were not part of our bunch. When any of the kids I played with was asked to babysit their younger siblings, there was an immediate protest. After all, we had more important things to do. We had to get to the railway station, and fight off the Indians!

When Declan was in his teens and at secondary school, things began to deteriorate even more. It all came out later. He was stealing cigarettes from our shop and selling them to his friends. He seemed to always know a quick way of dealing with authority. He told me in later years how one day when he didn't have his homework done, he decided to divert attention by fusing the entire electrical system in the school. He put silver paper into an electric bulb socket in his classroom. When the teacher came into the class and switched on the light, it short-circuited the whole school. That day he got away with not having his homework done, so to him it was a successful mission.

It was around this time that I was beginning to have serious feelings for a girl I had known from my earliest schooldays. My first memory of noticing this girl, who stood out from the others, was in First Class at St Catherine's Primary School in Ballyshannon. Sister Rosario used to have spelling contests every day, and the winner would receive a 'holy picture' as a prize. It wasn't much, but to a kid a prize is a prize. As I mentioned previously, these prizes were usually won by a little girl named Goretti Gallagher. The more she won, the less I liked her, but I did begin to notice her. She had a lovely freckled face surrounded by a mass of ginger curls, and she always had a contrasting coloured bow (in my memory usually green) in her hair.

When I was a teenager I became very aware of her presence again. Ballyshannon, being a small town, made us boys and girls really appreciate each other. At around thirteen I had gone to the pictures or out for walks with one or two girls from around the town. Yes, we were innocent, but it was a lovely innocence. Even at that age the girl I truly admired from afar was Goretti Gallagher. She was developing, like her mum, into a real stunner. She was very friendly with my close neighbour Dolores Daly, so she walked past our house every day in her green school uniform. Although she never would have known it, she had some kind of mystique about her that haunted me, and turned me into a 'Peeping Charlie' with only one fixation: her.

Our teenage years were always busy with one thing or another, but our social life was very important as well. We would regularly meet up on the way home from school, and, as I've mentioned, we often congregated in Coyle's Cafe, which had a jukebox. My 'other reason' to go to Coyle's was that Goretti and her friends would be there too. At the tender age of fourteen the urge within me to get to know her a little better just grew and grew. I was longing to ask her out, but I couldn't find the courage.

I got Goretti into serious trouble one time when I spotted her passing Coyle's Cafe. She had been sent down the town to get the meat for the dinner. As she passed Coyle's, I spotted her and ran out to call her back. We chatted for so long in Coyle's that by the time we were finished, the butcher's shop was closed, so there was no meat for the dinner that day. You can imagine the roasting she got from her mum.

One day the news began to circulate that Goretti Gallagher had contracted meningitis and was on death's door in the Sheil Hospital. The whole town was very concerned, and I was really frightened by the thought that this lovely girl could actually die.

Thankfully, she survived and slowly began to come out into the community again. I knew that I had to get her into my life, and eventually I summoned up enough courage to ask her out.

When I say I 'asked her out', you have to understand that I was only sixteen then, so I asked her friend Dolores to do the actual asking for me! This was how dates were arranged back then. You would ask a girl's friend to ask her if she would go out with you. It was still nerve-racking, and you were always worried that she would say no … but thankfully, she said yes. Our first official date was at the Ballyshannon Drama Festival, when we went to see Chekhov's *Cherry Orchard*. We had a great night and truly enjoyed being in each other's company. We were now girlfriend and boyfriend.

We kept in contact nearly every day after that. At this time I was playing music seven nights a week, so most of our dates would have been in the afternoons. In the band's third season playing in Bundoran, Goretti and her friends would go out to all the venues in Bundoran and would usually end up in the place where I was. This meant we got to be with each other twice some days. When I could, I would get off early and we would go to the Astoria Ballroom together. However, these were rare occasions. Goretti was very tolerant of my crazy music schedule, but we would try to be together as much as possible.

'I'd Stand in the Snow' (words and music by Charlie McGettigan)

I'd stand in the snow to be with you
Nowhere I wouldn't go … there's not a thing
*   that I wouldn't do*
I'd suffer the cold till I went blue
And I'd stand in the snow to be with you

I'd cross the ocean in a storm
Though the wind was blowin', the thought of you would keep me warm
In a force ten gale I'd make it through
I'd stand in the snow to be with you

There is no pain that I wouldn't bear
In the wind or the rain I'll be there whether it's foul or fair
I know it sounds crazy but it's true.
And I'd stand in the snow to be with you

There is no pain that I wouldn't bear
In the wind or the rain I'll be there whether it's foul or fair
So if you hear bad weather's due, remember
That I'd stand in the snow to be with you
I'd stand in the snow to be with you

CHAPTER 22

We All Did It!

These days we all take the clean air we breathe indoors for granted. If we are in a bar or restaurant, the prevailing smells will be coffee or beer from the bar. When I was playing in the pubs and bars of Ireland, there would have been smoke everywhere, although we didn't really notice it. Back then people smoked indoors, which was fine if you were a smoker, but vile if you were not. I was a smoker myself at the time. On a Monday after I had been playing music for the weekend, the smell that would hit me when I opened my guitar case was absolutely awful. Even I hated the stale smell of smoke or alcohol. It was truly abominable.

I remember we used to play a regular Saturday night in Conway's Corner House in Drumshanbo. It was a small pub at the time, with a big roaring fire behind us as we played. Not only did we get our arses roasted, but we could see a cloud of cigarette smoke over people's heads as they enjoyed their evening. I would light up regularly at a gig, and when I was playing I would stick the cigarette into the top of a guitar string while I sang a song, and take a puff or two when Brendan Emmett might be playing an instrumental piece. I don't know how the staff there, or anywhere else for that matter, who didn't smoke themselves tolerated other people's smoke all night. But nobody complained! It was just the norm. Some people would get very annoyed indeed with the owner of the premises if there weren't enough ashtrays on the tables. Imagine!

When I think about it now, I put our bad habit down to the power of advertising and the lack of good health information. How the limited information that was available at the time was taught to us was obviously also a problem.

Sometimes events in my life today remind me of how it was back then, and how stupidly we behaved sometimes. I suppose that is why we don't talk about it any more – we're ashamed! Take Christmas, for example. I remember after Christmas dinner we would all assemble in the front room of Goretti's family home, which wasn't a particularly big room. All the windows would have been shut tight, it being the middle of winter. Everybody would light up, usually between eight to ten people all smoking at the same time. Ashtrays would regularly have to be emptied as they overflowed with cigarette butts. No one complained. It was just the way it was. Mind you, it was very handy when you couldn't think what to buy Aunt Agatha for Christmas. A bumper pack of Sweet Afton in a special Christmas box was seen as an ideal Christmas present, and nobody considered that you were really taking a few years off poor Aunt Agatha's life.

Holidays are another time when I think about how smoking was all the rage when I was younger. If we went abroad on holiday we would buy our ciggies at duty-free prices, and indeed we would be expected to buy some for family members as well.

I remember the first time I smoked a cigarette. I was about ten years of age at the time. My friend Victor Fennell somehow got hold of a twenty pack of Gold Flake. We adjourned to the Station Rocks complete with a box of safety matches. I remember choking on the first pull, spluttering and coughing, and thinking I was going to die on the spot. Still, I persevered until I got the hang of it. We chain-smoked the whole pack that day and came home for tea as green as cabbages and stinking of cigarette smoke. Our parents very easily spotted our crime, and I'm sure some punishment was administered, but I can't remember. Smoking that first cigarette has always stuck in my mind, but the punishment didn't. I guess I must have thought it was worth it, because I continued smoking, albeit ever so much more carefully.

In our early teens we were less cautious about who saw us smoking. It was like a 'coming of age' thing to start smoking. Mrs Coyle in Coyle's

Cafe didn't seem to mind us assembling there to listen to the jukebox, and we all smoked openly. We didn't have the price of a pack of ten Carroll's, but Mrs Curran, who owned a tiny sweet shop on Castle Street, would sell us cigarettes singly for a few pence. Not only that, she would sell you two or three matches with a cut off the striking side of a match box. It was still not allowed by our parents – who smoked themselves, by the way – so, apart from Coyle's Café, most of our smoking took place outdoors in secret.

We used to go down the Mall for a smoke on dark November evenings, when we were supposed to be at the November devotions (a season of the rosary and benediction that took place every night in November). Well, if you're going to hell for missing November devotions, you might as well have a smoke on the way!

I remember one summer evening; Arthur, John Hannigan and myself were walking around the Mall enjoying our smokes, when who comes around the corner but Arthur's mum and dad. Arthur was wearing a lovely new tweed sports coat that he was after getting as special Sunday-only wear. John and I instantly threw our fags away, but Arthur was only after lighting up his, and he didn't want to waste it. He cupped the cigarette in his hand and put it into his pocket, still burning.

We chatted to his mum and dad for a while, but to Arthur it seemed like an hour, and he couldn't understand why we just wouldn't shut up. Neither of them spotted the cigarette, and as they walked away Arthur yanked his hand out of his pocket, letting go of the burning cigarette, and shouting obscenities at us as we laughed and laughed. It turned out that he had burned a hole in his lovely new jacket. Luckily one of John's uncles, who lived near the Corn Brae on the Bundoran Road, was a tailor who specialised in 'invisible mending'. He did a fine job on Arthur's sports coat, and nobody was ever the wiser … until now!

Nowadays, it would be very strange to see a pregnant woman smoking. Back when I was growing up, pregnant women were encouraged to smoke to help them 'keep their figure'. Imagine! People smoked in restaurants, bars and even hospitals. People would bring in cigarettes to smokers in hospital instead of Lucozade or grapes. I mentioned witnessing Father Gallagher setting fire to his hospital bed in an earlier chapter. I will never forget it!

There were so many different brands of tobacco available back then. For the hardened smokers who liked their cigarettes untipped, there were Gold Flake, Player's Navy Cut, Churchman's and Sweet Afton. For the poor man (or woman) there were Woodbines – or coffin nails, as they were called. These were tiny untipped cigarettes that were probably the cheapest ones going; 'coffin nails' was a fitting name. Then, for the more sophisticated, there were the upper-crust, posh tipped cigarettes, like Rothmans and Benson & Hedges. Women, at the risk of sounding sexist, liked to smoke menthol cigarettes. These had a fresh minty taste and I often smoked them myself. We loved the American brands as well, mainly Pall Mall and Camel. They had a slightly different flavour. My own preference was for Majors, a strong but short tipped cigarette.

I never smoked a pipe, but I did love the smell of them. Does anybody smoke a pipe these days, I wonder? There was something very special about watching the ritual of smoothing the tobacco in the palm of the hand before loading it into the pipe. The lighting process was special too, the match burning down to the very end as the smoker tamped the tobacco into his pipe with his brown nicotine-stained finger. The smell of pipe tobacco was absolutely gorgeous, and I would love to sit beside a man smoking a pipe. Very few women smoked pipes, but the older ones I do remember smoking clay pipes called 'dudeens'. A lot of the Traveller women smoked these, and you would see them sitting in their shawls on the street and lighting up.

I smoked myself right up until 1998, when I realised that smoking was definitely having a bad effect on my voice. I still can't believe it took me so long to admit the reality of what I was doing, but I just loved smoking. There was nothing like having a cigarette with a cup of coffee or tea after a nice meal. Having a smoke while I was driving the car was another favourite time for me. I'd planned to give them up for years, and then I quit for good on January 1st 1998. I haven't smoked a cigarette since then. It is the only New Year's resolution I ever kept.

It wasn't easy giving them up, as smoking was still allowed everywhere. Now it is the very opposite. Smoking has become a much harder habit to continue, because you can't smoke indoors anywhere. You must stand in shame outside the pub with your fellow weaklings, and you know what everyone who passes by is thinking.

CHAPTER 23

My Mother – Social Attitudes

My mother was a beautiful fair-haired woman. She was educated at the St Louis Convent School in Rathmines, and left school at around fifteen or sixteen years old. She contributed to the household income by working in Lee's department store in Rathmines. Although an only child, she had many friends and a good social life, mainly with her neighbours, her cousins and the people she worked with. Being big into dancing, she would talk about the big bands of the time, like the Joe Loss Orchestra and Victor Silvester's bands. It seems these and many others would play quite regularly in Dublin. They were the Westlife and Boyzone of the time.

She loved music, although she never played a musical instrument. I remember her singing songs from all the big shows around the house, but I don't remember her ever singing in public. As a child she would have been brought to all the shows in the then thriving theatre scene in Dublin, and would have danced at places like the Metropole Ballroom and Jury's Hotel in Dublin's city centre. I believe that my interest in music came from my mother's influence.

As a young woman she also regularly went to the theatre, and often talked about the great nights she had there. She loved the Theatre Royal in Dublin: a 3,700-seat venue that held 'all-in' Sunday night events, which included a film followed by Tommy Dando and his Lowry organ, which magically emerged from underground onto the stage amid loud applause. This would be followed by a live show featuring artists like Jimmy O'Dea, Harry O'Donovan, Maureen Potter, Danny Cummins, Noel Purcell, Micheál MacLiammóir, Cecil Sheridan, Jack Cruise, Paddy Crosbie and even international stars like Bing Crosby and Bob Hope. You got all this entertainment for something like five shillings (thirty-two cents). Good value or what?

Her other love was the cinema. The Stella Cinema in Rathmines was right on her doorstep, and she loved going there. It was a luxurious place with all the comforts of the 1940s. I remember queuing with my mum in the rain to see *Peter Pan* there. (These days the Stella has been restored to its former glory, and is doing great business again.) When my mother was at home in Dublin she was a voracious reader of novels and newspapers.

My parents seemed to run into difficulties very shortly after my mother moved to Ballyshannon. Granny Buckley considered my father a bit of a playboy. They never got on. As far as my father was concerned, there was just no way of pleasing his mother-in-law. The McGettigan family, behind all their apparent welcome, secretly could have felt that my mother was like some sort of fallen woman because she had followed their son (my father) to London, and lived 'in sin' with him there. That would have been seen as a highly scandalous thing to do in the 1940s. The Catholic Church made all the rules back then, so both sets of parents were outraged, each blaming the other's offspring.

In Ballyshannon, as time went on, my mother's mindset began to change. She went from being a quite industrious mother and housekeeper to a slightly reclusive stranger. She had a lot on her plate now, looking after her invalid mother as well as all her normal household duties.

Even as a kid I noticed how my mother was slowly drifting into a world of her own. When she stopped going to mass on Sundays I was ashamed of her, as I could not understand how she could disobey the rules of the Catholic Church. I had been totally brainwashed by the Church, and believed in all its doctrine. Not going to Sunday mass was considered a mortal sin, so I knew my mum was going straight to hell if she should die. She would spend all day Sunday in bed reading the newspapers, which just made things worse as far as I was concerned. Maybe she began to regret moving to the rural town of Ballyshannon, and leaving behind the more sophisticated lifestyle of Dublin. Whatever the reason, she began to retreat into a kind of twilight zone.

She had a few close friends, and she did join the badminton club, where she fitted in well, and made some friends, but slowly she began to retreat into her own world of books and magazines, which seemed to shield her from the rest of the world. I only gradually became aware that my mother seemed a little down a lot of the time. This would have been described as 'suffering with her nerves' back then.

My little brother, Declan, did not seem to notice any of this. At least I thought he didn't, but now I wonder if it affected him in a way that no one noticed. My dad just thought my mum was lazy. There were frequent rows and arguments about it, and I could not understand it at all. Things got better when she decided she would like to work in the shop. She had a definite skill in dealing with customers. Obviously her years working in Lee's in Dublin had given her aptitude for dealing with people. She liked them and they liked her, but they knew the family secret: apparently it was common knowledge around the town. I only heard the full details of this terrible situation in recent times, and it explains a lot about why my mother never really felt comfortable in Ballyshannon.

Gradually she descended into the depths of self-isolation, while my father's busy schedule continued. I had my own thing going on, so I was busy too. Declan was a busy little man as well, but we did not become aware of that until later. We were now in the mid-1960s, and attitudes were slowly changing. My grandmother had moved into a nursing home and this lifted a huge burden from my mum. The whole social system was changing too, and pubs and bars, which up to then were the domain of men, began to welcome couples. Husbands could bring their wives out, whether they wanted to or not! First it was to hotel bars and then to pubs and bars generally.

I put this down to the arrival of the ballad group scene. The Dubliners were seen regularly on television, broadcasting from places like the Abbey Tavern, with big enticing pints in front of them. As I have described, Bundoran began to open up to the 'singing pubs' phenom-enon. Women and men were out having the craic and enjoying the music and the company. I was making a few pounds entertaining them, so I wasn't complaining. At weekends especially, everyone seemed to take a break from the daily drudgery of life, and just enjoyed themselves.

My mother and father were no different. They were out socialising a lot more frequently. The Allingham Hotel in Bundoran was one of their favourite places to go. Paddy Farrell entertained there. He specialised in the songs of Jim Reeves, and my father became obsessed with him, because he loved Jim Reeves. They became friends. Paddy was a younger man than my dad and liked a drink, but my dad felt he could keep up with him. This involved lots of late-night drinking sessions and doing things like jumping into swimming pools when they were drunk, and other crazy stuff. I was well into my teens at this stage, and all I knew was that my parents *seemed* happier than they had been for a long time.

Having grown up in Ballyshannon, my father was really well known there, particularly in fishing circles. Every Sunday and Wednesday he would go fishing with pals, or sometimes alone, and my mother would be left at home. This didn't seem to bother my father. It was just what men did in those days.

One night I arrived home very late to find my mother unconscious and my father floundering around the flat in a drunken panic. I must make it clear here that my father never ever physically assaulted my mother, but his antics in Bundoran were obviously getting to her. I was the only sober one that night, so I immediately took charge and called Dr Quinn, who arrived quickly on the scene. He couldn't explain why my mother was unconscious, but he felt that she needed to be rushed to hospital immediately. They suspected an overdose, so she had her stomach pumped out. She was found to have taken twenty tablets after being out drinking with my father in Bundoran, on top of God knows how much vodka. Luckily she survived. They kept her in the Rock Hospital for a week for observation.

My father was genuinely frightened by what had happened, and so was I. We were both anxious to try to sort out the problem and get her whatever help she needed. Where had she got all the tablets? Marie Egan's chemist shop was across the street, and dad called over the following morning only to discover that my mother had run up a bill of over a hundred pounds there: a lot of money back then. Marie had been sending out bills each month, which obviously my mum was intercepting. Most were for codeine tablets called Veganin, which came in a red aluminium tube about six inches long. We all now know, or should know, how very addictive codeine can be.

My mother had a wardrobe that she always kept locked. No one ever questioned this until she took ill so suddenly. My father found the key, and to his surprise about a hundred empty Veganin containers tumbled out when he opened the wardrobe. These were available over the counter in those days. The Rock Hospital didn't have a laboratory at the time, so it was only when my dad found the containers that the nature of the tablets became clear.

It turned out that my mother had been using Veganin for her nerves for many years. My father quietly had a word with the three chemists in the town, telling them that she was not to be given Veganin or anything similar in the future. However, my mother would just buy it in chemist shops in other towns when we went shopping there. I had occasion to use Veganin years later to deal with the pain of a really bad dental abscess, and realised then how powerful these tablets were. I could see how easily one could become addicted to them, as they provide almost instant pain relief. They also gave you a sort of 'floaty' feeling that might be dangerously pleasant.

I was quite shocked by the whole incident, and could not understand how my parents had allowed this to happen. The only source of solace I had was my girlfriend, Goretti. She didn't seem as shocked as I thought she would be. She told me that she wasn't surprised by what had happened, and that it was a well-known fact around the town that my father and mother were having difficulties. How could I have missed all this happening right under my nose?

My mother continued to struggle with her addiction to codeine all through her life, and it eventually contributed to her death. If we knew then what we know now, we would have realised that my mother was suffering from depression and possibly menopause. The word 'depression' was never used back then. We didn't understand then that depression is an illness, and nothing to be ashamed of.

These days we don't attach the same kind of stigma to mental ill-health. Back then, staying in bed for days on end would have been regarded as slovenliness, and my mother would have been seen as a 'lazy cow'. Thankfully we now live in a more enlightened age and know that with the right treatment, great improvement can be made in the lives of those suffering from what can be a devastating illness. Sadly, I think the attitude of society back then to what we now call 'depression' served only to make the condition a lot worse for sufferers.

Very shortly after this, my mother decided that the family should get away from all this mad socialising and gossip. She decided to move to London as soon as she could, and my father agreed that he would follow her there once he had sold the shop. The business had not been doing well because customers were not paying their bills when they were due, and this left him with a cash-flow problem. He was finding it difficult to keep up repayments on the loan he had taken out to upgrade the shop. He had no option but to close down. The ironic part of all this was the local priest calling in to ask my dad not to sell the shop to a Protestant, when the priest was my father's biggest debtor, and one of the main reasons the shop was being sold in the first place.

My mother moved to London first and found a job as a chambermaid at the Strand Palace Hotel. She loved it there because of the anonymity London afforded her. By this stage I was working with the ESB in Dublin, so only my brother Declan and my father remained in Bally-shannon. Selling the shop took several months, and my father spent a summer season as a commercial salmon fisherman on the Erne Estuary. Eventually he moved to London to join my mother, with Declan in tow.

My father was a very talented man. The morning he arrived in London he spotted a job advert for a salesman in the window of a London Electricity Board shop. He walked in off the street and walked out with the job. The story of the adventures my mother, my father and Declan had in England is for another day, but eventually my parents returned to live in Ireland in the mid-1980s.

'Adieu to Bellashanny' (words by William Allingham, musical arrangement by Charlie McGettigan)

Adieu to Belashanny! Where I was bred and
*   born;*
Go where I may, I'll think of you, as sure as
*   night and morn;*

The kindly spot, the friendly town, where every one is known,
And not a face in all the place but partly seems my own.
There's not a house or window, there's not a field or hill,
But, east or west, in foreign lands, I recollect them still.
I leave my warm heart with you, though my back I'm forced to turn—
Adieu to Belashanny, and the winding banks of Erne!

No more on pleasant evenings we'll saunter down the Mall,
When the trout is rising to the fly, the salmon to the fall,
The boat comes straining on her net, and heavily she creeps,
Cast off, cast off!—she feels the oars, and to her berth she sweeps;
Now fore and aft keep hauling, and gathering up the clew,
Till a silver wave of salmon rolls in among the crew,
Then they may sit, with pipes a-lit, and many a joke and yarn
Adieu to Belashanny, and the winding banks of Erne!

The thrush will call through Camlin groves the live-long summer day;
The waters run by mossy cliff and banks with wild flowers gay;
The girls will bring their work and sing beneath a twisted thorn,
Or stray with sweethearts down the path among the growing corn;
Along the river-side they go, where I have often been,
O never shall I see again the days that I have seen!
A thousand chances are to one I never may return
Adieu to Belashanny, and the winding banks of Erne!

If ever I'm a money'd man, I mean, please God, to cast
My golden anchor in the place where youthful years were pass'd;
Though heads that now are black and brown must meanwhile gather grey,
New faces rise by every hearth, and old ones drop away
Yet dearer still that Irish hill than all the world beside;
Its home, sweet home, where'er I roam, through lands and waters wide.
And if fortune does allow me, I surely will return
To my native Belashanny, and the winding banks of Erne

CHAPTER 24

New Horizons

After I finished my Leaving Cert in 1968 I spent the rest of the summer playing nightly in the lounge bar of the Cavan House in Bundoran, a popular guesthouse owned by the Brady family, one of whom, Bernard Brady, played on the senior Donegal Gaelic football team. His brother Paddy was running the place then.

Jimmy Gallagher and I played there from 9.00pm till late (very late), seven nights a week. It was the usual lounge bar fare, and Jimmy and I knew what the customers who visited Bundoran every year wanted. We were singing songs like 'The Son of Hickory Holler's Tramp' and 'If I Were a Carpenter'. It was just Jimmy on his old red Egmond bass and me on a usually borrowed guitar.

I owned an Eko electric guitar back then, but it gave me so much trouble that I preferred playing a solid-bodied guitar owned by Ken Page or a Gibson Sunburst owned by a friend of mine, Joe O'Donnell. Jimmy's brother Sean loaned me his Fender Mustang occasionally. These were all really good guitars, and ones I could only dream of owning. I am forever indebted to the people who trusted me with their precious instruments. We put the bass, the lead guitar and the vocals through one solid-state amplifier. That was bonkers even in those days!

Brady's was a favourite place for other musicians to congregate after hours. Hugo Quinn was a trumpet player with the wonderful Clipper Carlton Showband and was on holidays for a few weeks, staying in Cavan House. Each night he would join us for a jam session. His big

Charlie's paternal grandparents – Joe and Nellie McGettigan – 1920's

Charlie's Mum and Dad on their Wedding Day 1948.

Charlie aged about 2 years at home with mum in Ballyshannon.

Photo taken by Dad of Mum and Charlie aged 4 years
on a family trip to Dublin Zoo.

Charlie aged 5 years with Dad who is proudly holding the 33.5 Ib Pike referred to in the book.

1979: Jargon – Winners at Enniskillen Song Contest. From left: Eamonn Daly, Charlie McGettigan and Brendan Emmet. (Fermanagh News)

1940's Aodh Rua GAA Club: Red Jack and his friends heading to Glenties 30 miles on bicycles to play in a match. 4th from right: Red Jack Gallagher. 2nd from right; Jack's brother Bob Gallagher. Centre standing: Charlie's uncle Dan McGettigan.

1962: Thomas Quinn Team won the Bakery Cup. Back row: 2nd from the right, Charlie aged 12 years. (Donegal Democrat)

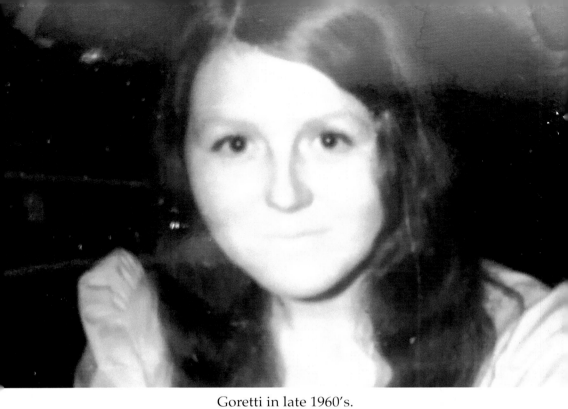

Goretti in late 1960's.

Charlie and Goretti in Astoria Ballroom, Bundoran 1972 / 1973.

Goretti with Yamaha guitar in early 1970's.

1980: Jargon early days at Ballysodare Festival; Back: Gerry Grennan, Front: Brendan Emmet, Charlie McGettigan (Sligo Champion).

Top row left: Charlie's school photo aged 10 years.

Top row right: 1972: Charlie and Goretti's Wedding Day. In the background is Arthur Greene and Carmel Gallagher (Goretti's sister).

Middle row: 1982/1983: Jargon Final Line up – Front: Gerry Grennan, Back: Brendan Emmet, Charlie McGettigan and Liam Gilmartin. (Photo by Lucy Johnson).

Bottom row: 1966: Summer Residency in Palace Bar, Bundoran. From left: Charlie McGettigan, Neil McBride and Jimmy Gallagher. (Flash Photos).

1982: Jargon with friends – Winners at Letterkenny Folk Festival. (Donegal Democrat).

tune was 'Cherry Pink and Apple Blossom White'. A guy who played nightly in the Holyrood Hotel would join us for many a great session as well: a ginger-haired fellow called Paul Brady. Paul was from Strabane, as was Hugo, and there were many marvellous sessions with Paul and Hugo leading the music.

Paul was an electric guitar player in those days, and could really rock it out. I remember hearing him for the first time in St Patrick's Hall, Bundoran, in 1966. We had organised a three-group session with our own group (the Reinbous), the Erratics and Federal Aviation. We were all showing off our guitar licks as we strutted our stuff on stage. I had learned the opening riff of the Stones' '19th Nervous Breakdown' and was feeling very chuffed with myself. Paul Brady came on stage later with his Fender Mustang guitar, and blew us all away. It was a night I'll never forget, and I have been a Paul Brady fan ever since.

'The First Time I Saw Brady' (words and music by Charlie McGettigan)

The first time I saw Brady
It was 1966
I was playing in a three band show
I was trying to show some tricks
He came on like a hurricane
Like a dervish in the night
The first time I saw Brady
Was the night I saw the light

He opened up with Elvis
And then he played some Chuck
I remember some Hank Williams
I was really thunderstruck
His voice was full of anger
His eyes were full of fire
The first time I saw Brady
I couldn't get much higher

He wore a Fender Mustang
Like a rifle in his hand
He was like a kind of gangster
He would challenge any man
We all just dropped our weapons
Our Egmonds and Connoisseurs
The first time I saw Brady
I really knew for sure

We walked home to Ballyshannon
Beneath the Easter stars
We had just received a lesson
In the strings of his guitar
I won't forget that evening
When he left us all behind
The first time I saw Brady
Is ever in my mind

When that 1968 summer season ended, Jimmy and I were kept quite busy playing in different combinations at dances and in pubs. I was working in my dad's shop during the day and playing music in the evenings. I was making about £30 a week, which was a little more than the average weekly wage at the time. Still, I began applying for steady jobs in the civil service, ESB, etc.

University was not an option for me. Education during my child-hood and early teens had meant the daily fear of getting a beating from the De La Salle Brothers and I was glad when that part of my life was over. I know from chatting with lots of other people over the years that there were many more men who felt the same. Securing a steady job was the next best option.

I had also been very heavily influenced by my grandmother. It was when we lived in 'The Wilderness' and my grandmother had come to live with us. She was soon the priority there. She had the best place at the fire in the wintertime, and kept my mother really busy dressing and undressing her, bringing her to and from the toilet, etc. She was in great pain most of the time, which understandably made her quite a cranky person. I could see the strain it was placing on my mother, and indeed on family life.

My grandmother had little regard for my father: whenever I was alone with her, she would run him down. 'Don't ever turn out like your father,' she'd say. At the time I had no idea what she was talking about. I think she was trying to say that I should get a good job, and not be tied to the long hours that my father had in the family business. Whatever it was, it coloured my view of working in the shop. I feel that without her influence I probably would have taken over the family business in due course.

I applied for a clerical officer job with the ESB, and was offered a position in October of that year. In my innocence I had no idea what a clerical officer was. My only reference for the ESB was the big hydro-electric power station in Ballyshannon. The people who worked there were considered a cut above the rest of us, so I was very happy to get any job with the ESB.

My mother came with me to Dublin, to help me get settled in. I was lodged in a boarding house in Herbert Place, where I shared a room with four complete strangers. My memories of that place are not good. It was a bed and breakfast arrangement, and definitely only suitable for a short stay. My job was in the ESB transport depot in South Lotts Road, near Ringsend. I was obliged to wear a shirt, tie and jacket every day, even though we had no contact whatsoever with the public. I soon found one consolation when I made a new friend, Jack Duffy. He was a jazz saxophone player, so we had a lot to talk about, mostly jazz.

Shortly after coming to Dublin, I hooked up with a friend of mine called Michael Travers: the Ballyshannon man who had taught me my first few chords. He lived in an apartment at the end of Leinster Road, and took me out one night to a place called Slattery's of Capel Street. They had a small lounge upstairs where live music was played every night.

Singing and playing that night were a collection of some of the best-known names in the world of folk and traditional music. The session opened with Frank Harte, a great singer, accompanied by Donal Lunny. My only awareness of Donal at the time was that he was a member of a famous vocal group called Emmet Spiceland. He and Frank played an amazing array of mostly Dublin songs, many that I had never heard before.

It got even better when the piper Liam Óg O'Flynn came on stage. I had never heard the uilleann pipes played live before. I had seen Seamus Ennis on television, when I was too young to appreciate what he was doing. Liam explained to the audience the mechanics of the pipes: the bellows, the chanter, the drones and the regulators. When he played in his beautifully disciplined style, it was like a full band playing.

After Liam, there was a singer/guitarist called Al O'Donnell. Al came on stage wearing a brown fringed suede jacket, with a long fringe of hair hanging over his face. He was playing a Martin guitar in a variety of tunings, and singing songs like 'Crooked Jack' and 'Sullivan's John' in his own unique way. It was his guitar playing that fascinated me most of all. It was a big, fat, resonant sound that filled the room. Up to this I had played nothing but electric guitar, but after hearing Al playing I was determined to explore the acoustic guitar.

I was like a kid at Disneyland for the first time, and all these people were a revelation to me. That night certainly had a big impact on my future career in music. From then on I was hooked on folk music and wanted to learn all about it. I was fascinated, and I still appreciate how lucky I was to be brought there that night by my good friend Michael Travers. Sadly, Michael passed away a few years ago at a very young age.

People often ask me how I got involved in the world of entertainment. I guess the answer is a combination of natural instincts, impressions, events I attended like the one at Slattery's, people from showbiz I met along the way (many before they were famous), but most of all it was hard work, with long hours of practice and performance. A little bit of good luck helps as well, but the truth is that I am hoping that by writing this book, I will discover the answer to this question myself.

While I was out enjoying the big city, my mum was working away on the phone at home trying to sort out accommodation for me. My cousin Catherine McMahon had connections with a family called Redmond who had a room to let, and they agreed to take me in. They lived in O'Connell Gardens, near Ringsend. It turned out that George

Redmond was a piano tuner who worked out of McCullough Piggott's music shop in Suffolk Street. He had a regular job tuning the piano at the RDS every Monday night. This was for a series of classical concerts featuring top international pianists. He would tune the piano before the afternoon rehearsal, then again after the rehearsal, and again during the interval. So once again I had made a new friend where there was a music connection. George was always a busy man, and in constant demand.

George's nephew, Willie Grey, and I became friends. Willie loved Irish ballads and every Friday night he and I would attend folk nights at Liberty Hall. Here again I discovered a whole other world of Irish folk music. A regular there was a singer called Bob Lynch who had been an original member of the Dubliners. Bob sang songs like 'Mrs McGrath' and 'My Nut Brown Maiden'. He also specialised in playing the flamenco guitar. The Wolfe Tones played there often, and Luke Kelly would arrive incognito, but he was unmistakable with his huge ginger Afro hair. Another singer, Hedley Kay, played a wonderful version of 'Buddy Can You Spare a Dime'. I loved his guitar style, which I immediately started to emulate. The Liffey Folk were also amazing, and their version of 'The Draft Dodger Rag' by Phil Ochs really hooked me. They would all adjourn to the bar next door after the concerts.

I had been trying for a number of years to learn all these acoustic songs on my old semi-acoustic Eko, but it was not working out well. I had noticed that a member of the Bards was getting a great sound out of a small Yamaha guitar. It looked very like Al O'Donnell's Martin in style. I set my mind on getting one of those. I found out it was a Yamaha FG140. Yamaha guitars were available in a shop called Danfay Instruments in Aungier Street. My dad sent me £29 to buy one, and my door to the acoustic guitar was opened. It helps to have parents who support you when they can see you are genuinely committed. It's like a vote of confidence and can mean a lot to any young kid starting out, no matter what their passion is.

Earlier that year, on a day trip to Dublin to visit Walton's Music Shop, I ran into Paul Brady again. He told me he had joined the Johnstons ballad group. I was horrified because Paul was always a 'rock 'n' roller' to me, playing his electric guitar. I was proved wrong when

I went to see the Johnstons around Christmas time in Liberty Hall. The line-up was the two Johnston girls, Lucy and Adrienne, Paul and Mick Maloney. They were fantastic! They sang really tight harmonies. Paul and Mick played the 'Ace and Deuce of Piping', a piping tune, on their guitars. They sang songs like 'Bitter Green', written by Gordon Lightfoot, famous for his big hit 'Early Morning Rain', and lesser-known songs like 'Julia', written by Jon Ledingham. They had a unique vocal sound.

My journey through the Dublin music scene was an inspiration. I spent most of my time getting as close as I could to the stage, so that I could see what the musicians were playing. I was desperate to get to practise the guitar licks I had picked up.

I saw an advert in the *Evening Press* looking for a singer/guitarist, so I applied. I got the job with the Broadsiders Ballad Group. My first gig with them was in the Embankment in Tallaght. I came on stage, tripped over a microphone cable and sent the microphone and stand hurtling onto a table of drinks belonging to the people sitting in the front row. I think they thought I was Frank Spencer of *Some Mothers Do 'Ave 'Em* fame. I wouldn't blame them if they did: I felt like Frank Spencer! My confidence was completely shattered, and my music career in Dublin virtually ended that night.

When I went to Dublin in 1968 to get a 'proper job', I really missed Goretti. She really missed me too, so in early 1969 she found a clerical officer job in the Department of Labour in Mespil Road. Shortly after, she went to work as a clerical officer with the Eastern Health Board. In those days there was no question of living together before marriage, so we tended to find accommodation close to one another in places like Sandymount, and eventually in Ranelagh, where she had a bedsitter in Mountain View Road. At the time I was living in a flat with three fellows from Portarlington. I called them the Offaly Gang.

I played just one more gig during the next six years of self-imposed exile from the music scene in Dublin: the 'Folk, Blues and Beyond' gig in Slattery's of Capel Street, with a friend, John Rockett. I stayed very much in the background, but I could feel my confidence slowly returning after every song, from the genuine warmth of the applause from the audience. You know what they say: 'If you fall off your horse, get straight back on again.' I can add to that 'Don't wait six years!'

Goretti was very tolerant as I dragged her to concerts by people like Rory Gallagher, Pentangle and many more during the six years we spent in Dublin, and we made some great memories together there.

CHAPTER 25

England and the Offaly Gang

Things in Dublin got worse. It wasn't only my music career that was on the slide; my trade union, the ESB Officers' Association, called a strike. I had been moved by this stage to Lower Erne Street, just off Pearse Street, to work in the ESB central stores. We knew that we were going to be on strike for a while, so six colleagues and I took the boat to Britain. The plan was to get work there for the duration of the strike.

It was my first trip out of Ireland, so in a way it was also an adventure. When we got to Euston Station, I remember being fascinated by all the black people working there. I was amused by seeing my first London 'bobby', complete with the classic helmet. I remember going on the huge escalator and looking at all the posters on the wall.

When we reached the top of the escalator, one of our group, a lad called Eugene McMahon, said 'Hey fellows, let's all pool together and buy *Playboy*.' Everyone laughed … but they all chipped in. Eugene was the 'character' in the group and always kept us amused.

We went to a Wimpy Bar for breakfast. Eugene had a conversation with the waitress that went something like this:

Eugene (in his best Clare accent): 'I'll have a hengburger and a glesh of milk.'

Waitress (in her cockney accent): 'You wah?'

Eugene: 'I'll have a hengburger and a glesh of milk.'

Waitress: 'You wah?'

Eugene: 'What kind of a kip is this?'

Waitress: 'Oh! You wanna kip? There's a B&B just up the road.'

I could see that Eugene was getting annoyed, so I asked the waitress to get him a hamburger and a glass of milk, and then everyone else gave their order.

The next day we quickly obtained work with a contract labour company called Welltrade: one of our colleagues had a contact there. The pay was three times what we were earning in Ireland. We were contracted out to various companies as labourers. One of the companies, Marconi, was delivering a radar system to the Iranian air force, and we were there to clean up all the equipment for an Iranian, 'Captain Zari', to inspect. He was so impressed with our work that he held an end-of-contract party. I got absolutely plastered on about ten Bacardi and Cokes, and had to be carried back to the B&B.

This was my very first experience of alcohol.

A guy called Patsy O'Connor and I left England sooner than the rest, because we were badly missing our girlfriends. We arrived back in Ireland just before Christmas, and found seasonal work at the Post Office sorting office in Sherriff Street. Patsy was always talking about his home place in Co. Cavan, a town called Bailieboro (also spelt 'Bailieborough'). Little did I know that in later years I would write a song called 'Bailieboro and Me', based on his reminiscences.

The strike ended shortly after Christmas and we returned to our jobs with the ESB in Dublin. My gross weekly pay was £11 but after deductions I ended up with £8, out of which I had to pay £4 for my accommodation. That left me with £4, on which I seemed to manage quite well. In England I had been getting 14 shillings an hour, which was a huge amount comparatively. I have to say the work was much harder over there, but for every 40 hours I worked I was getting £28.

I had got to know a really nice guy called Kevin St John while working in the ESB central stores. Kevin was an experienced drinker and took me under his wing as we drank our way through local pubs Larry Murphy's and McCauley's. We were working overtime for about six months after the strike to clear the backlog that had developed. We had lots of money and could afford to indulge ourselves. Kevin was from Portarlington; eventually I moved into a flat in Ranelagh with him and two of his friends, Dermie Egan and Murt Greene, also from Portarlington. This combination was a dangerous force when we hit the pubs of Ranelagh, and all I will say is that a lot of drink was taken and a lot of fun was had in the four years I spent living with the Offaly Gang.

One time that stood out was the Sunday in 1972 when Offaly won the All-Ireland Gaelic football title. I had been out with Goretti some-where, and when I arrived at the foot of Mornington Road, where the Offaly Gang and I were living at the time, I could hear loud singing, roaring and shouting, which got louder and louder as I approached our flat. When I reached the flat, the noise was so bad that I thought half of Offaly must be in there. When I entered, I saw Kevin, Murt and Dermie singing their hearts out and making the noise of fifty people.

We had some strange times in that flat. Hygiene was not a priority, and many days' dishes would regularly pile up in the sink. Dermie worked in one of the Quinnsworth supermarkets and was on his feet all day. The first thing he did when he got home was to fill a large basin with hot water and add some Radox; he would soak his tired feet for an hour or so. Often Kevin would arrive footsore from the walk home, and place his feet in the basin at the same time. I often came home and the two boys would have fallen fast asleep, both with their feet in the basin. I wish I had a mobile phone then, because it would have made a very funny photo.

At one point I could see Kevin scratching his feet a lot. 'Do you feel itchy?' he asked us all. Right enough, we did. We were all scratching ourselves to some degree. This went on for several weeks until I noticed that Kevin had literally scratched all the skin off his ankle. He went to the doctor, and was told that he had scabies. None of us knew what scabies was, but it didn't sound good. It seems that these little creatures get under your skin and plant their eggs there, and right enough we could see the little bumps not only on Kevin's skin but on ours as well.

The doctor had told Kevin that we would have to strip all the bedclothes off our beds, and take the lot, with our own clothes, to the launderette. We would also have to paint our entire bodies with soft pastry brushes smothered in a substance called Scabiol. We were horri-fied, as you can imagine, but followed the procedure to the letter. We had to paint each other's backs, which was not the most pleasant thing for us guys to be doing. The Scabiol smelled really horrible, and when we landed at the launderette the people there moved away from us due to the stench.

It wasn't long before our skin cleared up, and we never got scabies again, thankfully!

CHAPTER 26

Get Me to the Church on Time

Our social life in Dublin was great. We loved going out for the evening and visiting the pubs around Ranelagh. If the craic there was good, we could end up staying in one pub all night. It was only when you got up to go to the loo or the bar that you realised you might be getting a bit … unsteady. Still, you'd carry on and order 'just one more'.

Goretti and I also went to lots of concerts together: she was just as interested in the music scene as I was. Watching and listening to Rory Gallagher whenever he played the National Stadium was always a night to remember. Other favourites were the great music sessions at Liberty Hall. There was plenty of choice around Dublin, and we had the privilege of attending Thin Lizzy's very first gig, at the Star Club in South Anne Street. There were about forty people there, and we had no idea how significant Phil Lynott would become. We both worked hard during the day, and enjoyed ourselves as much as we could every evening. Our life together was perfect! In fact, it was so good that we decided to make it permanent.

I had got to know Goretti's parents very well by now, and I always enjoyed their company. Red Jack and Maria Gallagher were two wonderful people who had become a big part of my life. Maria – pronounced 'Mariah', as in the song 'They Call the Wind Mariah' – was born Maria McGuiney and raised in Donegal Town, in a small house opposite the Catholic Church. She had a sister named Agatha, and although the house was small they also kept lodgers. Such was life back then.

As they got older, Maria and Agatha loved dancing; being a good dancer was an important part of life in those days for a girl or a guy. They loved the quickstep, the foxtrots (slow and fast) and the waltzes (old-time and slow), and were equally comfortable with the Latin American dances like the tango, cha-cha-cha and paso doble. All men in their eyes were judged not on their looks or personalities, but on how good they were on the dance floor. Ballroom dancing was huge in all the big towns.

Red Jack Gallagher couldn't dance at all, and would be described as a 'hay foot, straw foot' kind of guy. Maria was, as people would say in those days, a stunner. She had beautiful red hair, was always immaculately dressed and loved clothes. It was ironic that she married a guy who couldn't dance at all, and even more so that he chose a girl from Donegal Town: he was a senior footballer from Ballyshannon, Donegal Town's bitter enemies on the field. But love has no such red lines.

Red Jack Gallagher was a football legend. Everybody in GAA circles had a story about him. He and his brother Bob played for the local Aodh Rua club team and for the Donegal senior county team. I enjoyed listening to Jack and Bob talk about their football days.

Someone in the Aodh Rua club had the foresight to make a video of the two men in their later years, and it's a joy to watch. They talk of the Ulster championship games and the journeys to and from matches. Jack was a man who called a spade a spade, as they say, and he was uncompromising in his criticism or praise of players, and the state of the modern game, as he saw it. In one section of the video the chat comes around to the subject of the new club dressing rooms, which had just been built.

'Do you know what they have up in the new dressing rooms?' asks Bob.

'What?' says Jack.

'Hairdryers!' exclaims Bob.

Jack is incredulous. When he was playing football there wasn't even a dressing room, and the idea of hairdryers was just bonkers.

I have a photo, which I treasure, of the Ballyshannon team, including Jack and Bob, heading off on bicycles to play a game in Glenties, which is over thirty miles from Ballyshannon. They would cycle to Glenties, play the game and cycle back. Bob said that the journey back always took longer, because they would have had a few drinks after the game and then wobbled their way home on their bikes.

It was the practice at the time that on polling day the parties would send cars out to known supporters to bring them to the polling stations. Imagine how embarrassing it was for poor Jack when a Fine Gael car arrived at their house to collect Maria, a staunch Fine Gael supporter all her life.

Regardless of the politics, Jack and Maria remained happily married for life. When you think about it, they cancelled out each other's votes when it came to an election. After I married their daughter Goretti, Jack and Maria became a permanent part of my life and one set of grandparents to my children.

Goretti and I were married in Ballyshannon in 1972. We had eighty-four guests at the wedding; my best man was my old school friend Arthur Greene. The atmosphere was full of warmth and genuine happiness for us. You could feel it! Everyone seemed to be enjoying themselves. I was on cloud nine, and so proud of my new wife, Goretti McGettigan.

There is a song ('Marie's Wedding') with the line 'going to a wedding is the making of another'. Remember I told you that I shared a flat in Dublin with the Offaly Gang? One of those guys, Dermie, met Goretti's sister Carmel at our wedding, and they went on to get married, so maybe there is something in that song.

The custom at the time was for the bride and groom to leave the hotel around 7pm to set off on their honeymoon. It felt strange as we drove away: like we were being thrown out of our own wedding! We stayed in the Great Southern Hotel in Sligo that first night, and got the morning train to Dublin the next day. On arriving in Dublin we went straight to the airport and got our flight to Amsterdam. I think this was the first time either of us was ever on an aeroplane.

We stayed at the Museum Hotel in Amsterdam, right beside the Rijksmuseum. I remember there were two single beds in the hotel room which we had to push together to make a double bed. The beds were on castors. In the morning it was like the room was haunted, because the beds would be far apart again! It was the Museum Hotel, after all … but eventually we figured it out. The floor was so shiny and well polished that, little by little, as you slept and moved around in your bed, it would move naturally.

During the days we explored the magic of the city of Amsterdam. There was a wide variety of restaurants, and some really interesting places to visit. We did the usual touristy things and really enjoyed it all.

I don't think it would have mattered where we went, because we were in love, and everything else for now was unimportant. I believe making good memories in life is so important, and I still try to make new ones every day.

'That's How It Is' (words and music by Charlie McGettigan)

You keep changing like the weather
One day good the next day better
I never know how you're gonna be
That's how it is with you and me

One day hot the next day colder
I keep lookin' over my shoulder
Sometimes you're really hard to see
That's how it is with you and me

That's how it is with you and me
We live our lives imperfectly
And though I love you totally
That's how it is with you and me

Every day a different colour
No one day like the other
A different song in a different key
That's how it is with you and me

CHAPTER 27

Where's Arigna?

After our honeymoon in Amsterdam, we arrived back to reality in Dublin. We were broke, and our immediate problem was wondering where we would get the rent for the flat we had rented at 24 Aungier Street. It had all been spend, spend, spend during the weeks beforehand, and now it was time to pay the piper. The bill for the wedding breakfast had been £110, which included a round of drinks for all the guests. The music group cost £15, which, even by the standards of the day, was very cheap (nowadays, a wedding group could cost as much as €5,000). But we needn't have worried. It turned out that £18 (the equivalent of two weeks' wages) that I had won in a work draw was waiting for me.

All through our marriage it has been like that. Whenever we wondered where the next week's food or whatever would come from, something always turned up.

Our flat was a glorified bedsitter at the top of a three-storey building, reached by negotiating eighty-four stairs. When you have to climb stairs like that every day, you count them at some point to pass the time!

It was an absolute death trap. There was no fire escape, and the stairs were entirely made out of highly flammable wood. The only good thing about it was that it was ours for now. We continued our friendship with the Offaly Gang and others from our time in Ranelagh. On Friday nights we would all meet up at the Wexford Inn for a drink and a bit of craic. Our drinking sessions in those days involved creating a pool at the start, rather than the round-by-round system. We each put in £2, and by the end of the evening we were all totally sozzled.

When Dermie, who was still working for Quinnsworth, was moved to its Drumcondra store, our Friday night session moved to the Cat and Cage in Drumcondra. This meant that the walk home afterwards was four miles to Aungier Street, and a little longer to Ranelagh for the others. Walking across Dublin city centre at midnight never worried us in those days (it's a much more dangerous place these days).

After a few months in a downstairs flat in Drumcondra, a new journey began for Goretti and me. I worked in the ESB central stores in Dublin for about five years. One day in 1973, on the noticeboard there I spotted an advertisement for a clerical officer in the Arigna ESB generating station. The bit that attracted me was 'Staff house will be provided.' I had no idea where the Arigna station was, but I immediately put in my application for the job. After extensive research I discovered that it was in Co. Roscommon, and generated electricity by burning coal from the nearby Arigna mines. The 'staff house' was in Drumshanbo, Co. Leitrim, about five miles from the station.

At my interview in Dublin, J. Kevin Kelly, the regional accountant, asked me what I thought the biggest item stored in the Arigna generating station would be. I immediately said the bleeding obvious: 'Coal.' I don't think it was the answer he was expecting, but as he scratched his head he said 'I suppose you're right!', adding, 'I meant in the store rooms of Arigna.' We talked about my experience in the ESB central stores for a while, and eventually he offered me the job. I am convinced to this day that my obvious but unexpected answer to his first question changed the course of my life.

A short time later I made my first visit to Arigna to see where I would be living and working. Angus Dunne, the Arigna station manager at the time, met Goretti and me at the train station in Carrick-on-Shannon. I think poor Angus was a bit taken aback when he saw this long-haired, bearded hippy getting off the train, but he didn't say anything. He treated us to lunch in Donnelly's Restaurant on the High Street in Drumshanbo. I thought the High Street was well named: it is about six feet higher than Main Street, and runs parallel to it.

It was November, and the weather was particularly bleak. After lunch Angus brought us to Grattan Avenue in Drumshanbo and showed us our future home. We were delighted with the house, which was in an eight-house estate owned by the ESB, on the outskirts of the town. Angus assured us that he would have the whole house painted before we moved in.

After that he brought us to see the Arigna generating station itself. My first impression was the predominant black colour. The station itself was a noisy place, covered in ashy soot. It had a huge chimney that belched out large volumes of smoke and ash into the surrounding countryside. Almost every member of staff I met there was covered in either soot or coal dust, but I was impressed with their friendly demeanour. The office I would work in was a bungalow structure away from the main station building. It overlooked the beautiful expanse of water that is Lough Allen. The weather was dull and wet that day, and Lough Allen wasn't looking its best, with large waves swelling up, fuelled by the howling winds.

I would be working with clerical officer Peggy Barry, whom I instantly liked when I met her that day. She was a dark, petite woman with a friendly smile, and she treated Goretti and me to coffee and biscuits. I felt at home straight away.

After a few hours in the generating station we headed in Angus's car to Carrick-on-Shannon, where we would get the train back to Dublin. On our way we saw, coming down a road at right angles to the main road, a large truck carrying about twenty miners, all covered in coal dust, with teeth that shone brightly in the headlights of Angus's car. These were the first miners I ever saw, and it was a strange sight.

A few years later I was brought down the actual mines to see them at work. It was a frightening experience for a guy like me, and you could not help but admire the men who worked in these dreadful conditions. Today the mine is closed, but you can take the same tour I was on, any day, by booking a visit to the Arigna Mining Experience. I highly recommend it because it is so interesting, and after your visit you will never complain about your working conditions again.

We reached Carrick just in time to catch the evening train to Dublin, and that ended my first visit to Arigna.

'The Life of a Miner' (words and music by Charlie McGettigan)

I think of the life of a miner
Who must work all his day underground
Where his lamplight is all that will shine there
And it's dark and it's damp all around
It is two or three miles to the coal face
And the tunnel is jagged and low
But he can't find work on the surface
So it's down in the mines he must go

Oh I know he's proud to be a miner
And he's proud of the face
But it takes a brave man to go down there
Down to that dark dank place

He will tell you he makes better wages
Which is more than most people can say
But conditions are like the dark ages
With his life and his limbs he will pay

And he prays that his son and his daughter
Will grow up in a world that's more kind
And he hopes they will find something better
Than a sentence of life down the mines

A few weeks later, Goretti and I arrived in Drumshanbo to set up house in No. 6, Grattan Avenue. Our belongings were so meagre that I can actually tell you what they were. We had a double bed, a table and four chairs, a wardrobe and two easy chairs. That was it! We had been living in furnished rented accommodation in Dublin, and hadn't accumulated much. When the furniture van left, we set about organising what little we had. Thankfully a cooker and fridge were provided, so at least we wouldn't starve.

After about an hour there was a knock on our door. It was Pat Maleady, the mechanical supervisor in the Arigna station. He called just to welcome us, and to say that there was going to be a bit of a session later in one of the pubs down the town, to celebrate the start of the shooting season. We would be welcome to join his wife and himself there if we felt up to it. We declined the invitation, as we were really shattered after our journey. Pat and his wife, Anne, would become great friends of ours in the following years.

I had a few days off before I started work, which we spent exploring our new home town. We quickly got to know all the neighbours. Paddy Smullen and his wife, Teresa, lived across the road with their large family. Paddy was music mad and Teresa was an excellent button accordion player. We were asked over for tea one day, and I was introduced to the legendary Packie Duignan, a flute player from Goberudda at the top of Arigna Mountain. Yes, Goberudda: what a great name!

I dropped a hint that I played the guitar sometimes, and soon I was in the middle of a music session with Packie and Teresa. 'I've landed on my feet here,' I thought. A few years later I wrote this song about Packie Duignan, who would play his flute at the drop of a hat.

'Why Wouldn't I?' (words and music by Charlie McGettigan)

Play for you, why wouldn't I?
Sure I'd play all night and day
And tomorrow do the same again
It would cause me no great pain
Hand me down me three-piece wallet
Beat your drum along in time
Play for you, why wouldn't I?
Give me one good reason why

I've played for them in Dublin Town,
In old Baggot Street so gay
They could fill a pint of porter
there that'd drive your mind astray
I played 'The Mouse' in that public house,
And 'The Bucks of Oranmore'
And women and men said to hear it again

They would stand to their knees in snow

The other day I played for them
In the county of Westmeath
I landed in Kilbeggan town
Where me friends invited me
In Edgesworthstown and Mullingar
I stopped to take me ease
And landed in a blaze of green
and met good company

There's famous men of music
Who have come to visit me
They're recording me for posterity
At least that's what they tell me
It seems I'm part of a dying art
Makin' history
But sure art apart I have the heart
To play for the likes of ye

A member of the ESB regional headquarters was sent to show me the ropes when I started my new job as administrative officer. I was in charge of purchasing and storing all the equipment for the station and monitoring the station budget, staff payroll, etc. The man they sent down was a very affable fellow, and we shared a few pints in the evenings in the local pubs. I was highly impressed with the easy-going nature of the job, and the slower pace of life here. Peggy did all the typing and operated the telephone exchange in the station. This was in complete contrast to my working conditions in Dublin: they were very hierarchical and a strict watch was kept on my every move. At least that's the way it felt in Dublin.

Friday was payday and I was told that I would have to go to the bank in Drumshanbo to collect the cash to pay the staff. My 'tutor' would accompany me. I was thinking 'Why do we both need to go?' I guessed I must be 'riding shotgun', like I had seen in Western movies. Just before we left, Peggy was asked to put a telephone call through to Terry McGowan's pub in Drumshanbo. 'Just ask Terry to put on two pints and say that we will be there in fifteen minutes,' said my colleague. This was at eleven o'clock in the morning!

Fifteen minutes later we were sitting on two high barstools with two beautiful pints in front of us. Terry's pints were legendary and he always took about ten minutes to pour them, hence the pre-order. I couldn't enjoy the pint because I was on tenterhooks all the time. I feared that some senior ESB official would arrive and catch us drinking pints at 11am on company time. We could get fired! Anyway, we collected the cash for the wages and everyone got paid correctly, despite our sojourn in Terry's pub.

Goretti, being a much better 'people person' than me, very quickly picked up on the social scene. It wasn't difficult for her, as she was out around the town all day. All the men living in the other houses in Grattan Avenue worked in the ESB power station, which meant that all the wives in the estate got to know each other naturally. Eileen McCabe was the wife of the station chemist, Ultan, and one of her first social contacts. Soon Goretti knew all the ESB neighbours in Grattan Avenue, as well as the jobs their husbands did.

Goretti also got to know a young woman (we were all young in those days) called Mary Giblin, who worked in Campbell's grocery and hardware shop. She became affectionately known as 'Gibby' and is one of our closest friends to this very day, as is her husband, Padraig McMorrow. Through Gibby she got to know Phil McGowan, who lived on the same street as her. Gibby was a native of Drumshanbo and knew the seed, breed and generation of almost everyone in the town. She and Phil took Goretti under their wing.

Gibby lived with her mother, Kathleen (known to all as Cissy), her sister Nuala and her father, Tom. Their house, right across the road from Campbell's shop, became an almost daily haunt for Goretti. Tom Giblin worked in the Arigna mines, but sadly he lost his life in a mining accident shortly after we came to live in Drumshanbo. By all accounts he was a great character, who also worked as a car-park attendant in the local Mayflower Ballroom. He had amassed a great collection of photographs, mostly of the showbands that played there. Tom's death was a sad blow for Gibby, her sister, Nuala, and Cissy, but they remained stoic throughout the funeral and mourning period.

Gibby, Phil and Goretti became very close friends. When I'd come home from work, Goretti would regale me with stories and craic she had in Cissy's house that day. Cissy's was a sort of open house where there was rarely a moment when someone wasn't in for a chat and a cup of tea. For such a small town, the amount of stuff they talked about was just incredible. It was a hot bed of stories, mainly about who was up to what in the town.

Even today, Goretti can go down the town for an hour and then spend two hours telling me all about it later: who she met and what the latest news or craic was.

CHAPTER 28

Leitrim Life and Jargon

I joined the Allen Gaels volleyball club in Drumshanbo in late 1973. They had a volleyball session every Monday night in a small indoor venue in the town. I was absolutely useless at volleyball, but I went along anyway hoping to make some new friends. In fact, I was no good at any sport. As my father-in-law, Red Jack, used to say, 'He couldn't kick snow off a rope.'

That first night I spotted a guy who had long hair and a beard, just like me. I thought he looked like a kindred spirit, so I went over to chat with him. I had seen him before in Ballinaglera Hall, at a concert where he sang 'Jake the Peg with His Extra Leg'. I thought at the time it was very brave of him to have a go at a comedy song, but he carried it off really well.

We got talking and quickly realised that we had a lot in common. His name was Eamonn Daly. We had grown up listening to the same radio programmes, and we both liked everything from the Goons to Maureen Potter. I told Eamonn how the night I had first seen him in Ballinaglera had almost ended in tragedy for me.

After the concert, some of us had adjourned to Mulvey's pub nearby for a few drinks. The few turned into a lot. I got quite drunk and eventually needed to pee. I was directed to the outside toilet by the barman. In those days, the toilet facilities in country pubs were usually outside.

It was dark when I went out, and almost immediately I walked straight into a low corrugated iron roof, giving my head a terrific bang.

I was stunned for a moment, but I think being drunk somehow dulled the pain, so I just completed my ablutions and returned to the bar. It wasn't until the next morning – when Goretti, seeing my head, screamed 'What happened to you last night?' – that I remembered banging my head on something, but I couldn't say what at the time. I had a lump about half an inch high on my forehead, and as the day went on I began to remember the incident on the way to the loo. So for me that gave a whole new meaning to the phrase 'I hit the roof'!

As we laughed and chatted, Eamonn asked me if I was going to compete in the 1974 GAA Scór competition, which was coming up. I didn't know what it was, so he told me that it was a talent competition run by the GAA to keep members occupied during the winter months. Each club in the county would submit participants for a wide range of cultural competitions: ballad groups, quiz teams, novelty acts, recitations, etc.

Tony McGowan was the chief bottle washer in the Allen Gaels GAA club, and a member of the Leitrim GAA County Board. He was the most optimistic man I ever met. Tony had decided that I should represent the club in two competitions: 'solo ballad' and 'ballad group'. He told me that Eamonn Daly would join himself and me for the ballad group section (Tony was a really fine piano accordion player).

I was happy with that, but I had heard Peggy Barry singing around the ESB office, so I proposed that she could join us, along with Anne Maleady, who was also a fine singer. It was all agreed. Now I was part of a ballad group. That's how things happen!

I took it all very seriously, as usual, and began rehearsals in my house almost immediately. I decided on a couple of songs for us to sing. I was determined that we would have lots of harmonies. For starters I picked 'Only Our Rivers Run Free', a song written by Mickey McConnell. It was very popular at the time, sung by Christy Moore and Planxty. I also chose 'Tunnel Tigers', a Ewan MacColl song I had heard the Johnstons singing.

I had a 'no nonsense' approach to rehearsals, and taught Eamonn and the girls their harmony parts. However, Tony was a different matter. He was an extremely busy man, and made it to only one rehearsal. He didn't even have an accordion of his own at the time. Tony was very politely sacked: nothing personal, but you were either fully in or fully out. Just in case you might think that that was the end of Tony and me, he became one of my closest friends in later years. We even played together numerous times at various gigs.

After taking part in a few heats of the Scór competition, we won the Leitrim ballad group final. That gave us the chance to represent Leitrim in the Connacht finals in Castlebar. Reaching the final of anything at this stage in my life constituted the pinnacle of my success to date. I was buzzing with delight.

The final in the Traveller's Friend Hotel (now the Royal Theatre) was a huge event, and a very nail-biting affair. Anne Maleady was very close to the end of her pregnancy, which added to the tension. A real star could have truly been born that night! Thankfully, Anne came through the contest with flying colours, but we were pipped at the post by a Sligo ballad group. Nonetheless, I was very happy with our performance and delighted to have had the chance to compete at this level.

I must add that I didn't get past the first round in the solo ballad competition, because I sang a song called 'Old Maid in a Garret'. It was a Scottish song, and therefore broke the rule that all songs had to be Irish in origin. I brushed off my mistake and decided to concentrate hard on the ballad group section.

Our group continued for a few months, but the two girls gradually drifted from the ranks. I was a tough taskmaster, demanding a lot of rehearsal etc., so I didn't blame them. Eamonn and I continued to sing together at various events, purely for the fun of it. We just loved singing together. We entered a new RTÉ Radio talent show called *Top Talent*, and qualified to take part in a heat in my old stomping ground of Bally-shannon. It was held in the Imperial Hotel (Dorrian's) in May 1974. This was our first radio appearance, so as you can imagine we were full of fear and trepidation.

At this stage we had put a name on our little duo: Jargon, a name I had already used for a duo I was part of in Dublin with John Rockett. I always liked the name, and still do. We sang a Cat Stevens song called 'Sad Lisa', and I thought we did a great job with it. Larry Gogan was the compère. It was the first time I met Larry: he was a huge star on radio and television at the time, and when you met him in person he was no different from how he was on the airwaves. He was a lovely, friendly man and a joy to be with, and he was quick to put everyone at ease.

All the contestants, production crew and audience got together after the show for sandwiches and drinks. Larry spent his time chatting and mingling with everyone. Everything was going great until Goretti's father, Red Jack, arrived. He had a few drinks on board, and made straight for Larry Gogan.

'Hello, Gay,' says Jack to Larry. (Gay Byrne was the biggest TV star in the country at the time.)

'I'm not Gay,' says Larry.

'Yes you are,' says Jack. Nothing would convince Jack that he wasn't talking to Gay Byrne.

For the rest of the evening, every time Jack met Larry he would say something like 'Listen, Gay' and Larry would shout back 'I'M NOT GAY!' It was a bit like Trigger in *Only Fools and Horses* calling Rodney 'Dave' all the time. I still laugh when I think of Larry shouting 'I'M NOT GAY!' It would be even funnier today!

The *Top Talent* show was broadcast a few weeks later. I thought we did well, but Rosaleen Linehan, one of the judges, commented about our song: 'I really like the boys, but all I can say about the girl in that song is … it's a good kick in the arse she needs.' She might have been right, but after her comment I knew we had no hope of winning.

Still, we were satisfied to have got through our first ever broadcast on national radio in a reasonable fashion. After that, all we wanted was to get better and better. At this stage Eamonn and I were in big demand to play at concerts and events in the Drumshanbo area. We decided we'd try our music on the pub and cabaret circuit. To do this we would need some PA equipment, so we purchased our first system, consisting of a Marmac 60 watt amp, two Marmac speakers, three Shure microphones and two microphone stands. The whole lot cost us £384, which was a huge outlay at the time. Luckily, Noel Henry, the manager in the Northern Bank, had heard us playing and was so impressed that he loaned us the money without hesitation. Full of confidence and expensive gear, the new Jargon was now off and running.

We began to get bookings in bars and lounges within a forty-mile radius of Drumshanbo. In the 1970s there was a huge pub scene in

Ireland. The *Leitrim Observer* advertised the pub venues in the area every week, so it was easy for us to research where we might play. Two full broadsheet pages were devoted to small ads for pub and cabaret venues alone, and another two to the ballroom circuit.

There was a lot of live entertainment in those days. I don't know where people found the money to go to all these venues, but somehow they did. The summer marquee scene alone had people out dancing five or six nights a week. Of course in those days a pint of Guinness cost one shilling and eight pence. You could get nicely sozzled for less than a pound (€1.27).

Jargon, I have to say, weren't everyone's cup of tea. We died on stage quite often in those early days. Our programme was all acoustic music, and we only had one acoustic guitar and two harmonious voices. We played the songs of Simon and Garfunkel, the Beatles, James Taylor, Planxty, etc. Back then the most popular music in pubs was country and western. We learned quite quickly that we should be more selective about the venues we chose to play in. In certain venues we were exactly what people wanted. Paddy Matthews, who ran a bar in Carrick-on-Shannon called the Silver Swan, took a chance and gave us a booking. After that he filled our diaries: sometimes we played there four nights a week.

Other venues that suited us were The Parting Glass in Mohill and The Bamboo in Manorhamilton. Noel Henry, our favourite bank manager, recommended us to the owners of a venue in Lisnacusha in Co. Longford called Rakish Paddy's. We didn't know at the time, but this was to become the most important venue we played in. We got to play support to a lot of the biggest artists in the country there. Christy Moore was a regular, as were De Dannan, Paddy Reilly and the Bothy Band. Other national icons such as Paul Brady, Donal Lunny and Andy Irvine played there, as well as international artists like Julie Felix and Pierre Bensusan. I remember Christy Moore arriving at Rakish Paddy's in his Renault 4 van and erecting his own PA system. That's how it was back then.

The venue was run by the Farrell brothers, Luke and Peter. Luke was the music lover and Peter was the businessman. One afternoon an elderly lady called at the pub and introduced herself, then asked for a booking. Peter didn't recognise her, and asked how much she would need. 'A hundred pounds, my good man,' she said. Peter laughed and said he wouldn't be interested at that price. I suppose £100 would have been the equivalent of €1000 nowadays. 'Right,' says the woman, 'I'll tell you what I'll do. I'll take whatever is taken at the door: that way you won't have to be worried about the cost.' Peter agreed to the arrangement and included the woman in his advertising for a Wednesday night.

The night came, and Peter couldn't believe what happened. The venue was packed to capacity and the door takings amounted to a massive £250. The woman was Margaret Barry, the great ballad singer. Everyone knew her except Peter. We were the support act and it was a most enjoyable evening of music and song as Margaret and her sidekick, fiddler Phyllis Ní Catháin O'Malley, regaled us with their stories and songs. Peter had a quite serious expression at the best of times, but on this occasion it was positively dour. Yes, he was making money on the drink, but he could have been making a lot more.

The next time I saw Margaret Barry was many years later when she played to a packed house at the Ulster Hall in Belfast. It was then she told me about her deal with Peter that night.

The pub scene back in the 1970s was quite varied. There were very few places where people actually listened, so we became a kind of background music. It was very disheartening for musicians who wanted people to listen to their music. It was also a period of great strife in Northern Ireland, and we were constantly asked to sing rebel songs, which we always politely refused to sing. Those kinds of songs just weren't our thing. Some publicans who booked us never booked us again because of it. One publican told us that we were the worst group she ever heard.

In some pubs there was a regular Sunday session from 12 noon until 2pm. At one such session, Eamonn was standing at the bar behind two guys chatting.

'Who's on in Jackie Doherty's tonight?' One guy asked.

'Them Jargon bucks,' the other answered.

'Well, I wouldn't go from here to the counter to hear them fellas,' was the reply. 'Never listen in to other people's conversations' was the lesson Eamonn learned. Today, I think the equivalent would be 'Never look at the social media comments made about you.'

I often wonder what the criteria is that make some music acceptable to some people and yet unacceptable to others. I would say that most of the time our music did not exactly appeal to the masses, no matter what way we presented it. When Eamonn and I met we had some kind of natural love for the same kind of music. We had both grown up in small towns during the 1960s, and our tastes in music were quite similar.

However, there was one thing we could never agree on, and that was who was the better group, the Stones or the Beatles. I was still very firmly in the Beatles camp, and Eamonn was equally firmly in the Stones camp. A few years earlier he had seen them play live at a famous concert in Hyde Park, London. In the end we agreed to differ, but even to this day the issue of Stones versus Beatles arises regularly in our conversations.

We had enough in common otherwise, because we both loved traditional Irish music, folk music, pop music, rock music and even the blues. Singer/songwriters like James Taylor, Don McLean, Bob Dylan and Paul Simon were heroes to both of us, and we also liked Christy Moore, Paul Brady and groups like the Bothy Band and De Dannan. In the world of pop music we enjoyed the Hollies, the Everly Brothers and Irish groups like the Freshmen and the Plattermen. With all these similar influences we came together as a duo very naturally. If I sang a song, Eamonn would immediately find a harmony, as I would do for Eamonn's songs. Neither of us had any formal training in music, and yet we instinctively gelled harmoniously. Later Eamonn began to add a little comedy to our act, with verbal pieces like 'Piddling Pete' and 'Finnegan's Wake'. They were a great success, so we started adding comedy songs like Jake Thackray's 'Sister Josephine' and John Prine's 'Dear Abby', which we changed to 'Dear Angela': a reference to Angela McNamara, who had an agony-aunt column in the *Sunday Press*.

Sometimes, real comedy moments crept unrehearsed into our act. We were playing in a bar called The Kon-Tiki in Rooskey (I never understood the name, which, it turns out, refers to a 1947 raft journey across the Pacific led by Norwegian explorer Thor Heyerdahl). It was what one might call a 'theme' lounge. The stage was on a little island in the middle of the venue, surrounded by water and Hawaiian palms. A lovely guy who was a friend of Eamonn's brought us up two pints of Guinness. He wasn't aware of the layout, and walked straight into the water, sending the pints flying. The audience erupted in laughter, and it was impossible for us not to join them. It was so funny at the time. At the end of the gig a woman came up to us and asked, 'Do ye have your man with the pints with ye every night?'

Another night we were playing in a pub called Ging's in Carrick-on-Shannon. The final few songs were usually very upbeat, with everyone singing along. In the middle of our final song, amid all the excitement, my denture flew out of my mouth and landed on the floor about three feet away. I quickly retrieved it while continuing to play my guitar, hoping nobody had noticed. I got it off the dusty floor, dipped it in my pint, reinserted it, and continued singing. Similarly to the Kon-Tiki incident, a woman came up after the show and asked me seriously, 'Do you do that thing with your denture every night?'

We took our music very seriously, regardless of whether people liked it or not. We added to our little duo a few years later when a colleague of mine in the ESB, Brendan Farrelly, joined us for a while with his banjo and an eight-string instrument called a cittern. Brendan, the station chemist in the Arigna power station, was a lovely looking fellow who drew women like a magnet without ever really trying.

However, when it came to commitment, Brendan didn't understand the meaning of the word. He was the kind of fellow who would say 'I'll meet you in that pub across the street in five minutes,' and you might eventually meet him in the pub three weeks later. That was Brendan, and bit by bit he became less and less of a feature in Jargon. We remained close friends on a personal level, and I continued playing with him in traditional music sessions for many years after Jargon had disbanded. He was a great musician and a very friendly character, with his curly red hair and winning smile. Sadly, he died a few years ago.

Jargon continued as a duo, but shortly afterwards life changed for me in the best way possible when my first child was born.

CHAPTER 29

The Bedpan Shuffle

I t's hard to believe, but we didn't have a car when we came to Drum-shanbo; indeed, we spent the first twelve months cadging lifts from whoever was kind enough to offer them. A car pool was established among those who were on day work in the power station, so I got a lift with whoever was on the rota. I remember that it seemed to rain every single day of that first year, so my umbrella was in regular use.

Jimmy McBrearty, a mechanical fitter in the station, gave us a lift to Ballyshannon and back whenever we wanted. Jimmy was from Bruckless, near Killybegs, so Ballyshannon was on his route home. We regularly thumbed a lift to Dublin to meet our Dublin friends, even after Goretti fell pregnant in that first year.

I remember the first time we thumbed, a Toyota HiAce (they spell it funny) van pulled up. Goretti was suffering severe morning sickness at the time. The van was covered in blood on the inside and there was a stale meaty smell. This was our first encounter with Dermot Doherty, a butcher. He brought us all the way to Dublin: how Goretti survived is still a source of wonder to me.

When she became pregnant we were delighted. She attended Dr Deasy, a large Kerryman who seemed gruff but was actually a great doctor. There were all kinds of stories about him. It was said that one patient – a very old man not long for this world – had howled 'I don't want to die, doctor!'

'Don't worry, my good man,' said Doctor Deasy. 'When you're dead for a while you'll get used to it.'

At one point during Goretti's pregnancy she was lucky to survive a threatened miscarriage.

One of our neighbours, Nancy Forde, heard about Goretti's near miscarriage. She went down to Mrs McKenna in the post office, who had previously been a nurse, to discuss the matter.

'She should stay in bed till noon,' said Mrs McKenna, 'so she'll need one of these.'

Mrs McKenna produced a large shiny bedpan from under the counter. She gave Nancy a piece of newspaper to cover it up, and Nancy left the shop.

'It's a bedpan for Goretti McGettigan,' Nancy said to everyone she met on the way to our house: a little too much information for the citizens of Drumshanbo. Goretti was raging when Gibby told her about it afterwards.

Drumshanbo was to be our home for the next fifty years, and we still live there. We've had so many wonderful adventures there, and I know that had I not moved there, my musical career would not have turned out as well as it has.

'Drumshanbo Town' (words and music by Charlie McGettigan)

If ever I'm down Leitrim way I spend a little time
In a hidden jewel of Old Ireland's crown
Just a few miles out of Carrick it's a spot that's just sublime
A little place they call Drumshanbo town

In the shade of Sliabh an Iarann down beside Lough Allen's
*   shore*
Where the Shannon River flows from higher ground
It nestles 'neath Arigna where the miners mine no more
A little place they call Drumshanbo town

And even when I'm far away it's always in my mind
That someday I'll return and settle down

In that little piece of heaven where my dreams are all enshrined
A little place they call Drumshanbo town

Just to walk by Aughagrania, Aughacashel and Bencroy
Where the colours of the countryside abound
And to visit Aughnasheelin where I rambled as a boy
And then make my back to Drumshanbo town

And people come from far and near to seek a silent prayer
In a place where peace and quiet can be found
And they know the sisters in the little convent of Poor Clare
Will pray for them down in Drumshanbo town

So if ever you're down Leitrim way you should spend a little time
In a hidden jewel of Old Ireland's crown
Just a few miles out of Carrick it's a spot that's just sublime
A little place they call Drumshanbo Town

CHAPTER 30

Tara

On 14 August 1974, Goretti wasn't feeling too well and, being near to her time, decided it might be a good idea to have a chat with her doctor. Dr Quinn in Ballyshannon had been both our families' doctor down through the years. As we had no car, Goretti's brother Sean, who worked in Manorhamilton, was summoned to bring us to Ballyshannon in his tiny Mini. I don't know if people realise how close to the road you were when travelling in a seventies-era Mini, but it was approximately six inches and not very comfortable.

In those days a wife went in to see the doctor alone, and her husband sat in the waiting room like an innocent eegit who had nothing to do with it all! Goretti came out to tell me that she was being admitted to the Sheil Hospital for 'observation'.

Having got Goretti settled in at the Sheil, I went to her parents' house nearby in Bishop Street, where I planned to stay the night. At this stage the family had moved to a beautiful new bungalow on a hill called Mullinashee, otherwise known as the Hill of the Fairies. It had wonderful views of the Erne Estuary and the hills around Bally-shannon. It was actually the place that William Allingham wrote about in his poem 'The Fairies', which I mentioned earlier:

Up the airy mountain, down the rushy glen,
We daren't go a-hunting for fear of little men.

Nothing would do Red Jack, Goretti's father, but we'd go for a few drinks in the nearby Thatch pub. Let's say that I had a skinful, and that's all I remember of the night. The next morning I was still sleeping it off when I became aware of two female voices chatting outside the bedroom I was in. I heard one of them say something about seven pounds and four ounces.

I quickly realised that they were talking about a baby, and that baby was mine. I was the father of a baby girl! I was so excited ... and then for a second I thought that maybe they were talking about some other woman who had had a baby. When I came storming out of the room and heard the word 'Congratulations!', I didn't need to hear any more.

I rushed to the Sheil Hospital to find Goretti in great spirits, and my new daughter safe and well. It's hard to explain the feeling: I can only say that I was relieved that both had come through the birth safely and everything seemed fine. We were so lucky to have the Sheil in those days, and such wonderful staff to look after us.

We had spent the previous nine months debating what name we would give our new baby. Eamonn Daly, my partner in music, had suggested Lara, after the character in *Doctor Zhivago*, but we eventually settled on Tara. So now here we were, the three of us: Goretti, me and Tara McGettigan. We were a couple up to that day, but now we were a family.

A lot happened in the following week. Goretti was kept in hospital for about five days, during which I purchased my first car. I remember bringing Tara home in my new (to me) white Renault 4. I was still a novice driver, but we made it safely to Goretti's home in Mullinashee. That night I reversed my new car into a car owned by her Aunt Mary Rose, leaving an ugly scrape on my own car. Luckily, Mary Rose's car seemed undamaged.

The following day we left Ballyshannon to attempt to drive all the way to Drumshanbo. Tara was in a carry cot on the back seat, and little did she know that she was taking her little life in her hands by being a passenger in a car with a dad who was a very inexperienced driver. However, we reached Drumshanbo safe and sound.

I knew nothing about the practicalities of being a dad. All kinds of baby stuff started to appear in the house like magic. Goretti had been building up a stockpile of equipment over the previous nine months – sterilisers, bottles, nappies, etc. – and I hadn't noticed at all.

That first night Tara slept in our bedroom with us, and every time she moved or made any kind of noise, we would sit up immediately to check that everything was OK. I certainly wasn't aware of all the feeds in the middle of the night or anything else. How uneducated we men were back then.

Somehow we muddled our way through, and it was sheer joy to both of us when we could see that Tara was beginning to recognise us and her surroundings. Gradually, her own little character began to appear. I became a dab hand at changing nappies, bottle feeding and all the rest of it. Eamonn Daly used to be horrified to see me changing nappies, but I was so proud of myself for managing to master the art. Little did he know that he would soon be in the same position?

Drumshanbo is an ideal place to raise a family. As soon as Tara could walk and talk, she was out playing with several other children who also lived in Grattan Avenue. She became best friends with a lovely girl named Suzie Maleady, and they were both able to play safely and happily around the avenue. They were enrolled in St Patrick's School: literally around the corner, a mere two minutes' walk from our house.

When they start their first day at school, it is a special moment for them and for you. Tara the little baby was now a little girl. She was a bright student with a natural talent for music, so we arranged for her to have some piano lessons, first from a piano teacher called Mrs Roberts in a draughty old room beside the Church of Ireland church, and later with Siobhan Talbot in Carrick-on-Shannon.

Tara's summer holidays were mostly spent around Acres Lake in Drumshanbo, with many trips to places like Cormongan and Corrie Strand, both on the shores of nearby Lough Allen. She learned to swim at a very early age, and went on to represent Leitrim at the Community Games in Mosney, Co. Meath. She also excelled at piano and, after a year in the vocational school in Drumshanbo, continued her secondary school education at boarding school: the Convent of Mercy school in Tuam, Co. Galway, which had a great music faculty.

Tara was quite a shy girl but all that changed when she got a summer job in McTernan's pub in Drumshanbo. She suddenly transformed into a confident young lady. I'm convinced that the experience of working in that very popular bar served to develop her social skills. She loved the customers and they loved her. To this day, strangers often come up to me in the street and say 'How's Tara getting on?' These would be customers she served in McTernan's.

At one point Tara was offered a place as an au pair in Belgium. She wanted to explore the world and different cultures. She really enjoyed her time there, living with the family who created the Belgian cartoon story *The Adventures of Tintin*. It was a good experience for her, and she often talks of the kindness of the family, and how well she was treated.

To us as parents, it was a worrying time at the beginning. We no longer had a little girl who depended on us for everything. We had a daughter who was independent and wanted to make her own life. I'll never forget the complex feeling the day we watched her enter the departure lounge at Dublin Airport, knowing that anything that might happen to her now was beyond our control. It was very emotional, and the only way I could express my true feelings was in a song. It's called 'If Anything Happened to You'.

'If Anything Happened to You' (words and music by Charlie McGettigan)

If anything happened to you
If my worst fears should ever come true
I'd have no reason to carry on through
If anything happened to you

I cannot imagine a world
Without you around me to hold
My days would be empty
My pleasures be few
If anything happened to you

If anyone took you away
Or somehow you wandered astray

There's nowhere I wouldn't pursue
If anything happened to you

So promise me you will take care
It's a wicked old world out there
I'd be devastated
Be broken and blue
If anything happened to you

CHAPTER 31

Shane

I continued a very busy schedule, having a full-time job with the ESB and playing my music with Jargon, over the next couple of years. On September 9th 1976 I brought Goretti out for a meal to celebrate her birthday. We enjoyed our meal very much and then relaxed with a few drinks afterwards. Goretti was pregnant so she was careful what she had to drink, although back then a few drinks during pregnancy didn't seem to be a problem medically.

We went to bed as usual and I was fast asleep when I started getting a nudge from Goretti. It was almost dawn and she was feeling that her time had come. She had her bag packed, as many women do, so off we set with a little urgency for Sligo General Hospital, with our two-year-old daughter, Tara, in the back seat. There were no such things as car seats for children back then, or even seat belts. Imagine that!

We arrived at the hospital at about 8.30am and left Tara waiting in the car for the short time it took me to see Goretti safely into the maternity ward. When I arrived back at the car I found that poor Tara had had a little accident and was soaked through. Was it any wonder? We went to Dunnes Stores and got her some underwear, a top and a dress.

When I had her fitted out and she was all clean and fresh, we returned to the hospital to discover that Goretti had already given birth to a baby boy. Both mother and baby were fine and in good health. Tara could barely understand what was going on, but she did know that Mammy had gone to the hospital and got a new baby for her to play with. I was stunned that it had happened so quickly. All I could say was 'Missed it again!' Goretti had been further on in her labour than she thought, and it was such a close call that she nearly had to have our baby in a bath because there was a shortage of beds, but luckily she got one in time.

The following afternoon I was driving down the hill of the Mall in Sligo after being with Goretti and our new baby, Shane, still in that world of my own. When I put my foot to the brake the car wouldn't stop. Luckily, Goretti's brother Sean was with me, and had the presence of mind to tell me to turn the car towards the pavement, which put a halt to it. I was really lucky that there was no damage to the car, because I had just traded it in for a brand-new Toyota Corolla which I was collecting the following Monday. Had there been any damage, the deal would have cost a lot more.

Later that evening I was playing with Eamonn Daly in Dunne's Pub in Carrick-on-Shannon. It was not where I wanted to be, but I had made a commitment. When we finished playing we started 'wetting the baby's head' in a big way, and then adjourned to John and Vera Timlin's house for just a few more. We had Sean with us, and somewhere in all the fun he found the going tough, so we put him to sleep upstairs. I spent the night in Eamonn's house.

The next morning I was in my office at the power station as usual. Around 11am there was a gentle tap on the door. 'Come in,' I said. It was Sean. 'I've just had a very strange experience,' he said. 'I woke up in a strange bed with a man on one side of me and a woman on the other. I didn't know where I was or who I was with.' Sean did look pretty shook up. It turned out that when John and Vera went to bed they couldn't wake Sean, so John got in on one side and Vera on the other, leaving Sean in the middle, completely oblivious. It was a funny story to hear at the end of two extraordinary days for me.

Shane suffered from reflux for about three months, always from 5pm until 8pm each day. The only way to comfort him was to carry him around the house. The poor little fella was in dreadful pain. He became very familiar with my Toyota, because I regularly used to take him for a brief drive around the town at maybe three in the morning, with him in his carry-cot on the back seat. This generally sent him off to sleep. Thankfully his reflux gradually disappeared, as did his middle-of-the-night insomnia. Shane grew into a very likeable little boy, and it wasn't long until he was running around Grattan Avenue with Tara and all the other children.

He attended St Patrick's Primary School, where he was good at everything, and eventually after a year in '7th' class he was awarded a scholarship to St Mel's Secondary School in Longford as a boarder. We are ever thankful to his teacher, Paddy O'Keeffe, for his dedication to Shane's tutoring. He had stayed the extra year in primary, but under protest. He had started playing football and idolised the brother of his best friend, Barry McGuire, who was a pupil in St Mel's.

Most of his friends went directly to St Mel's, so this meant that he was a year behind them. He had also studied piano with Mairin O'Keeffe and was her first pupil to receive a distinction in his piano exam. When he went to St Mel's, however, he found that the football was on the same day as music, so the piano was abandoned and football took precedence.

He continued to play piano regardless. How he played it is beyond me. He had to have his hand X-rayed after a football injury. When we looked at the X-ray we discovered that several of his fingers had been broken previously and had reset naturally but completely crookedly.

Shane went on to represent St Mel's at all levels in football and also played with Allen Gaels, his home club in Drumshanbo: he obviously got the football from his grandfather, Red Jack. He was one of those people who were good at almost any sporting activity, from pool to tennis. Shane and his best friend, Seamus McGuire, used to organise little tennis tournaments during the summer holidays at the courts beside Acres Lake in Drumshanbo. There would be a small entry fee and all their friends would compete for the prize, which would be the sum of all the entry fees. Invariably it would be Shane and Seamus who reached the final. These tournaments could last days, and of course Seamus or Shane would pocket the winnings.

He loved football. I remember one of his mentors, Eamonn McGowan, saying to me when he was about fourteen, 'Shane's a great player but he tends to hold back a bit and could do with being a bit more aggressive on the field.' I told Shane what Eamonn had said, and after that if anything he was over-reckless on the field.

He had a very short career in hurling, however. An experienced hurler was brought to Drumshanbo to show the youngsters the rudiments of the game. They were all given new Hurley sticks. As they were running out on to the pitch, the guy in front of him hit Shane with his hurley as he swung it back (totally by accident), and he had to have stitches in the resulting wound. That was the end of Shane's hurling career. These days they would all have been wearing helmets, but not back then.

Shane progressed through all the levels of GAA football with his club but also with the Leitrim county squad, and eventually ended up on the county senior panel. At club level in the 1990s he was part of the very successful Allen Gaels team. This was a golden era for both Allen Gaels and the county senior team. In 1994 Leitrim won the Connacht final for the first time in sixty-one years, so every player in the county wanted to get his place on the team. Understandably, we were very proud of Shane when he was picked for the minor county team and eventually the senior team.

I had one of my proudest moments of all a few years later when Shane ran out in Croke Park for a game against Dublin. One of the Dublin players was Paul Clarke, a policeman at Dublin Airport, where I had met him earlier that week. I told him that Leitrim would knock the socks off Dublin the following Sunday. It was just a bit of banter, but when the game started that day, the first player Shane came in contact with was Paul Clarke. Shane gave him the mother and father of a shoulder to announce his arrival. He was trying to intimidate the opposition, and had no idea that I knew Paul at all. I don't know if Paul knew who Shane was, but it was a moment I'll never forget. It was obvious to me that Shane was now a fully confident young man in his own right.

Not all moments were fun. Shane had gone to the funeral of a relation of a friend of his one day. He was booked to babysit that night for our neighbour Mary Rudel, so when he didn't arrive home after the funeral we wondered where he was. After a while the phone rang. It was one of Shane's friends, Kieran McWeeney.

'Hello, Mr McGettigan,' said Kieran (parents were all known as Mr or Mrs at the time). 'Could you come down to McTernan's pub and collect Shane?'

'OK, I'm on my way,' I said, not knowing what was going on.

I drove down to McTernan's, only to find poor Shane lying motionless on the pool table and out for the count. Drink had obviously been taken. Eventually I succeeded in waking him up, and got him into the car. He wasn't making a lot of sense, but what drunken man does?

At the house he felt sick and wanted to throw up. A little stream ran beside our house, so he leaned over the small wall to get sick into it, and almost fell in. He actually toppled over the wall, and I was just quick enough to catch him before he fell into the water. I brought him straight upstairs to bed so that his mother wouldn't see him in this condition. He slept it off and was none the worse for wear the next morning. It's amazing how much a good night's sleep can benefit a person.

He went to college at Dublin Institute of Technology, where he did media studies. I remember going up to Dublin with him to find accommodation, just as my mum had done for me so many years earlier. We eventually found a flat, which he decided to share with his pal Seamus McGuire. It was a small and pokey place, but clean and tidy.

The one time Goretti and I visited, there were leaves sticking out of one of the presses. On opening it we found a bag of potatoes: they'd been there so long they had begun to sprout! I guess when they bought the spuds they were full of good intentions. We just laughed, because we knew 'boys will be boys', as they say.

Later Shane moved into a basement apartment on Rathmines Road, which he shared with a girl he knew called Grainne Timlin. She was the daughter of the aforementioned John and Vera Timlin, in whose house I stayed the night he was born. Grainne's dad passed away very shortly after she and Shane moved in together.

I remember he took his bike up to Dublin to save money on bus fares, and chained it to the fence outside the apartment. That's where it remained, and remained and remained: he never used it again. It rusted away to a wreck, and we had to have it removed.

At one point, Shane's media studies in Dublin involved photography. He had a project to create a photo essay of a book he was reading. The main character was a tramp. He asked me, with a big smile on his face, if I would pose as the tramp. I was a bit shocked and imagined myself asking my own dad the same question. I asked Shane if he thought I would be suitable to pose as a tramp. 'Oh yes,' he replied. 'You'll make a hell of a good tramp!' I'm still trying to work out if that was a compliment or an insult, but it made me laugh and I agreed to be his muse.

A few days later we went to Dublin to make the photo essay. In an attempt to look more like a tramp, I dressed in some dirty raggy clothes and dirtied up my face with dry mud. We took loads of photographs on the streets around Harold's Cross. Shane made all the decisions, and I was happy to let him. It was a nice feeling to be directed by my own son for a change.

In one shot I was standing on the street while Shane was taking photos from the other side. Suddenly a car screeched to a halt and a woman got out. As she approached me, I realised it was a friend of mine, Maxi, who was a radio and television star on RTÉ.

'Are you OK, Charlie?' she asked, all concerned, as she looked at this dishevelled version of her friend in front of her. She obviously thought I had hit bad times.

'I'm fine, Maxi,' I said. 'I'm dressed like this for the camera. I'm acting as a tramp.'

'The camera?' Maxi was more than surprised. 'What camera?'

I pointed and said 'Over there, see! My son, Shane'.

We had a great laugh when I introduced her to Shane and explained what we were doing.

I wonder if you remember that moment of hilarious fun, Maxi.

We lost Shane in August 1998 when scaffolding he was working on in Boston collapsed, and he and a work colleague, Ronan Stewart from Dundalk, fell to their deaths. He had gone to Boston to play football with a team there, and had found a job with a construction company which sadly didn't observe health and safety regulations. I could fill three books with my thoughts on this tragedy, but the family and I just try and live day by day with the pain of our loss.

We had some wonderful times with Shane during his short life and made memories that we will cherish forever. We regularly meet people we don't know who had met Shane in different situations, and all their stories show him to be someone we are rightly proud of. Many of these people tell us about Shane being very kind to their own sons during his days at St Mel's Secondary School in Longford. Indeed, many of his contemporaries there have talked of his supportive attitude, and of how he helped them through rough periods in their lives.

We often wonder how his life would have turned out – the 'What if?' factor. The Allen Gaels football pitch where Shane spent so many happy times is now called Shane McGettigan Park, which means his memory will last for ever in his community. Below is a song I wrote when Shane went off to college.

'In Your Old Room' (words and music by Charlie McGettigan)

In your old room there's a pair of old socks
Some broken toys in a cardboard box
And I remember all the trouble you took
Fillin' in that old colouring book
And on the wall there's a football team
And every face has a hope and a dream
And I remember how you won your first game
You made me feel so proud

In your old room I used to tuck you in
Tuck in your blankets right up to your chin
Now I know I'll never do it again
I suppose you're just too old
Your old room is full of memories now
When they were happening I just don't know how
I never noticed you just suddenly grew
Now you're a full-grown man

In your old room at the back of the door,
There hangs an old jacket you wore
You know the one that you don't wear any more
It's got a tear in the sleeve

Shane

In your old room there's a character
In every little thing that I find there
These are the only things that I've left to share
Sitting down in your old room

CHAPTER 32

Ciara

O ur youngest daughter, Ciara, was born in 1979. I can honestly say that she was the easiest of our three children to take care of. Maybe we had become experts at child-rearing, or perhaps she was just a happy little child. She had lovely fair hair that used to get almost white in the summer sun. We were still living in Grattan Avenue when she was born, and as she grew up she quickly made friends with Sarah Barry, the daughter of one of the first non-ESB residents in Grattan Avenue. Sarah was a musical child who came from a very well-known traditional music family, the Wards. She still plays the concert flute to this day. The two little girls played happily on the avenue as often as they could, and, just like her older sister and brother, Ciara went to school in the nearby St Patrick's National School.

I always think of Ciara as a very independent child, who knew her own mind from an early age and did not suffer fools gladly. I always wonder when a child has older siblings if they have to have a little extra resilience to make their own space within the family. Ciara certainly has it.

As time went on she had a friend named Lorraine, the daughter of friends of ours, Tony and Phil McGowan. We talk about the McGowans a lot: they are very special friends. One Christmas Santa brought Ciara a Fisher Price cassette recorder, and she began to show her creative side. I don't know how aware she was of my own songwriting activity, but she and Lorraine started writing songs of their own, and recording them on the Fisher Price recorder. I was so impressed when I heard them, and I marvelled at their sheer courage. It's not an easy thing to write songs and then allow other people to critique your work, even if they are family. I should know! We still have the recorder and indeed the cassettes she recorded, and they're not bad at all.

I'd play music a lot in the car when Ciara was very young, and she would be quick to give me her opinion about my tastes. I would always be scatting along with songs or pieces of instrumental music. One day she shouted from the back seat: 'Dad, all you seem to play is that ooma, balooma music!' It was a new one on me. I was stunned at how her little mind was processing what she was hearing, and I kept thinking about it for ages.

That phrase of hers – 'ooma, balooma' – kept going round and round in my head. I had to do something with it, so I wrote this song, which is on my *Family Matters* album.

'Ooma Balooma' (words and music by Charlie McGettigan)

Well I know a little lady who keeps singing a song
Something about it got me singing along
It doesn't have any meaning, it's got nothing to say
It just goes Ooma Ballooma Balay

Singin' Ooma Ballooma
Singin' Ooma Ballay,
I tried to fight it but it won't go away
It doesn't have any meaning, it's got nothing to say
It just goes Ooma Ballooma Balay

In the quiet of the evening when I go for my snooze
I put my feet up and I kick off my shoes
I am tired, I am weary, it has been a long day
Then she goes Ooma Ballooma Balay

She sings this melody all day
No other melody, it just goes Ooma Ballooma Balay

Well this crazy little lady got me going insane
She keeps doing it again and again
It doesn't have any meaning, it's got nothing to say,
It just goes Ooma Ballooma Balay

It's a happy little tune, and always brings back memories to me of a happy little child in the back of my car.

We have a large cassette collection of songs from musicals, but none of us could remember where the cassettes came from. They would have been collected over a period, in one of those weekly magazines that always seemed to come on stream in early January. We now know it was Ciara, but it doesn't seem like her choice of music.

She had a big collection of dolls. She was always very protective of her toys, but I guess she had to be. I remember she had to spend some time in Sligo General hospital just after Christmas one year. We brought some of her new Christmas toys to the hospital with us, but when we were going home she said 'Take my toys home. The other kids will want to be playing with them, and then they'll get lost.' She was always a cautious soul, our Ciara.

Ciara's determination was a quality that stood to her very well all through her life. When she was a young child, we used to have these little endurance games. The idea was that you would take some small item like an orange, and see who could hold it at arm's length the longest. You would think this would be easy because an orange doesn't weigh a lot. However, after even two minutes it starts to feel heavier, and after three minutes your arm begins to flag as the orange feels really heavy.

I remember telling Ciara that I would give her a £5 note if she could hold the orange out for fifteen minutes, thinking she wouldn't last anywhere near that length of time. I was quite amazed when she lasted five minutes and completely gobsmacked when she lasted ten, but, lo and behold, she held out for fifteen minutes! She was almost in tears and her face was flushed, but she didn't give in.

As it turned out I didn't have a fiver on me at the time, and somehow or other I never gave her that fiver. As I discovered many years later, it wasn't about the money as far as Ciara was concerned. It was about beating the odds. To this day she enjoys letting me know that I still owe her that fiver.

Ciara was always well organised in her school work, and did very well in her exams. However, when she became a teenager, her personal organisation at home was a different matter entirely. She's the only person I know who could transform a tidy space into something resembling a bomb site in a matter of minutes. She had the uncanny knack of spreading her belongings over a wide area in seconds.

Equally, when she started coming in late from nights out, we would awaken to the sound of her banging the front door closed with a thundering crash. You would then hear a thump, thump, thump as she made her way up the stairs in her high heels. Two loud bangs as each shoe was taken off and tossed to the floor. This was the typical arrival home routine of our Ciara after a disco.

She inspired me to write another song, this time for the parents of teenagers. It's called 'Teenage Daughter'. I recorded it on my album *Another Side of Charlie McGettigan*. Here are the lyrics, which might remind you of someone you know!

'Teenage Daughter' (words and music by Charlie McGettigan)

I've got a teenage daughter in my house
I've got a teenage daughter in my house
She sits around and moans
And stretches out her bones
This teenage daughter in my house

She's got a ghetto blaster in her room
And its principal feature is volume
It seems to make her proud
To play the damn thing loud
Or she's got hearing problems I presume

Her room is a disaster area
It's got stuff all scattered everywhere
And underneath her bed,

Several things are dead
As well as last week's dirty underwear

Her boyfriend, he's a funny kind of bloke
He's the kind of guy I'd like to choke
He wears such funny clothes
He's got four earrings in his nose
And he seems to be permanently broke

She'll be a woman before long,
And I suppose I'll miss her when she's gone.
I'll miss the sleepless nights
The arguments, the fights
And all the reasons why I sing this song

OK, I took a lot of poetic licence: she didn't have a ghetto blaster and her boyfriend didn't have nose rings, or any other characteristic I mentioned. This song is not about Ciara personally, but it was inspired by how teenagers in general were at the time.

Ciara went to the Convent of Mercy in Tuam, just like her sister Tara, and enjoyed every minute ... more poetic licence! She loved travelling and spent her summer holidays in places like Edinburgh, where she worked in a fast-food outlet. We visited her there and she showed us all the highlights of the city, including a pub called The Last Drop. In bygone days it had a public scaffold outside, where many people were hanged. We stayed there about a week and enjoyed all the atmosphere of the Fringe Festival. We have never been to Edinburgh since, but it is on the bucket list.

In other years she went to the Isle of Man, where she worked in a Chinese restaurant, and to New York. I remember she was about three weeks in New York and hadn't found a job. She rang us at home when she was near the end of her tether. She had done an interview the day before and was told they would call her.

'They still haven't called!' she sobbed.

'Be patient, they'll call. Anyway, don't worry, you'll find something,' I reassured her.

'But I'm here three weeks and I still can't find anything.'

'No pressure! Give it another few days and we'll chat then.'

She got the job the next day, and had a wonderful summer in New York.

Mind you, the job was in a clothing outlet in Manhattan, and she said 'If you saw the sweaty bodies that try on blouses and tops, you would never try anything on in a shop again!'

CHAPTER 33

Eamonn Daly Calls It a Day

Jargon continued as a duo, until a very important character came into view. I had become aware of Brendan Emmett a few years earlier when I heard him playing at a venue in Sligo called The Trades Club. It was one of the few 'listening' venues in our area. This meant people actually listened to your music, rather than using it as a background to their own chatter.

Brendan was a quiet guy with long straight hair, and wore spectacles. I was immediately impressed with the precision of his finger-picking guitar style. He was playing Joplin rags, which would originally have been played on piano: his thumb would play the notes that the left hand would have played on the piano, while three fingers played the melody and middle accompanying notes, normally played with the right hand on the piano. It sounds complicated, but it amounted to a really talented musician producing a sound that was a truly wonderful listening experience. He also played the music of Leadbelly, Doc Watson, John Renbourn and many others.

He and his friend Damien Killoran, who lived close to him in Ballyfarnon, Co. Roscommon, played on the same circuit as us, as 'Emmett and Killoran'. Brendan played guitar and mandolin; Damien sang and played guitar. I knew I would have to get to know Brendan. We spoke occasionally here and there, and I remember inviting him to have a session with me sometime.

The opportunity came when RTÉ Radio came to Drumshanbo to spend a week in the community. They were broadcasting programmes from a mobile unit, featuring the best of music, poetry, short stories, etc. about the town and its environs. This would have been the first 'local' radio, I suppose. Eamonn Daly and I were asked to present a programme, and I immediately thought this would be an opportunity to introduce Brendan to the world of radio, so I asked him to come along and perform with Eamonn and me. He came reluctantly and brought his beautiful Martin guitar with him. I came to know Brendan very well in the years following that, and in fact we lived in each other's musical pockets for almost thirty years.

Brendan grew up in Ballyfarnon, where his 'larger than life' father, J.T., owned a tyre remoulding plant called Emmett Remoulds, as well as many other varied businesses. After spending a year in college in Galway, where he learned his first few chords on a borrowed guitar, Brendan returned to work with his dad in the family business. He bought his first guitar, a Yamaha FG180, in Galway, and immediately started to explore the world of guitar playing in the only way he could … very intensely. He also developed an interest in the mandolin, and bought his first Martin mandolin shortly after that. Through a series of accidental encounters he teamed up with Damien, and eventually found himself playing around the pubs and cabaret venues of the region.

Brendan didn't do things by half. He bought the records of musicians like Ton Van Bergeyk and Stefan Grossman, and had a great collection of vinyl albums. Whenever you visited Brendan's house in Ballyfarnon he would play for you his latest purchases, which he usually bought from the mail-order sources he had discovered in *Frets*, a monthly American music magazine devoted to acoustic music. *Frets* also featured tablatures of a lot of the tunes he was listening to. Brendan would follow these 'tabs' assiduously, and practise the tunes until he had them just right. I was fascinated by what he was playing and I became a devotee of his music.

At that time during the mid-1970s, Brendan was quite introverted and shy, and initially didn't want to play publicly at all. He was a purist in the best sense of the word, and just enjoyed playing the music.

When Brendan Farrelly wasn't available to play with Eamonn and myself one night, I asked Brendan Emmett to stand in. Reluctantly he joined us, and it was really good. By this time he was a very proficient mandolin player as well.

Brendan Farrelly was gradually easing himself out of the band, and Brendan Emmett played with us at more and more gigs. His confidence playing to an audience was growing all the time. When Brendan Farrelly eventually left Jargon officially, Brendan Emmett was his natural successor. As one Brendan left, another Brendan came in. I seem to know a lot of guys called Brendan, and yet another completely different Brendan will become very significant in my life.

Anyway, I was delighted to have Brendan Emmett with us on a more permanent basis now, not just for his musicianship but also for that second harmony voice I was hoping he could sing. Brendan had never sung in his life, and was astounded when I said 'And now your vocal' to him. He had no idea that he would be asked to sing. Thankfully, he took to singing like a duck to water, and thus expanded the musicality of Jargon immensely.

Jargon continued with that line-up until 1979. However, I think the intensity of the work we were doing was beginning to take its toll on Eamonn Daly. He was also a teacher in the vocational school in Carrigallen, Co. Leitrim, and was soon appointed vice-principal there. This, of course, increased his school workload, and the late nights and long distances we were travelling were no longer feasible.

I think the straw that broke the camel's back for Eamonn was a gig we played in Letterkenny, Co. Donegal, in the winter of 1979. My brother-in-law Sean Gallagher had set up the gig at a renowned venue, The Continental Music Lounge, on a Wednesday night. The snow was so bad that we had to turn back after twelve miles, and the gig didn't happen. Sean rescheduled it for a Wednesday night two weeks later. Unfortunately, the snow was just as bad, but we persevered and reached Letterkenny after a nearly four-hour journey. We had a lacklustre gig because we were shattered after the long journey, and there was a very small crowd due to the weather. To be honest, I was surprised there was anyone there at all that night, but I am grateful to those hardy souls who came along.

After the gig we emerged onto Main Street to find that there had been even more snow: it was at least six inches deep at this stage. Eamonn, carrying a microphone stand in each hand, lost his footing and fell backwards into the snow. His dignity suffered more than his body, but it was not a nice experience.

We were travelling in two cars: Brendan had brought his own car, and Eamonn Daly and I were in my car. The snow was so deep that it was difficult to know whether we were on the actual road or in the fields on either side. The cars kept losing traction, so we had to get out and push them when we couldn't climb the hills. I don't know how we got anywhere at all, because Donegal is a very hilly place. At one point Eamonn took off his socks and put them over his shoes to gain some kind of traction when he was pushing the car.

Four hours later we reached Ballyshannon after what should have been a one-hour journey maximum. We decided to sleep in Goretti's parents' house, and continue the journey in the morning. This meant that Eamonn didn't arrive in school until noon the following day. Eamonn was often late for rehearsals and even gigs, but he had *never* been late for school. Very shortly after that, he announced that he was leaving Jargon.

I have to say that when Eamonn left Jargon I was quite depressed. We had been playing together for five years. Eamonn was always the front man, and I mostly assumed a back-up role. He was not only a musical partner but a great friend. However, I had to bite the bullet and accept his decision to withdraw from the band, which left Jargon at two members still standing, namely Brendan Emmett and myself.

We had been playing quite a bit around Sligo in places like Coolera House, Heneghan's and Beezies. Coolera House was the stomping ground of a great band called Pumpkinhead, which featured the late Thom Moore and his wife Kathy, as well as Rick and Sandi Epping. I was a big fan and in particular loved the songs Thom wrote. They were a huge influence on my own songwriting in future years.

I remember on one occasion in Heneghan's, on my way back from the toilet, I found a guy with his leg jammed up in the doorway, blocking my way. I politely asked him to let me pass, but he refused to move. I gently pushed his leg away from the door, and he collapsed in a heap on the floor. 'He's drunk,' I thought to myself … but I was wrong. It turned out that he was stone cold sober, but could only stand up by using crutches. I was mortified, and did my best to get him onto his feet, in front of the entire audience. We just about survived until the end of the gig.

CHAPTER 34

Bailieboro and Me

We began to notice a young guy who regularly turned up at our gigs and often came to chat with us afterwards. It turned out he was the younger brother of a legend around the Sligo folk scene, Tommy Grennan. Tommy was a great bouzouki player, and also made his own musical instruments. Gerry was his brother, and bit by bit we got to know him and to appreciate his guitar and bouzouki style, which he had obviously learned from Tommy. He was ten years younger than me, but his musical taste was roughly the same as Brendan's and mine. I don't remember how he ended up joining Jargon, but he had a great singing voice, which made him an ideal replacement for Eamonn Daly.

Around this time I was beginning to write my own songs, but rarely had the courage to sing them in public. Now, with Gerry on board, I became more assured, and began to throw a few of my original songs into the Jargon repertoire: songs like 'Same Old Places' and 'The Singer', a song inspired by Janie Cribbs, the lead singer with Thom Moore's new band, Midnight Well. Our harmonies were getting better and better, and we seemed to be getting gigs further afield than ever before. One highlight was when we were asked to play at the Ballisodare Folk Festival, possibly the first really big summer music festival in Ireland. We even got our picture included in the programme leaflet.

It was the most terrifying gig of my life thus far. Backstage, I was literally pissing myself with nerves when an American artist (I'm not sure, but it could have been legendary folk singer Dave Van Ronk) came up to me and asked if I was all right. I said 'There are eight thousand people out there … and I'm a bit frightened.'

'Don't forget to enjoy it,' he said.

'I hadn't thought of that,' I answered.

We went on stage and started to play, and the crowd's reaction was great. I really enjoyed that night, so ever since, before I perform, I remind myself 'Don't forget to enjoy it.'

Around this time, late 1970s and early 1980s, there was a thriving folk club scene in Ireland and we were lucky to play on that circuit. I always felt that we needed a bass player to really solidify our sound. I suppose I was harking back to my Bundoran days when I was playing with Jimmy Gallagher. (Indeed, Jimmy was to help us out in making demos a few times.)

Gerry had a friend who lived around the corner from him in Jinx's Avenue. His name was Liam Gilmartin. Although he was a really good lead guitarist, would he be interested in playing bass with us? Luckily he was interested, although I think when he saw me he wondered what he would have in common with an ageing hippy. Gerry and Liam were about ten years younger than me, so age was a factor. However, he fell into the bass really easily and as far as I was concerned, Jargon now had a complete line-up. It turned out that Liam was an excellent harmony singer as well, and this expanded our repertoire enormously.

Looking back at my diaries from the early 1980s, I was double-gigging with Jargon and an ensemble called Sheebeg. Sheebeg was a mainly traditional music band that featured one of the most talented flute players in the country, Tommy Guihen, and my old pal Tony McGowan on piano accordion. Tony, who was a teacher in the Drumshanbo vocational school, had discovered Tommy when he was a pupil of his. Tommy lived just out the road in a place called Mountallen.

Tony was totally daft about Irish traditional music, but doubled with a wedding/pub band called the Rocky Mountain Rangers. It was like that in those days. Indeed, I often played with the Rocky Mountain Rangers too when they needed me. Sheebeg was a lovely alternative to Jargon. Tommy, Tony and I had a wonderful time together, and the boys were a joy to play with.

In those days the Troubles were raging in Northern Ireland, and every Saturday night the local Sinn Féin people would arrive into the pubs selling *An Phoblacht*, a political paper. Not being a supporter of the Provisional IRA, I always refused to buy it. Tommy, however, was a diehard supporter of the armed struggle: he always bought a copy, and couldn't under understand why I didn't. We nearly split up over it, but sense prevailed and we agreed to differ.

In the meantime, Jargon was starting to spread its wings. One of our favourite venues was the Copper Kettle Folk Club in Enniskillen. The man in charge there was Galey Quinn, and the audience came along to listen. It was a great chance for me to play my own songs and for Gerry and Brendan to play their favourite 'Americana' instrumentals. Indeed, Brendan was writing some wonderful tunes with great titles. 'Farnon City Stomp' was one that referred to his home village of Bally-farnon, which was nothing like a city. 'Bedpan Shuffle' was another of his tunes. We did a lot of support gigs around then with people like Jim McCann and Ralph McTell.

I started to make some studio demos (demonstration recordings) around 1979/80. My first was with Dick Keating in Dublin. Dick was a legendary session musician and had a small studio at the back of his house. Fred Meyer was his engineer: an old-style analogue engineer who knew how to record most voices and instruments really well. I was writing a lot of songs at this time, although I was still only starting to explore this aspect of my life, and making demos to send to RTÉ for the National Song Contest. I realised that for some songs I would have to record quite sophisticated demos.

There were lots of song contests going on around Ireland at the time. We had won the Enniskillen Song Contest in 1979, when Eamonn Daly was playing with us. The song was called 'Leaving Enniskillen' and the prize was £250, so this win encouraged me to enter more.

The Cavan Song Contest was a really good one. They had a full orchestra featuring musicians from the RTÉ Light Orchestra under the baton of the late Earl Gill. We qualified for the final of this one with a song called 'My Home in Old Breifne', again with Eamonn Daly in the line-up, and we came third. The real star of the contest that year was Thom Moore: one of my favourite songwriters, as I have said. Thom won with his beautiful song 'Cavan Girl', sung by him with Janie Cribbs and Rita Connolly doing their quite unique harmonies. I remember Thom was being managed at that time by none other than Paul McGuinness, who became famous as the manager of U2.

We entered the Cavan Song Contest again the following year with a song called 'Bailieboro and Me', and this time we came second. The following summer we entered a folk music contest as part of the Letterkenny Folk Festival. This contest had a broader remit in that it was about musical performance. I think we had to sing a few songs, one of which was 'Bailieboro and Me'. The judges included Canadian singer Joyce O'Hara; Robin Hall, who was in a popular folk duo with Jimmy McGregor; and the head of PolyGram Records, John Woods. It was a very exciting event to be involved in, and even more exciting when we won. Part of the prize was a recording contract with PolyGram, which resulted in the release of Jargon's first single, 'Bailieboro and Me'.

'Bailieboro and Me' (words and music by Charlie McGettigan)

I once knew a lad of this country
Who cherished the place he came from
Where it seemed like the sun shone on every
*   tomorrow*
And laughter was in everyone
And the smile that came over his sad face
When thoughts of it came to his mind
Would brighten dark corners in this lonely city
When we ever fell to repine

He said I'm from Bailieboro, land of my childhood dreams
Bailieboro, calling me home
Bailieboro, one day I'll take you there
We're close as the shore and the sea
Bailieboro and me

He talked of the heathery hillsides
Where wild duck and pheasant would fly

With his dog and his gun he would stroll of an evening
Away from a world rushing by
Though we spent pleasant evenings in London
I knew they could never compare
With the fond recreation he found down in Cavan
Where he always longed to repair
I haven't laid eyes on him lately
Our paths have gone different ways
But I wonder if he ever settled in Bracklin
Or travelled the road to Corleigh
Do his thoughts ramble on through Virginia?
Is he finally there with his own?
Oh the pictures he painted of loving trips homeward
To harvest the seeds he had sown

CHAPTER 35

Jargon – Success at Last

My musical journey through life kept opening new doors for me, each one bigger than the last. I guess there were other factors at play, which I feel are best summed up in those words made famous by C.J. in the *Reginald Perrin* series on BBC television: 'I didn't get where I am today …' without the support of some very influential people, a lot of hard work and the most essential ingredient, a good dollop of luck!

Someone who reached out to support us was Nuala O'Connor, who was a producer with RTÉ radio. She put in a word for us with all her colleagues, and we really benefited from her influence. Philip Kampf, producer of the *Gay Byrne Hour*, was very supportive. Willie O'Reilly, John Keogh and many others in the RTÉ organisation were also very decent to us during this period. John Cadden, with his great handlebar moustache, helped us enormously. I cannot be thankful enough to all these people who encouraged us and showed confidence in Jargon.

P.J. Curtis, an important man at the time, also helped out, by inviting us to sing backing vocals on Maura O'Connell's version of Thom Moore's 'Saw You Running'. He was producing people like Freddie White and Stockton's Wing, and was also involved with the Bothy Band and others. He got us a lot of television shows on BBC Northern Ireland.

P.J. was very friendly with BBC producer Tony McAuley, who was a folk singer himself and loved what he was doing. If P.J. recommended anybody, Tony would make it his business to go and see the act, with his trusty sidekick, Maeve.

He set up an audition for us in a back room of the Celtic Hotel in Enniskillen, where we played for about half an hour. The great thing about Jargon was that we didn't need any PA or amplification: we could just get out our instruments and play on the spot. This impressed Tony, and he immediately booked us for his annual TV series *As I Roved Out*, which featured acts from the world of folk music. We were over the moon with this, and it went very well when shown. We ended up playing on many of his later TV shows as a result.

Appearing on a show like *As I Roved Out* was a big step on the success ladder back then. The programmes were made at the King's Hall in Belfast the week after the annual Northern Ireland agricultural show took place. This meant that there was a smell of cow shit lingering in the air throughout the show. If anyone had said to me at the time that we were shit, I had my answer ready – 'No ... that was the cows' – but I never got to say it, thankfully.

We were put up at the very posh Europa Hotel in the city centre. It was the most bombed hotel during the Troubles in Northern Ireland, so security was paramount there. We did two shows with one of my heroes, Ralph McTell, of 'Streets of London' and 'Clare to Here' fame. He is a genuinely nice man, and we had some great craic with him back at the hotel, as well as on the show. I remember he asked us to sing the Patsy Cline classic 'I Fall to Pieces' with him on the show. It went down tremendously well, and was one of the highlights of my career at that point.

Working for the BBC in those days was like working for the ESB. It was a large semi-state company with a strong workers' union, so every programme was made by the book. The show took two days to produce. We would stand on the beautiful set to rehearse and go through our songs many times. It wasn't until the tea break that we realised how many people were involved – electricians, lighting technicians, floor managers, etc. – when about thirty people converged on the canteen together.

I remember at one rehearsal Brendan Emmett couldn't hear his mandolin in the monitors. I pointed this out to the sound technician, and he sent one of his minions to see what we wanted. I told him we couldn't hear the mandolin. He went back to his boss to tell him this. After a few minutes he returned and asked 'Which one was the mandolin?' He was so serious … and we couldn't answer with the laughing, so we just pointed it out.

This was after two days' rehearsing, and we knew that all the efficiency that impressed us so much was purely on the TV production side. They may know that side of things extremely well, but we know the music side. It was the first time I realised that we artists are a very small but a very important part of a huge production process.

Our appearances on TV in Northern Ireland were quite beneficial. We began picking up lots of concerts in Belfast and Derry, and other places in that region. We were aware of the Troubles, but music was our main focus. The checkpoints in the middle of the night slowed down our journeys home and reminded us of where we were, and we breathed a sigh of relief when we crossed the border in Belcoo. We were always glad to be back in the Republic.

We decided to team up with P.J. Curtis for our second single in 1983. P.J. was very thorough and came down to our part of the world to listen to our repertoire. Eventually we decided to record a song I wrote called 'The Singer'. As I have mentioned, it was inspired by the singing of Janie Cribbs, the vocalist in Midnight Well. For the B side we selected a song written by Gerry Grennan called 'How Long'. (Everything was still on vinyl back then, so there had to be a B side.) We went to the famous Windmill Lane Studios in Dublin to do the recording. It was released on Dara Records, and it was all financed by the wonderful Shay Healy. Shay was another great mentor for the group. He was still riding on the crest of a wave at the time, after his song 'What's Another Year?' won the Eurovision a few years earlier.

At the studio we were joined by Paul McAteer on drums and Richie Buckley on saxophone. Frankie Lane also joined us on 'How Long'. Recording our songs that day was an amazing experience, and one I will never forget. I remember coming home from Dublin and playing the recording to Goretti, over and over again, until our neighbours John and Rita Casey began banging on the wall because of the noise.

Everything had to be listened to at full volume in those days … and some kids today think it still has to be, despite the advent of headphones!

Our little group, Jargon, was definitely on the way up, and with Marcus Connaughton, our new publicist, looking after the PR we were on the RTÉ radio playlist again, which meant we were getting up to four plays a day on the station (these days you'd be lucky to get four plays a month). We were being asked to do more and more work on radio and television, which was creating great status for the group commercially. Success at last … we had made it!

CHAPTER 36

Hey Mister Dreamer

In July 1983, Noel Kelehan, the conductor of the RTÉ Light Orchestra, asked me if I would be interested in spending a week in Knokke in Belgium, singing with a sixty-piece orchestra at a song festival. It was a huge vote of confidence in me, and I immediately jumped at the chance. Jazz singer Honor Heffernan and a Dublin singer called Mary Downes were also invited. We sang every night with this very professional orchestra, and it was really exciting to perform some of my songs with this impressive group of musicians. I noticed that Noel was always referred to as 'Mr Kelehan' throughout the week; such was the high esteem his fellow conductors and musicians held him in.

Knokke is a seaside resort, and the weather was perfect all week. To be honest, it was a lonely week for me during the daytime, because I was not in the holiday mood. This was a serious opportunity, and I did not want to let 'Mr Kelehan' down.

Noel proved to be a really thoughtful travelling companion. He was so supportive to me, knowing I was like a fish out of water. There was a jam session every night after the shows at our hotel, and Noel would play piano until the wee small hours, with a cigarette permanently hanging from his lips. He was a kind gentleman, a wit and a fantastic musician.

On a different note, Mary Downes received a different kind of attention some time later, when she and a few other women swam naked in what was hitherto a male-only swimming spot, the famous Forty Foot in Dublin Bay. Fair play to them!

On our arrival back from Knokke we were delighted to have another song I wrote included in an RTÉ compilation album called *Sounds Promising*. It was 'Man on a Stage Alone', a song inspired by Marcel Marceau. We had recorded it at the Greenfields Studio in Headford, Co. Galway with an engineer named Gerald O'Donoghue. The man himself, Marcel Marceau, heard the song and arrived at my dressing room one night when we were on the same show, to thank me and tell me how much he liked it. He was the famous mime artist, but I was the one who was speechless that night!

At this point we were beginning to get used to having our songs on record, even though it was a really big deal in those days to have even one record out. There were no home recording studios back then; everything was done in a fully professional studio like Windmill Lane or Lombard Studios, and it was a very expensive process.

I began to write a lot of my own songs from then on, encouraged and inspired by the success of our first two singles. I decided to enter the National Song Contest in 1984 and was picked for the final with a song called 'Bebop Delight', a whimsical little number. This was the first time I would get to sing with the full RTÉ Light Orchestra, conducted by Noel Kelehan (in Belgium it had been an international orchestra). It was great to work with Noel again as well as heroes of mine like guitarist Des Moore, bass player John Drummond and Desi Reynolds, a brilliant drummer. Noel did the arrangement of the song and it sounded really magical. Linda Martin was the winner and earned the chance to represent Ireland with a great Johnny Logan song called 'Terminal Three'. It came third that year to a song I honestly can't remember now.

We were planning to record our third single when I heard a demo of a song by a singer named Jane Cassidy. She had made it in Shaun (known as 'Mudd') Wallace's studio in Randalstown, Co. Antrim. I was very impressed with the sound, so we decided to record our third single there. Our song, 'Hey Mr Dreamer', was inspired by a short story by Thomas Hardy. Honor Heffernan had shared it with me on the plane home from Knokke. We augmented the group for this recording by having Don Ponsonby play the drums.

Working with Mudd Wallace was a unique experience, because he was such an eccentric character. He was also an amazing sound engineer of the old school, having trained at the BBC. He could be quite abrasive to those working with him, but we got on well enough. The poor tape operative had a dreadful time trying to please his master, but in the end Mudd always got the job done really well. I have never met anyone like him since.

Recording sessions ran into the wee small hours, and were sometimes interrupted by daft parties and some serious smoking of cigarettes that you couldn't buy in the shops. I was to get to know Mudd even more when I recorded my first solo album with him in 1984/85.

'Hey Mr Dreamer' was a great success, and again it received massive airplay on both RTÉ and BBC Radio Ulster. We were working harder than ever, and things seemed to be going from strength to strength. I couldn't believe our luck!

We were getting really well known at this stage, which meant we were very busy chasing up and down the country, doing concerts and public appearances. We appeared frequently on RTÉ, BBC and UTV.

Gay Byrne had us on his radio show regularly, and he always impressed me. All the people working with him knew that he didn't suffer fools, and held him in high regard. I was to work with him many times in later years, and I have always regarded him as the ultimate broadcaster. His *Late Late Show* on RTÉ was the prime TV show to appear on back then, and it still is to this day, albeit with a different host. Jargon made two appearances on the *Late Late*, and it was very exciting. It was as prestigious in Ireland as the *Ed Sullivan Show* was in America. We were guaranteed the biggest audience in the country, so it was a huge step forward for us.

Gaybo, as he was affectionately known, was always charming, and he treated us like his protégés. He ran a tight ship, and involved himself in every aspect of the programme. I remember on one occasion he wandered into the studio during rehearsals, and a particular artist was not coming up to scratch. With a very subtle wave of Gay's hand to the producer, the artist was immediately dropped from the show.

We also appeared on a TV programme called *Festival Folk*, recorded at the National Stadium, Dublin. This was another great show for us, because they put a couple of our original tracks on the RTÉ album that followed. We toured the country in 1985 with Chris Rea. I remember the four of us in Jargon travelled in Brendan Emmett's Vauxhall Astra with our instruments, our baggage and Liam's bass amp, but the car never let us down. It deserves to be in a museum.

Brendan was unwell throughout the tour, but he struggled through it. All our dreams were coming true, so nothing would daunt us. Brendan also managed to tour with Tommy Makem and Liam Clancy that year, which was a great bonus for him. On top of that he got to work with one of his heroes, Arty McGlynn, and Arty's wife, Nollaig Casey. The saying 'It never rains but it pours' comes to mind.

When I look back through my diaries for this period – 1982 to 1985 – I am astonished by the energy we all seemed to have. I had a fulltime job with the ESB, not to mention a wife and a family, and the other members had fulltime jobs as well … so how did we all manage to be involved in a group that had such a heavy workload?

I was blessed in having a wonderful wife. As a parent to our children, Goretti was and still is just unbelievable. In their early years she was there for their little demands and seemed to fall into parenthood instinctively. We were very lucky, and despite all the activities I was involved in, I still managed to spend lots of time with them.

Goretti kept them on the straight and narrow road of education, particularly when they reached secondary level. She was a wizard of the dreaded CAO form, where children had to map out their college careers. She became a consultant not only to our own children in this regard, but to other parents in the town. She encouraged our children in all their activities, ensuring that piano practice was done every day, that they attended swimming practice and all the rest. I joined all the other proud parents when our children represented Leitrim in the Community Games. They loved swimming and choral music best.

I sometimes forget what an intelligent person Goretti is. Her memory is amazing. She not only remembers our now extended family's birthdays, but the birthdays of most of the people we know. She has a trick of associating different events with each other. I'm a divil for forgetting people's names and, more importantly, their partners' names. So many times I have found myself asking Goretti what so-and-so's wife's name is, in case she answers the phone when I ring. Mind you, she gives me hell when I don't introduce her to someone we might meet out: 'You left me standing there like an idiot. Why didn't you at least introduce me?' I'd have to answer 'I couldn't remember their name.'

I never had any problems in life like alcoholism, mental breakdown, depression or even burnout; I always seemed to cope with whatever life threw at me. Without a doubt I was transformed in so many ways by my relationship with my Goretti. She has always been a very wise counsellor in my life, and has helped me make so many important decisions. She has a very musical mind, and I always use her as a sounding board for my songs and performances.

She has a very clever way of letting me know if she isn't impressed with something I have done. I might, for example, have spent a long day in the studio working on a new song. I would be feeling very excited about it, and dying to hear what she thought of it. I always knew if, after I'd played the song for maybe twenty or thirty seconds, she said something like, 'Do you know what Ciara did at school today?' that I needed to go back to the drawing board. Goretti is always very measured in her appraisal of my music, not unlike the editor of a book. She will point out sections that won't make sense to the listener, and on occasion suggest better ideas. I think for any artist trying to make their way, the support of a good partner and loving family means the most.

Goretti is always in demand for quiz teams, as her general knowledge is excellent. She reads the daily newspaper from front to back, whereas I usually skim through it. She is also an avid reader of literature, a passion we share. We both enjoy going to the cinema and watching our favourite shows on TV.

Goretti has a huge interest in music, and we have both been members of the Drumshanbo adult choir for nearly forty years. Unlike me, she can read music notation, as she studied piano for many years. This has been a valuable asset to us. Goretti has guided our children through their music education, and they in turn have guided our grandchildren on their musical journeys. We always had similar musical tastes since the days we played the jukebox in Coyle's Cafe back in Ballyshannon all those years ago.

We also share an interest in drama and enjoy going to the theatre as much as possible, and particularly talking about the plays we have seen. In our home, family always comes first, and my ever-evolving career took second place to that.

CHAPTER 37

Songs of the Night and Other Stories

As the 1980s progressed, I was writing songs that wouldn't necessarily suit Jargon, and bit by bit I found myself working more with other artists. Brendan Emmett was working with people like Makem and Clancy and Frances Black, and touring both here and abroad with them. Also, Gerry Grennan and he were travelling to Europe as a duo, so the concentration on Jargon was waning all the time. Liam Gilmartin was working with Stockton's Wing and Ray Lynam.

Although we had gone our separate ways musically, we kept together spiritually all the time. I often think what a great group of musicians Jargon members were. We never officially split up; I think it more like fizzled out. Indeed, we tried to put Jargon together again about twenty years later, but it didn't work. The magic was gone!

I began doing concerts and events either on my own or with Brendan Emmett when he was available. I recorded my first solo album, *Songs of the Night and Other Stories*, with Mudd Wallace. That was an experience in itself. Mudd, who sadly is no longer with us, was an excellent engineer, as I have referred to earlier. He was a genius at work, and he engaged a fabulous selection of musicians for my project, including members of the Ulster Orchestra, Billy Brown of the Freshmen, Keith Donald of Moving Hearts, and indeed Vivian Campbell of Def Leppard. Well … I did say I was writing songs that wouldn't suit Jargon!

Vivian arrived in Randalstown in his Mazeratti, and insisted I go for a spin with him. There was only room for the two of us, and when it took off it was like a rocket. I had never been in such a car before, and haven't been in one since. We hit the M1 in about ten minutes (normally half an hour) and were travelling at 140 miles an hour on the motorway. I couldn't enjoy the spin because I was praying silently to myself all the way. I was never so glad to get out of a car. Vivian was the ultimate rock star and insisted on prancing around the studio as he played. But man could he play.

Keith Donald was someone I had admired as far back as 1967, when I heard him with another great showband, the Greenbeats. Back then the showbands were not allowed to play dances during Lent, so some of them played concerts instead. The Greenbeats came to the Abbey Ballroom (now the Abbey Arts Centre) in Ballyshannon, and played a sit-down concert. 'Penny Lane' by the Beatles had come out the Friday before, and there was a fantastic piccolo trumpet solo on the record. Keith played this solo note for note on the alto sax. I was hugely impressed by his skills then, so having him in the studio now playing saxophone on my songs was incredible. He turned out to be a very pleasant fella as well.

The Freshmen were my favourite Irish showband. I'd seen them several times live, and Billy's own songs were right up there with Burt Bacharach and Jim Webb. I sort of idolised him. Now he was helping me make an album with the other top talent we had assembled.

I went to meet him at the railway station in Antrim, and was mildly shocked to meet this elderly-looking man with a stick. Could this be Billy Brown? I suppose it might have been ten or fifteen years since I had seen him on stage, and the years had obviously not been kind to him. However, in the studio his musical skills had not aged one bit. He was a joy to work with, and added so much to the album and to the conversation.

The album finally came out on Bus Records, and Marcus Connaughton, co-owner of the record company, had me appearing anywhere and everywhere to promote it. Jeanette Dunne (now Burke) designed a wonderful cover and the album was a huge critical success. It never reached number 1, but it did OK.

I remember a particular televised concert at the Cork Opera House. The band I was working with were from Northern Ireland and were running late, so they missed the rehearsals. We had cleaners and anyone else who was available stand in holding sweeping brushes for guitars. People have no idea about the crazy lengths we musicians go to to make the performances they attend the best we can! In the end the musicians arrived just in time and the concert went really well.

While all this was going on I was working with Maura O'Connell, about whom I'll talk more in the next chapter. Her manager, Maurice Cassidy, had us playing all over the place. We had augmented the show at this stage, and I was to end up working with another great hero of mine, Arty McGlynn. I recall standing at the foot of the stage in the Astoria Ballroom in Bundoran, watching Arty play with various showbands back in the 1960s. He was an incredible musician, and I felt so chuffed to be working with him. His wife, violinist Nollaig Casey, and he came as a package. We also had Aidan McGuigan, a friend of Arty's, on bass. We were sounding pretty good and played everywhere from small venues to the National Stadium, and even the Cork GAA stadium, Páirc Uí Chaoimh. I was having a ball.

In the late 1980s I started to get interested in American country music, and began writing songs in that genre. I was picking up a few more covers (other people recording my songs) with people like Ray Lynam, and folk singers Frances Black and Eleanor Shanley. Song royalties started to come in, and whether it's one euro or a million euro it doesn't matter. Just to get your first royalty cheque for writing songs is a very special feeling. It's like a validation of your effort, and it feels very good indeed!

When I think about it now – how busy I was, playing with all these people – I can't understand where I was getting my energy from. In 1990 I recorded a country-influenced album called simply *Charlie McGettigan*. Again we recorded this with Mudd Wallace, using mostly country musicians from the North of Ireland. I think people were surprised with this album as it was a much cleaner sound, and had none of the 'kitchen sink' elements, like strings and wind instruments, that we had used on my first album.

'The Guy Who Lives Next Door' (words and music by Charlie McGettigan)

I wish I had a car like the guy next door
I wish I had a power drill
I wish I had a shower, an electric lawnmower
And an infra-red grill
If I only had a bike I'd go anywhere I like
If I only had a yacht like the one my neighbour's got
A TV in every room a camera with a zoom I could be like him

The guy who lives next door
He's got so much he's such a bore
He really makes me want to roar
The guy who lives next door

He's got carpet wall to wall where he rolls his golf balls
Into paper cups
He's got a hi-fi stereo and you can hear it next door
With the volume up
He's got a wife with a machine
Who keeps everything so clean
She looks ever so serene just like in a magazine
And if I only had his clothes, hair below my nose
I could be like him

The guy who lives next door
He could eat his dinner off the floor
Cos his little lady does her chores
The guy who lives next door

The guy who lives next door
He doesn't fart he doesn't snore
He runs five miles a day and more
The guy who lives next door

I've got a drafty old house with a cat and a mouse
And a leaky tank
My old paint is getting loose and my wife calls me a goose
And I owe the bank
He goes vacationing to France, I think I've been away once
He goes drinkin' at the club with the guys on the way up
And whenever I feel low, I console myself and know
I couldn't be like him

CHAPTER 38

The Maura O'Connell Years

There were some great Irish bands around during the 1970s and 1980s in all genres of music. Rock bands like U2 were making it big all over the world, not to mention Van Morrison, Rory Gallagher, Thin Lizzy and many more. The Boomtown Rats had a UK No. 1 hit with 'Rat Trap', and Bob Geldof went on to be globally renowned for his work with Live Aid in 1985.

Irish folk bands like the Dubliners were known worldwide, and the likes of the Chieftains, De Dannan, Planxty and the Bothy Band were also making big waves in the sea of popularity during those years. Musically, I was keeping my feet firmly on Irish soil with Jargon and trying to give my songwriting endeavours more of my concentration.

When a singer called Maura O'Connell joined De Dannan in 1981, they had a huge Irish hit with a song called 'My Irish Molly-O'. I was delighted for Maura because I knew her personally. I had first met her some years earlier at a session in the Colliers Folk Club in Carrick-on-Shannon, when she and Mike Hanrahan, under the collective name Tumbleweed, came to play. I was absolutely gobsmacked by her performance, which consisted mostly of country songs from the likes of Emmylou Harris.

The next time she came to play, I had a cassette with me of a song I had written that I thought might suit her, called 'Let Me Know About It'. It was hard to get her to listen to it because she was so busy, but she did get to hear it eventually. I was hoping to enter the song in the upcoming Cavan Song Contest, so I brazenly asked her if she'd be interested in singing it there. I couldn't believe it when she said she would like to sing it. I'd love to say we won, and the rest is history … but we didn't win, despite her great performance. That's part of the music business as well: learning to lose sometimes, whether writing or performing.

Soon after that a very well-known impresario, Maurice Cassidy, took Maura under his wing. He knew talent when he saw it. He sent herself and P.J. Curtis off to Nashville to record Maura's first solo album. The album was very impressive, with all the top Nashville session men playing on it, and it was a huge success when it hit the music shops. It included a song I had written called 'I Don't Know How You Do It', so I had a more than special interest in it.

The following year Maura decided to live and work in America, but she would still come home to Ireland and do tours about three times a year. My phone rang one day and it was the impresario himself, Maurice Cassidy. He asked me if I would be interested in touring with Maura as a duo when she was here. I was shocked, to say the least, but absolutely delighted, so I immediately said yes.

Maura came down to Drumshanbo to explore the musical possibilities of this project. She stayed with my wife and me for a week, during which time we put together a set of songs to feature in our act. I was very worried that Maura's fans would expect her to have a big band with her, and yet she was happy to be going out on the road with just 'little old me'.

Our first gig was in Drogheda and I was extremely nervous, but the nerves were unfounded. She tore the house down, and not one person complained about the simple show we gave them: they all loved it and went home happy. Even we were surprised at how well we were received, so from that point I was part of the Maura O'Connell and Charlie McGettigan duo. We toured for about two years in all, augmenting the act when required, with people like Arty McGlynn on guitar, Nollaig Casey on fiddle, Aidan McGuigan on bass and Peter O'Hanlon on guitar. We played every possible kind of venue. One night it would be an intimate theatre gig; the next night we could feature before a late-night disco.

It was always fun, but sometimes it was weird. We were booked to play at a hotel in Co. Kerry in September 1984. When we arrived, we immediately noticed a very strange musty smell as we checked out the stage area. We couldn't figure what it was, but it smelled like a dead body or something. Following our noses, we traced it to a large storage room at the back of the stage. Slowly, we pulled the door open, not knowing what we might find. We knew it was something rotten, and it had that human smell about it for sure.

Suddenly, a deluge of smelly roller-skate boots fell out on top of us. The hotel had just thrown about 200 pairs of sweaty boots into this big storage room without cleaning them first! During the summer months they held roller discos, and here was all the gear. Imagine 200 pairs of sweaty socks packed into your cupboard with the door closed on them for any length of time. It was weird, and that was only the start of a totally weird day altogether.

Eventually we got to go on stage. The venue was packed, and the gig was going great when I noticed that Maura's attention had been drawn to a few women at the front of the stage. She was shaking her head quite sternly at them. We continued singing, and I felt something hitting my face. Then it happened again. People were throwing coins at us!

I had often heard of people throwing tomatoes or other rubbish at stage performers to show their unhappiness with the show, but this was a new one to me. Throwing coins must mean they loved it!

'What's all this about?' I asked Maura.

'They wanted to get up and make a speech, and I said *no*!'

All I could say was 'What?' as the coins were now coming at us relentlessly. I knew they would soon run out of coins, and we were near the end of the gig, so we continued regardless for all the people who did want to listen.

When we got back to the dressing room, I asked Maura, 'What was that all about?' It turned out that a shipment of arms destined for the IRA had been intercepted by the gardaí earlier that day near Banna Strand. Several people were arrested and taken to Dublin for questioning. It seems that one of the women who wanted to make a speech was the wife of one of the men who were arrested. Who knows what she wanted to say?

I agreed with Maura in not allowing that on our show. People were there to enjoy the night, and it was not the time or the place for political speeches. We got paid as agreed, but on the way home I said to Maura, 'We should have got them to gather up all those coins fired at us during the show. We deserved them as well, and there must be a fortune scattered around the stage.' We both laughed and kept the joke going to shorten the road. 'Do you think, Charlie, we should have each been given a brand-new pair of roller blades as well, for putting up with the stink?' was the next quip, followed by more uncontrolled laughter.

On reviewing my notes for the time, I'm amazed at just how much work Maura and I were doing together. Towards the end of that year I began to drift away from Jargon, as I've described in a previous chapter: not in any deliberate way, but I could not be everywhere. I had to make choices, and I was influenced by the fact that Maura had a really good management team. I was spending most of my time with her anyway.

In January 1985, Tony McAuley asked me to appear again on *As I Roved Out*, this time with Maura O Connell. It was lovely. Maura had become really well known at this stage. A month later I was back on the TV when Jargon appeared on a BBC show, *The Entertainers*, which was recorded at the King's Hall in Belfast. The lads knew by this time that I was heading down a different road. My days with them were now few and far between.

Maura kept telling me that I should come out to America and make a record, so eventually I did.

CHAPTER 39

New York and Nashville

I travelled to America for the first time in early 1985. Maura O'Connell at this time was living in Nashville and was recording an album there, with her then partner, Béla Fleck. To describe Béla as a banjo player somehow sounds belittling: he was a multi-instrumentalist, and introduced the banjo into a wide range of music, including jazz and classical.

It's ironic that a bunch of us acoustic music fans in Drumshanbo and Ballyfarnon were already aware of people like Béla, Sam Bush and others, long before Maura met Béla. He was possibly the most exciting banjo player in the world, and still is. So you can imagine how excited I was at the prospect of being in the recording studio with him.

Before going to Nashville, Maura and I had a few gigs in the Boston area, and also a week at Tommy Makem's Irish Pavilion in New York. Yes, the Big Apple – and I was going to get a taste of it! When we were there we stayed in the apartment of a lovely Scottish woman called Maggie Cadden – a concert promoter that Maura had become friends with – on East 84th Street, within easy walking distance of downtown New York. I remember asking Maggie (a veteran of New York) where I could get a map of the place. 'You won't need one,' she said. 'It's just streets and avenues in blocks. You'll find your way around no problem.' She was right. However, it all felt very strange to me that first night. After all, I was a long way from Drumshanbo and Ballyshannon.

Maggie took us to a really lovely Chinese restaurant that first night. She was friendly with this very humorous man whose name I can't recall, and he made up the foursome. As we settled in for our meal, an elderly man and his wife sat down with a younger couple at another table: I assumed one of the younger couple was their offspring. All was going fine until the elderly man suddenly stood up and proceeded to thump the elderly lady in the face.

I was horrified, and made to intervene immediately, but the droll man with Maggie stopped me, saying 'Let them be! She's probably used to it.' With that the elderly man sat down, and the family continued their meal as if nothing had happened. I turned to the guy I was with and asked 'What do you mean, she's probably used to it?' He told me it was a common occurrence over there and nobody ever interfered, adding 'You could get stabbed, you know!' He then asked me, 'Does that not happen back in Ireland?'

I had no answer, but it made me think and, more importantly, become aware of domestic violence. Eventually, I wrote a song called 'Why, Why, Why?', loosely based on a Tim Edey melody, in which I tried to figure why domestic abuse happens. It's one of the songs on my *Man from Twenty* album. Here are the lyrics:

'Why, Why, Why?' (words and music by Charlie McGettigan and Tim Edey)

Why, why, why, do you make her cry, cry, cry?
You say that you love her; you think the world
*   of her*
But I ask you why, why, why?
Pain, pain, pain, you give her pain, pain, pain
Try to confuse her, batter and bruise her
Do it again, and again and again?

You lose control, assume a new role
Go to some dark and dangerous hole
You hit her hard then you try to console her
But I ask you why, why, why?

Time goes by; she gives you one last try
Maybe it's over, maybe you'll never
Make her want to cry, cry, cry
But she sees that look in your eyes
That look that she despises
She sees the stranger, she sees the danger
And I ask you why, why, why

One minute love, the next minute hate
First you are tender then you're irate
You go on some bender then it abates
I ask you why, why, why

Why, why, why, do you make her cry, cry, cry
You say you love her, think the world of her
But I ask you, why, why, why?

The next morning we took a taxi to check out Tommy Makem's Irish Pavilion. We were stopped at an intersection when I noticed a pedestrian walk in front of a cyclist, then push the cyclist to the ground. The pedestrian ran, opened the door of our cab as we came alongside, and jumped in. 'That guy is going to kill me!' he was yelling. The cab driver braked to a halt and replied, 'Not in my cab he's not, get the hell out!'

Just then the cab door opened again: the cyclist was trying to attack the pedestrian, and also trying to push his bike through the open door. In typical Irish fashion, we scooted out the other door and left them to it. 'What about my fare?' yelled the cabbie? 'Get it off those two!' I shouted back as we ran. I don't know what happened after that, but if it was today someone would have it up on YouTube.

Despite this chaotic first experience of New York, the rest of the week at Tommy's Pavilion went extremely well. We played three sets a night and went down a storm. The atmosphere was electric, and we always left the stage on a high. One thing that has stuck in my mind is a huge picture of Tommy Makem himself that hung on a wall at the back of the venue: one of those pictures that would be looking at you no matter where you were in the room. It certainly kept the staff on their toes.

Maura O'Connell's friends De Dannan were in town that week as well. Maggie Cadden was organising their concert, so I had to move out to make room for them. Luckily, Sean and Olive Conlan and their family from Drumshanbo lived just a couple of blocks away, and they gave me a bed for the night. They had come to one of our concerts in Tommy's and given me their number. Olive was a private nurse and Sean was the caretaker of the apartment block they lived in, which entitled them to a free apartment. It was in the basement, and all you could see out of the window was an endless procession of legs as they passed by on the pavement above. The apartment was beautifully decorated, and I was surprised when they proudly told me that they had furnished it almost entirely from skips. It seems that this was normal in New York.

Maura told me about a great bar we should visit: a place called Brandy's, directly underneath Maggie's apartment. What she did not tell her naïve friend from Ireland was that it was a gay bar. The music there was terrific: the musicians were out-of-work Broadway singers, comedians, actors and dancers, waiting for their next big gig. There was a huge goldfish bowl on top of the grand piano, where you put your dollars to tip the performers. The talent was truly amazing, and of course there was a huge camp element to the audience.

It was a great evening until the MC asked where everyone was from. 'Ireland!' Maura called out, pointing at me. The MC then insisted we sing. I figured we'd go down like a lead balloon in this environment that was so different from what we were used to, and I felt really intimidated by the quality of entertainment that had been on before us. Thankfully they loved us, and we seemed to fit in perfectly.

After our week in New York we took a plane to Nashville. I stayed with Maura and Béla in their house, and soon realised why Béla was the best banjo player in the world. He practised all the time: I'm talking a minimum of four hours a day.

Béla was producing Maura's second album, *Just in Time*. Jackie Daly, the accordion player, was also over from Ireland, and dubbing on some tracks. I was singing some backing vocals, along with this demure woman whose name was Nanci. One of the songs Maura was recording a song I wrote called 'Feet of a Dancer'. It sounded great and I was happy with her interpretation of it. When we finished for the day,

Nanci asked me if I would like to go to the Cannery that evening, where she was launching her new album. I didn't need to be asked twice.

All the music royalty of Nashville were there, and I was mesmerised by the whole affair. It transpired that the Nanci I had been singing with all day was the now famous Nanci Griffith. Some members of one of my favourite bands, the Newgrass Revival, were there, and I remember their guitarist Pat Flynn asking Maura if she had made her Easter duty, like confession, mass and communion, before Easter Sunday. I thought he was joking but he was deadly serious. It was some night, and there was I in the middle of it all, trying to look cool.

Another night we went to see the Nashville Bluegrass Band at the Station Inn: they had a great sound and were very talented. Jackie Daly was with us, and I enjoyed having him around. He's a very humorous man who doesn't hesitate to speak his mind, and it was good to know I wasn't the only one feeling like a fish out of water.

I met many of my heroes during those few days: Jerry Douglas, Sam Bush and Russ Barrenberg, to name but a few. I also spoke to Emmylou Harris on the phone, although I didn't know it was her at the time. She called looking for Béla and when he wasn't there, and said 'Tell him Emmylou called' as she hung up!

Béla very generously introduced me to several publishers, and I soon realised two things. Publishers take their business very seriously in America, because they don't know if they are going to hear the next number one song when a songwriter walks into the room. And at any one time, something like 75,000 songs are in circulation in Nashville: a sobering thought.

We returned to New York for a few more days, and I went home shortly after that. It wasn't long before Maura was back in Ireland as well. I never played in Croke Park, but we did play in Páirc Uí Chaoimh, on a bill with John Denver and Kate and Anna McGarrigle. We played the Ulster Hall in Belfast as well as the Belfast Opera House, and the Olympia, Gaiety and Abbey Theatres in Dublin. One Friday night I was playing with Jargon at the Gaiety Theatre, and had to rush away to play another gig with Maura at the Wexford Inn. Such was life in those days.

Working with Maura opened up many and varied venues to me. She and her management team treated me really well during those two years. What I learned about the music business has stood to me well, right up to the present day.

'Feet of a Dancer' (words and music by Charlie McGettigan)

I hope you find the feet of a dancer
I hope you can sing in the rain
I hope you find all the easy answers to your pain

It won't be easy. What can I say?
There will be trouble on the way
Around every corner, terror and tears
But always remember that we're here

And I hope you find the feet of a dancer
I hope you can sing in the rain
I hope you find all the easy answers to your pain
I hope you find love and affection
I hope you find someone who'll care
I hope you find all the right directions everywhere, everywhere

A shoulder to cry on
Whenever you're low
You can rely on us you know
There's nothing too crazy
Nothing too dear
Always remember that we're here

Even when the rain comes falling down, and oh it's falling down on you

And I hope you find the feet of a dancer
I hope you can sing in the rain
I hope you find all the easy answers to your pain
I hope you find love and affection
I hope you find someone who'll care
I hope you find all the right directions everywhere, everywhere

CHAPTER 40

Eleanor Shanley

I am living in a hotbed of traditional Irish music here in Co. Leitrim, but there is also lots of contemporary music. The place is full of wonderful musicians and singers, and I feel right at home here. The Lennons from Rossinver spring to mind, as does the McNamara family from Aughavas.

Just up the road from me in Keshcarrigan, a well-known singer called Eleanor Shanley was reared. It was the late Tony McGowan who first introduced me to Eleanor. Tony was a teacher in Drumshanbo Vocational School, and he heard her singing at a school concert. Ever the enthusiast, Tony figured he had Leitrim's answer to Joan Baez. He was right! Eleanor started to turn up at music sessions we used to have in various places when we weren't officially playing anywhere.

I was immediately struck by her voice: she had a great range and powerful projection. We might be playing in a very noisy pub, but Eleanor could silence the place with her rendition of an unaccompanied song like 'Raglan Road'. She had a voice that once you heard it, you wanted more.

We didn't see her as much after she went to work for a government agency called FÁS, because she was based in Dublin. She became involved with the Tops of the Town variety shows there, and represented the Wild Rose team from Manorhamilton, Co. Leitrim. Each team had to present a full-length variety show, and the finalists got the opportunity to appear at the Gaiety Theatre.

The next thing we knew, Eleanor Shanley was announced as the new singer with the then high-flying traditional group De Dannan, following in the footsteps of Dolores Keane, my good friend Maura O'Connell and Mary Black. This put her on a different level, with many TV appearances, and she gave up her FÁS job. We were all really proud of Eleanor's success.

Eleanor had recorded a few songs with De Dannan, and one day she called me and asked if I had any songs that might suit her. 'Yes,' I said, 'I've written lots of songs! Come and take your pick.' She picked a song I had just written, inspired by my daughter Tara flying off to Belgium to work as an au pair for the summer. I remember thinking as Tara entered the final departure area at Dublin Airport, 'If anything happened to you my life would be unliveable.' That was the inspiration for the song. Eleanor recorded 'If Anything Happened to You' with De Dannan. I was absolutely thrilled.

After a few years Eleanor decided to go solo, and asked me if I would help her out. This was yet another extension to my already crowded musical activities, but I was happy to say yes. In the following years we played all over Europe at various festivals. One that stood out was Tønder Fest in Denmark, a huge festival where Eleanor would get four or five standing ovations for her singing. In Europe when they want more, they do what we here in Ireland call a 'slow handclap'.

We added some good musicians to our ensemble, including people like my old Jargon friends Brendan Emmett and Liam Gilmartin. I remember playing in a really small venue in Tønder, the town where the festival was held, for Queen Margrethe II of Denmark. We didn't know what to expect, but it turned out to be a big success. The queen sat smoking constantly in the front row and was a very unassuming person. She was on an official visit to celebrate Tønder's 500th anniversary.

On another occasion Eleanor's suitcase went missing, and the airline gave her an emergency kit that included toothpaste, toothbrushes and two pairs of paper knickers. Whether she wore the paper knickers we will never know, but we all had a great laugh teasing her.

Eleanor was always up for a laugh, but was also well able to stand her ground when needed. If there was ever an argument about money or conditions with a promoter regarding a gig, she would make sure we got what was due. One time I saw her take on a guy who was mugging a neighbour of hers outside the apartment block where she was living in Dublin. She ran down to the ground floor and confronted the mugger, who didn't hang around too long!

Eleanor has worked with well-known Irish artists as well as many international ones. I remember at one stage she had two Black gospel singers from Harlem with her. I saw their show in a small theatre in Carrigallen, Co. Leitrim: it was pure magic, and Eleanor was well able to hold her own in the gospel and blues elements of the music. These were powerful singers from America's top gospel choirs.

We all adjourned to a local pub after the gig. As is usual in small pubs in Ireland, there were two or three auld bucks smoking their pipes and minding their own business. I'll never forget seeing their jaws drop when these two very confident Black people arrived in the pub. It was like aliens had just landed and walked in.

The bar filled up very quickly with members of the theatre audience. A rousing sing-song started, and everybody was having the time of their lives. Suddenly there was a loud banging on the pub door, and two gardaí arrived and started taking names and addresses, including those of our two friends from Harlem. (You can be prosecuted for being in a pub after hours.) Also, two nuns from a local convent, dressed in regular clothing, had been at the concert and arrived in for the craic and a couple for the road. When the Gardai got addresses like Saint Veronica's Convent or Main Street, Harlem, they knew there was no point in going any further.

Later Eleanor worked for a number of years with Ronnie Drew of Dubliners fame. They were as different as chalk and cheese, but worked really well together, Ronnie with his gravelly voice and Eleanor with her dulcet tones. They released a song called 'A Couple More Years' with the line 'I've got a couple of years on you, baby, that's all' … and Ronnie certainly did.

I've worked on and off with Eleanor, and indeed still do on occasions. She has always been a pleasure to travel and work with. We have shared many adventures, both musically and socially. She is a fine singer but she always kept her feet firmly on the ground. Sometimes promoters would call from distant European locations and Eleanor's late mother would tell them that she couldn't come to the phone because she was over the fields chasing cattle. I don't think Irish mothers are well known for the diplomacy skills!

That was the reality of Eleanor's home life. She remains one of my favourite singers, and I sometimes have to pinch myself to confirm that I am actually standing on stage with her. Long may she continue singing!

CHAPTER 41

Paul Gurney – A Lifetime in Music

On a cold night in Carrick-on-Shannon in 1979, I first met Paul Gurney, a man who has been a very important part of my life ever since. I was auditioning for a TV show called *Trom agus Éadrom*. (You can see the show on YouTube: just search for *Trom agus Éadrom*.) It had been so snowy that day and night that Paul had to use his accordion case as a sled to get him out of his home place in Kiltyclogher, Co. Leitrim, and down to the road, where he got a lift into the town. It wasn't much warmer in the audition venue either, I can tell you. We met briefly, but I liked him straight away. He was that kind of fellow, friendly and very affable, with a twinkle in his eye.

Our paths didn't cross again until I was asked to produce a recording of one of my songs, 'People Are Telling Me', for a band called Lightning Strikes in Mudd Wallace's studio in Randalstown, Co. Antrim. Paul was one of the musicians, and I instantly remembered him. Again this was a brief encounter!

The next time we met was when Paul was operating out of a small studio in Earl Street in the centre of Longford town in 1989. He was recording an unknown singer called Cathy Jordan, who was recording one of my songs. Cathy was to become the lead vocalist in a traditional Irish music band called Dervish. They achieved worldwide success, and were picked to represent Ireland in the 2007 Eurovision Song Contest with a song called 'They Can't Stop the Spring'. I could see then that Paul was not only an excellent musician but a very skilful sound engineer as well. He was determined to get the very best sound possible, to enhance Cathy's voice.

When I decided to record my third studio album, *In Your Old Room*, I remembered Paul and his engineering abilities. I phoned him and asked to meet up; he invited me to his new studio in Longford. When I arrived I discovered that he was now working in a state-of-the-art studio owned by himself and a guy called Larry Keogh. He had come a long way from that snowy night all those years ago, through sheer hard work and a passion for music.

I decided that this was the place I wanted to record in. I like to lounge about between takes, so it was a bonus to find he had a lovely big green leather settee in the control room where artists could relax. It was one of the best decisions I ever made, and since then I have recorded six albums with Paul.

As I got to know Paul on a more personal level, he told me that he came to live in Kiltyclogher when his parents decided to leave London to take over his grandmother's shop there in 1969. His dad was a very athletic man who had served in the British army during the Second World War, and was wounded. His mum was a nurse. Paul was six years old at the time, and one would have thought that the culture shock of moving from London to a little village in Co. Leitrim would have been dreadful, but Paul always says that he instantly fell in love with the place. However, he did experience a little bit of anti-British sentiment because he had an English accent. He recalls that he lost the accent within about six weeks in order to blend in with his peers.

'Kilty', as it is known, is a tiny village in north Leitrim that is steeped in traditional music. The world-renowned Lennon family lived there at the time, as did the Shanley family, both of which were hugely important in influencing and focusing Paul's obvious musical talent. Ben Lennon, a master fiddler, his son Maurice, who was a founding member of Stockton's Wing, and Charlie, a renowned fiddle and piano player, are all highly respected traditional musicians. Michael Shanley taught Paul a lot of his Irish traditional music, and the Michael Shanley Traditional Music Festival is held in Kiltyclogher every year.

Paul had played a little piano in England, where his parents had an old upright in the front room. He never had lessons, but his sister Claire remembers him playing 'Alexander's Ragtime Band' on the old Joanna (that's what they called pianos) at the tender age of six. On arrival in Kiltyclogher Paul was exposed to Irish traditional music for the first time, and immediately warmed to it. He started off on the tin whistle and progressed to the piano accordion.

Soon he was entering the Fleadh Cheoil events himself, and he won the all-Ireland piano competition in 1978. Paul had the rare ability of playing jigs, reels, etc. with his right hand, using the left hand as his accompaniment. The piano at the time was mostly used only as an accompaniment instrument in traditional music; very few played it as a complete instrument. It is a difficult art to master, but not for Paul's natural talent.

He was sent off as a boarder to St Patrick's College in Cavan for his secondary education. Here he was exposed to pop and rock music, and played a borrowed electric guitar. Incidentally, the guy who loaned him the guitar was none other than my great friend John Hannigan. It's a small world!

Paul loved the electric guitar and formed a little rock outfit in St Pat's: they found themselves supporting professional bands like Reform from Limerick and Mama's Boys from Co. Fermanagh. He was a big fan of Pat McManus, who was also a multi-instrumentalist, in Mama's Boys, and others like Gary Moore of Thin Lizzy fame, and Johnny Fean of Horslips.

Paul went on to study electronic engineering in Sligo IT, and completed his City and Guilds. He soon found himself with lots of work as a television and radio engineer in Longford, where he moved after his studies. His love of rock 'n' roll took over again, and he began playing in professional bands. The professional music scene was a tough business, with many long hours not just playing but also travelling all over the country. It was not a life for everyone, but Paul persevered and became a much sought-after musician. He played for almost ten years with Lightning Strikes and many other bands. Finally he settled down with his wife Edel in Longford, where he now combines his years of experience as a musician and his training in electronic engineering in Real World Studios. I love going there.

It's hard to explain, but Paul has a great way of making me feel comfortable in the studio. I am not the greatest musician technically, but somehow I play and sing at the top of my game when I'm working with Paul. These days we instantly gel when I present a new song to record. He knows instinctively what is needed to record my songs. Over the past twenty-five years or so, we have rarely raised our voices above normal conversation level during our sessions, and that's rare in the music business. There are always artistic differences, but Paul is a patient man and I respect his opinions. Usually he does know better!

Paul is proficient at almost any musical instrument you ask him to play. He is an amazing rock electric guitarist, but can be equally amazing playing tunes from the traditional canon on acoustic guitar. He's a really super piano player, and is very proficient in producing all the varied keyboard sounds we use these days in the recording studio. There are lots of good musicians and lots of good recording engineers, so finding someone who is good at both might be enough. With Paul, it's the third element he has that makes him so special. He can listen to a song and know exactly what's needed to enhance it, and to get the best out of all those who come to his studio. That's an art in itself.

Paul has had the cream of Irish musicians working in his studio. From the world of traditional music, people like Matt Molloy, Frankie Gavin and De Dannan spring to mind, while Shay Healy, Marc Roberts, Paul Harrington and others from the wider world of entertainment have also benefited from working with Paul. Then there's me!

One day I was telling him about how my mother-in-law was afflicted with Alzheimer's disease. Paul's mother was suffering similar symptoms. We chatted about the difficulties of ageing and more, and eventually we decided to write a song. I think it is one of our best efforts, and I have a lot of fans who think so as well. It is called 'Sometimes'.

'Sometimes' (words and music by Charlie McGettigan and Paul Gurney)

I called to you the other day; you looked much the same
You didn't know what day it was; you didn't know my name
We talked about the good old days and how they'll be no
　　more
You asked for friends whose lives had ended many years
　　before

I spoke to you about my wife; you said you never knew
I spoke about my children and you said 'Children too?'
You talked about your mother as if she was still here
I told you she was dead and gone but you didn't seem to hear

Sometimes you're in a happy place
Sometimes frustration reigns
As I watch you look off into space and I wonder where you've been
Cos it hurts to watch you struggle with those demons in your head
And it hurts to watch your tortured face as you try to find the thread

I see the person who looked after me in childhood years
I always knew that you were there to wipe away my tears
And though I see you sitting here I know you're far away
In some demented state of mind; where that is, who can say?

We try to make some sense of it this family of ours
We try to come to terms with this disease that just devours
We wish that you were back with us, just like you used to be.
But we know that all that's left for us is some sweet memory

Paul has his own Eurovision claim to fame. He was the pianist in Marc Roberts's band when Marc represented Ireland in 1997 with 'Mysterious Woman'. They came second.

CHAPTER 42

And Then There's Christmas

'**D**id you hear the racket on your roof last night?' I asked young Shane McLaughlin from next door one Christmas morning. 'What racket?' asked Shane?

'Ah, sure, you must have heard it. Santa's sleigh broke down on your roof last night. The whole neighbourhood heard it. The reindeer were all in your back garden, grazing on the carrots you left out. Santa was in an awful quandary about being late for the Carrick-on-Shannon children, so Junior McGowan repaired one of the rotors on the sleigh wings as quickly as he could. I never knew there were wings on his sleigh myself, but Junior was well able to fix them.'

Shane's eyes were all agog as I told him the story. A couple of cows had strayed into his garden the night before, so I used their hoof prints as proof for my story. Shane was only about six years old at the time, so in his eyes this was all possible. He was sorry he missed it, but happy that he had left out plenty of carrots for Santa's reindeer.

I love Christmas! It is the most wonderful time of the year, as the song says. When I was a child, Santa used to visit every year and throw us handfuls of sweets as we crowded around him. We knew the real Santa only came on Christmas Eve, but we enjoyed these other Santas even though they had false beards and fake suits. Stephens's shop on Castle Street, Ballyshannon would have toys displayed in the window for the entire month of December, as would Paddy O Neill's at the Bridge End.

Each had a 'Toyland' that we would visit whenever we could, to pick out we wanted the real Santa to bring.

Christmas Eve was always a magical time for children, and still is. We would go to bed early that night, secretly determined not to sleep so we could get a glimpse of Santa for ourselves. Some kids were successful and would tell us about it the next day, as we sat in amazement. They would describe in great detail how they had seen Santa leaving their presents and having the snack they left out for him, while all the time they were pretending to sleep. The rest of us would have to admit that we had the same kind of plan, but unfortunately we didn't stay awake.

Christmas morning was the end of the wait, and all the children were excited to see what Santa brought. Our presents would be at the foot of our beds when we woke up, but we weren't allowed to open the parcels until everyone was up and about. The waiting would be excruciating. Presents in those days were things like cowboy suits for boys and nurse's outfits for girls. There would also be books – annuals, as they were called – like *Dandy* or *Beano* for the boys and *Bunty* and *Judy* for the girls. Another favourite was the Christmas stocking that held sweets and bars of chocolate and sometimes even cap guns.

We would all be marched off to Mass at 11am, where nearly every boy would be wearing a cowboy suit and every girl a nurse's outfit. Other kids would come to church on roller skates, and some better-off kids would arrive on brand-new bikes. We rode home from mass on imaginary horses, shooting each other with our cap guns, or stood on the square facing up to each other to see who the fastest draw was. If you lost, you had to lie motionless on the street for a few seconds to show you were dead.

My father used to talk about a kid in Dublin who enjoyed this so much he refused to grow up. He became famous around the city as an adult, because you never knew where you would meet him. Out of the blue you would hear 'Bang! Bang!', and when you looked around there he would be, pointing a big key at you. If you didn't fake having been shot and injured, he would shoot you again: 'Bang! Bang!' Everyone loved him, and he became affectionately known as 'Bang Bang'. What a great character he was.

When I was a teenager, Midnight Mass on Christmas Eve became the focal point. It was actually held at midnight back then, not like today. I loved listening to the Christmas hymns and carols, and watching the drunks staggering up to receive Holy Communion. Occasionally one would light up a Woodbine and would have to be forcibly removed from the church. It was always good fun to watch and snigger.

After mass we would congregate in John Hannigan's house on the corner of Chapel Street and Market Street for tea with bread and jam. That was a treat to us back then. John's dad, Donald, had a great bass voice and would burst into that lovely hymn 'Adeste Fideles' at the drop of a hat. We would all join in, and salute him with our mugs of tea when he finished.

Pope John XXIII lived on the other side of the street from John's house. His real name was Josie Donagher, and he owned a pub that locals called 'The Vatican'. Josie looked uncannily like the Pope, so he was always known as 'the Pope', and very proud he was of it. If someone was a bit under the weather on Christmas Day, they could always get in the side door to 'The Vatican', and Pope John would serve them up some miraculous cure. At home their wives were engaged in their own miracle, getting the Christmas feast ready.

Christmas dinner was always a big deal, and we children looked forward to all the special treats. The turkey and ham with sage stuffing was so special, I get hungry every time I think of it. However, the same argument came up every year when I refused to eat the spuds and Brussels sprouts. I didn't like either, and still don't.

My favourite was the dessert. My dad would soak a sprig of holly in whiskey, then insert it in the Christmas pudding. He would light it, and a lovely blue flame would light up the table. There was always sherry trifle for those who didn't like pudding. After that the Christmas crackers would be brought out, and soon we would all be sitting around in silly paper hats. Usually the stuff inside the crackers was rubbish, but there were little riddles on small pieces of paper in them as well.

They gave us some fun for a while, but I remember one year someone had provided really expensive Christmas crackers, and the contents were great. Some of them had small fireworks and sparklers that could be lit indoors. I never found out where they came from, but I never forgot them either.

At around six o'clock the Christmas cake and mince pies would be produced, and turkey sandwiches provided for those who fancied them. When I think of it, my mum did so much to provide the best fare possible, and we took it all for granted. She would have baked and iced the cake with both almond and sugar icing weeks before. Lots of fruity ingredients were mixed in, plus lashings of John Power's whiskey.

Making the plum pudding was an even harder job. She would always let us lick the mixing bowl after she put its contents into a large bowl covered with two layers of grease-proof paper secured with twine. This was put into a big pot and boiled for hours. It was a couple of months' hard work for sure, and all the wives and mothers got was January 6th as a women's day off in recognition.

After tea, as it was called then (because dinner was at lunchtime) we would play games as a family. Someone had always received a compendium of games, or maybe a draughts board. As we grew older, games of Monopoly became the big one, and rows invariably broke out as interpretations of the rules were questioned. Monopoly games could go on forever, and most weren't finished before we all grew tired. We would retire to our beds, happy little children, and as Goretti's dad would say in later years, 'Christmas is as far away now as it ever was.'

When my own children came along we got to enjoy it all again, from a different point of view. We kept to all the same traditions we had experienced as kids. One year I ordered a home-reared turkey from a colleague, Bernie McCauley: 'No bigger than twelve pounds' weight,' I told him. Bernie delivered the turkey on Christmas Eve fully gutted, with the giblets in a small bag. When Goretti tried it for size in the oven on Christmas morning it wouldn't fit, so we had to cut it up into smaller pieces. Bernie had given us an eighteen-pound turkey, but only charged us for a twelve-pounder. Goretti stuffed it with the kind of stuffing that only she can make, and eventually it was ready to cook.

She still makes the stuffing for both our daughters these days. I know many people who still swear by their granny's stuffing, pudding or cakes. I think it shows how much they enjoyed all their Christmas feasts when they were children themselves.

I always enjoyed it when Goretti's parents came to visit us in Drumshanbo. Red Jack was a great storyteller. I remember one Stephen's Day when Jack was engaged in conversation with another GAA great, our friend Tony McGowan. As the whiskey was consumed, the tales got taller and taller. Jack was talking about a particular day when a game was on in the Brothers' field in Ballyshannon. Someone took a haymaker of a kick, and the wind carried the ball into the River Erne. This was a common occurrence, as the pitch wasn't too far from the river.

'And wait till I tell ye,' said Jack. 'I was fishing down the channel a few months after and I caught this huge salmon. When I cut open the salmon, do you know what we found inside?'

'What?' said Tony.

'The bloody football!' said Jack, laughing his head off.

Another story I loved Red Jack telling was about the great snow of 1947. There are various descriptions of how deep the snow was that year, and many photographs on Google showing houses submerged in it. Jack would say, 'I was walking through the town on the day after the big snow and I tripped over something.'

People would ask 'What was it?'

'Well, I pulled the snow off the object and found it was a cross.'

'A cross?'

'Yes. It was the cross on the steeple of the church.'

These were the kind of innocent yarns that were spun when you were in Jack's company.

I remember them coming up to stay with us for a week once. Jack lasted only three days before he yearned to return to Ballyshannon. They were very happy there, and were not much for travelling.

CHAPTER 43

Black Pudding for Christmas

Down the years, Christmas was always a busy time for me as far as music was concerned, with office parties, carol-singing events and Christmas concerts. One of the most joyous events to perform at was the RTÉ Television Christmas Eve concert, which was and still is a huge part of Christmas for the public. Highlights would be sharing the programme with artists such as the Chieftains and Chris de Burgh. They were generally presented by RTÉ favourites like Mary Kennedy and Anne Cassin, and held in places like Maynooth Seminary Chapel. They were recorded a few weeks in advance, so I had two separate kinds of Christmas experiences every year, and both were terrific.

The excitement on Christmas morning in our house was palpable, as the children opened their presents with sheer delight. Whatever they got, it was great, and they didn't have to wait until we got up to open them. They would rush into our room at six or seven in the morning, and sometimes earlier, to tell us the news about what Santa had brought. We were amazed, of course, and equally excited for them.

There was always that Christmas morning panic when something was missing, like batteries for toys, or some element of the Christmas dinner. Poor Joseph Mac used to be tortured on Christmas Day, opening his shop on his one day off in the year to provide last-minute things forgotten by families.

Goretti and I liked to have a glass of wine with our Christmas dinner. One Christmas the panic set in when we couldn't find the corkscrew, so I called down to Michael and Noreen Breen, who lived three doors down from us, to see if I could borrow one. They would have been in their fifties at the time, and didn't have children. Mick opened the door in a black tuxedo, complete with white shirt and bow tie. Noreen, standing behind him, was in a lovely sparkling evening dress. They invited me in, and I was charmed to see their beautifully decorated front room. I felt like I was in Buckingham Palace. Mick was a mechanical fitter in the power station, but the way he looked that day he could have been Prince Philip, and Noreen could have been the Queen. It's a memory I'll always cherish.

Television had come a long way by the time my children were kids, and their Christmases revolved around shows and films like *Willy Wonka and the Chocolate Factory* and *The Christmas Morecambe and Wise Show*. We did all the usual things, but sometimes Tara ended up going off to the piano room in a huff over some board game or other conflict. She would pound the piano for half an hour and come back as if nothing had happened. Shane and Ciara loved getting her going, but she always settled herself down with music. Even the little rows between kids were a joy to observe at Christmas, as their individual characters began to shine through.

Talking of television, a man I came to know very well, Red Jack Gallagher, used to tell us about the first television in Kildoney, a remote townland between Ballyshannon and Rossnowlagh. The owner was a man called Joe Morrow who was knowledgeable about most things, and was known to sing a song every now and then. He had a huge TV set installed where the dinner table used to be in his kitchen, regularly ate his meals off it, and always referred to it as 'Her'. 'There was great stuff on *HER* last night,' he'd say.

Joe considered himself an authority on most things but in particular about music. He was often heard after a few pints singing in a high tenor voice songs like 'Come back Paddy Reilly to Ballyjamesduff' or 'Johnston's Motor Car'. No one ever told him that he *wasn't* one of the finest singers in Ireland, so he continued to believe he was. He was asked one time what he thought of the famous Irish tenor Count John Mc Cormack.

'Yerra…. He's not bad' he answered.

On one occasion, the assembled masses of Kildoney were in Joe's house watching the Miss World contest. The girls were introduced with their 'vital statistics' (a term we rarely hear now), i.e. their bust, waist and hip measurements: for example 'Miss Canada, 36–22–36'. One of the neighbours asked 'What are those numbers they're calling out, Joe?'. 'Them's their muscles,' Joe replied.

Another time, the neighbours were in Joe's kitchen to watch the second Muhammad Ali–Sonny Liston heavyweight title fight from the USA. This would have been at about three in the morning due to the time difference. Joe always had his special seat beside the fire, and no one else would dare sit there. The excitement was huge.

Just as the fight started, Joe turned towards the fire to relight his pipe, and by the time he got it lit, it was all over: Ali had knocked out Liston in one minute and fifteen seconds, and Joe had missed it. He was furious, but with the craic and sing-song in the house, he soon calmed down.

Both Jack and Bob were very involved in local politics, being staunch Fianna Fáil supporters. The enmity between Fianna Fáil and Fine Gael would come to the fore at election times. Jack and Bob would canvass with the Fianna Fáil candidates, and would spend many hours putting up posters and distributing other election paraphernalia.

Music always played a big role in our house. Not only would I be performing for various Christmas TV shows and other events in the weeks prior to the big day, but Goretti and I still sing with the Drumshanbo adult choir, as I have mentioned, and have sung at Midnight Mass for nearly forty years now. Orla Daly, Eamonn Daly's wife, is the choir's musical director and has the patience of a saint. She organises a Christmas carol service every year around December 20th. It's always a very special event when our own choir joins forces with the children's choir and the folk choir, plus special guests. We've had Michael Harding, Seamus O'Rourke and singers like Eleanor Shanley and Sandy Kelly. We had the Strabane Silver Band one year and they were sensational. We normally start rehearsals in mid November, refreshing the arrangements of our favourite Christmas songs and carols. I love it! I could sing Christmas songs all year.

One year Aonghus McAnally, producer of the *Gay Byrne Hour*, brought 'Gay's Christmas Show' to St Patrick's Church in Drumshanbo. We had a full orchestra, and guests like tenor Finbar Wright, Juliet Turner and the wonderful soprano Virginia Kerr. Our choir sang beautifully, and I sang a brand-new Christmas song I had written called 'Johnny's Coming Home for Christmas', accompanied by the wonderful National Youth Orchestra. It's hard to describe what it feels like to hear your new song in a setting like St Patrick's Church. It was live, with the whole country tuning in.

This was Gay's last Christmas show, and he joined the congregation for a knees-up after it. He was so friendly and spoke to everyone. We presented him with a lovely hand-crafted wooden sculpture of a vintage microphone made by Drumsna wood sculptor Jim Gannon. It was an honour for us all to be with Gay on his final Christmas radio show.

I was also part of the Gay Byrne Christmas Eve Show a few times. This was usually in Grafton Street, and once again it was a treat to watch Gay in action. He would be based on the balcony at Bewley's restaurant, and in place at about 7am to make sure everything was up to scratch. Like most professionals, he could make his presentation seem almost spontaneous, whereas in reality a huge amount of work went into it.

The atmosphere on Grafton Street on Christmas Eve was always special. Some were rushing around last minute panic buying, while others were just strolling around soaking up the good vibes. I would usually perform a new song on the show, which increased the adrenaline rush for me.

As my children grew older, the Christmas priorities changed. They wanted to spend a lot more of their time with their friends. The usual arguments arose, like whether or not they would be let go to the Christmas disco. Invariably everyone was going to the disco except them, so they usually won, because we were mostly too exhausted to argue with them. That's not entirely true: it was mostly because we were kids ourselves at one time, and in some ways still are.

Down the years I've always managed to keep Christmas Day free to be at home with my family. On Stephen's Day we often went out with the Wren Boys. This involved dressing up in ridiculous costumes and masks, and then going around to pubs and houses singing and playing seasonal songs. We would have traditional musicians and singers all in disguise, and the craic would be mighty. Many of the pubs would treat us to a seasonal Christmas drink, which we never refused. We would be quite tipsy at the end of our little tour. Still, we raised lots of money for charity and it was all just so much fun.

For many years I organised a 'black pudding' evening in aid of North West Hospice in one of the local pubs. 'Black pudding' referred to hackneyed songs, but it also meant that we would serve actual black pudding to all the patrons. I was blessed to have really great guest artists like Tommy Fleming, Marc Roberts, Seamus O'Rourke and Eleanor Shanley. In the year we won the Eurovision, Paul Harrington and I topped the bill. These were very special events not just because we made thousands of Euros for the North West Hospice, but because they showed the heartfelt generosity of my musical friends, who gave their time free of charge.

Midnight Mass these days is at 9pm, which means we can adjourn to one of the local pubs after it's over. The usual drunks make an appearance at mass in every town, even at 9pm. As they stagger towards the altar for their Christmas communion, I always smile and think to myself, 'some things never change'.

However, other things do change. Your kids become adults with partners, and now the kids in the house are your grandchildren. Our grandchildren have given Goretti and me a new lease of life. We have been so lucky to be able to spend endless hours in their company, and we are really proud of them. They are all different and have unique characters of their own.

Our first daughter, Tara, went on to study for her BA in music at Maynooth University and, shortly after qualifying, met her husband-to-be, Seanie Bennett, when they had part-time jobs in a pub called The Roost. She now lives in Johnstownbridge with Seanie and their three children. Tara brought Padraig, Siofra and Cathal into our lives.

All three are members of the Dublin Youth Orchestra, where they play violin. They have played with the DYO for many years, in venues all over the country as well as many performances at the National Concert Hall.

Padraig is also an accomplished guitarist (I wonder where he got that from) and released two singles that received airplay on radio stations throughout the country, including RTÉ Radio One. He has also co-written a short opera which was performed by the DYO with guest singers. Padraig conducted the orchestra. Not bad for an eighteen-year-old! It has been my privilege to play with him on national radio and we have regular jam sessions, which I always enjoy.

Cathal is a fine singer and has been in the recording studio as well. To date he has recorded three pieces of music with the help of the guiding hand of the multi-talented Paul Gurney in Longford. He also plays piano and ukulele, and he is only thirteen years of age. I hope he makes waves in the music industry as he gets older.

Siofra, possibly the most musical of the three, does not like the limelight. She is a wonderful violinist and is now learning to play the cello. I don't know where she is going to take her music, but she will always be able to count on my support.

My younger daughter, Ciara, works as a legal librarian these days, and she and her husband Ray have given us three more lovely grandchildren, Olivia, Leo and Eoin. They live in Dublin and we love them all dearly.

Ciara's three have gravitated towards sport. They also have a passion for the visual arts. Olivia and Leo are very promising artists and I love seeing their creations, especially at Christmas. Eoin is still very young, but tries to do everything his older siblings do. I love watching them all develop.

Olivia's latest love is rugby, and she has joined her local team in Terenure. When Olivia gets interested in something she gives it her all, so I look forward to watching her play for Ireland one day. I think Leo's game is going to be tennis, but he has such a natural sporting instinct that he will be good at whatever he chooses. We are always teasing Olivia about her support of the Dubs, but she does have a soft spot for Leitrim too. She even wears earrings with the Leitrim colours.

These days we spend Christmas Day with Tara, her husband, Seanie, and their children, who are growing up now much faster than I would like. We spend Stephen's Day with Ciara and her husband, Ray, and their children. What a treat it would be to spend Christmas in the future with my great-grandchildren … well, you never know!

We have been so lucky to have had such lovely children. Tara and Ciara, and their families, are such an important part of our lives. We can chat to them on the phone, but what we enjoy most is when they visit us here in Drumshanbo, or we visit them in their homes in Dublin and Kildare. Of course someone who is ever present in our minds, especially at Christmas, is our beloved Shane. He was a light that shone brighter than any Christmas tree, and he is and will always be a huge presence in all our lives.

They have all left home now, so it is just Goretti and me. We have been in love for the bones of sixty years. I didn't know love could get better as the years went on, but it has, and continues to get better and better. I love to see her in a crowd and to feel our eyes connect. This happens again and again, mainly because she always stands out in a crowd for me. I know she has always been the one stabilising feature in my life, and I feel so lucky to have spent so many happy years with her.

I wrote a millennium song in the year 2000 for our local children's choir. It was called 'Merry Christmas and a Happy New Year', and since then I have had nothing but joy singing the song with them at every Christmas Day Mass.

In 2020 we made a video of me, dressed as Santa Claus, and the children singing my song. We used it as the theme for a Go Fund Me campaign in aid of the autism unit at St Patrick's School, Drumshanbo. We raised over €20,000 and the children were very proud of themselves.

'Merry Christmas and a Happy New Year' (words and music by Charlie McGettigan)

It's that time of year again
When we forget all the trouble that's been
And the children look for snowflakes in the sky
And the people passing by wish you the best for the season
And no one has to ask the reason why

So many years have come and gone
Since he sent his only son
And Jesus Christ was born to save us all
And all around the world there's gonna be a celebration
And Jesus is the reason for the call

So Merry Christmas and a Happy New Year
Let's make this Christmas go without a tear
Let's understand, hold out the hand of friendship without fear
So Merry Christmas and a Happy New Year

As we greet the coming year
And a brand-new year is here
And the old one disappears into history
Let's hope in a thousand more, we'll celebrate this great occasion
The birth of Jesus Christ on Christmas Day

In this modern world it's so nice to see every year that same sparkle of the Christmas magic in the children's eyes, which we all had in ours so many years ago. You don't have to have a lot of money, and you don't even have to have kids yourself, to share in that Christmas magic. Goodwill is free, and I for one want to see more of it, especially at Christmas.

Pops at Bushy Park with granddaughter Olivia.

Our children at home in the early 1980's: Shane and Tara with our youngest Ciara in front.

Pops reading a bedtime story to Cathal, Siofra and Pádraig (Tara's children).

Nana Goretti reading: Leo, Goretti, Olivia, Eoin and mum Ciara.

14 June 1998: Shane McGettigan of Leitrim during the Connacht Senior Football Championship Semi-Final match between Leitrim and Galway at Páirc Seán Mac Diarmada in Carrick-On-Shannon, Co. Leitrim.
(Photo by Brendan Moran/Sportsfile)

Family together: Back: Charlie, Siofra, Ciara, Pádraig, Ray, Eoin, Seanie. Front: Cathal, Tara, Olivia, Goretti, Leo.

CHAPTER 44

The Songwriter – Brendan Graham

On my musical journey through life I've met many people. You never realise how important some of the people you meet might become later in your life. One such man was Brendan Graham.

I first met him at the Wild Rose Song Contest in Manorhamilton, Co. Leitrim back in 1974. I could see he took the dress code very seriously, as he wore a tartan dinner jacket. He is a big tall fellow and was looking very smart indeed that night. I was immediately drawn to his very friendly personality, but we were engaging in a song contest battle so there was a slight rivalry.

In the end the best song won – 'Sing Me an Old Irish Song', written by Brendan and sung by Frank McCaffrey. Song contests were all the rage back then, and we songwriters kept running into each other at the different events. Brendan had won the Wild Rose Song Contest so many times that eventually he disqualified himself from entering, but he would still turn up as a guest. The last song I entered was called 'I Stayed at the Heartbreak Hotel'. I'm sure you can guess what that was about. The contest was cancelled that year, which was a real disappointment, because I felt it was my best chance of winning to date.

Song contests were great vehicles to showcase newly written songs. It was always interesting to hear other people's appraisal of your work, good or bad. It was a learning curve and quite an achievement in itself to qualify for the finals in any of them. There was always a live band, and the songs had to be arranged to suit the band. Saxophone player

Gay McIntyre from Derry was the band leader at the Wild Rose contest, and the band featured jazz guitarist Norman Watson, a regular on a UTV series called *Teatime with Tommy*. I was slightly in awe of these musicians, not just because they were great players, but because I had often heard my father and mother talk about dancing to their music back in the late 1940s and early 1950s. They always spoke very highly of them as musicians.

Brendan and I kept in touch from then on, mostly by letter. We would plan to meet up at a particular song contest, but also met by chance at various events. Brendan, like me, was a very consistent song-writer, constantly writing and getting demos of his songs made. In the 1980s and 1990s we started writing the occasional song together, one of which, 'By the Time the Leaves Are Brown', was recorded by Sandy Kelly and American singer Hal Ketchum. To get even a nibble from an American artist in those days created huge excitement for us.

Brendan would occasionally send me rough demos of new songs he had written, and I would send him a demo or two of my own songs. I valued his opinion, and I like to think that he valued mine. In 1992 he sent me a rough recording of a song called 'Rock 'n' Roll Kids'. I was a big Don Williams fan at the time, and when Brendan asked me to do a demo of the song, the version I did definitely had a Don Williams influence. We both liked it, but it really wasn't going anywhere.

The following year he sent me a different demo of 'Rock 'n' Roll Kids', sung by a Dublin singer called Paul Harrington. I had heard Paul singing on the radio and enjoyed his style. This demo was just Paul singing to his own piano accompaniment. I told Brendan that it was a fantastic version of the song and that I'd eat my hat if it wasn't picked up by some international artist and make him a fortune.

'Rock 'n' Roll Kids' then took on what seems like a life of its own. The same year, 1993, I was asked to be a judge of the preliminary entrants in the Irish National Song Contest. There were 300 or 400 entries. Back then, judging was done under very strict rules. All the entrants had a pseudonym so the judges wouldn't be swayed by knowing the artists or the songwriters. Accountancy firm KPMG supervised the whole process very sternly, with a member of their staff sitting in.

All was going well until this very familiar song came to us. It was 'Rock 'n' Roll Kids'. I had to say that I had heard the song previously, and I knew who the songwriter was as well as the singer. It was decided to put the song aside, and the KPMG representative took a note of my statement. The song didn't qualify for the 1993 contest as a result.

I told Brendan what had happened, and I knew he would be disappointed, which he was. I was also feeling bad for him, but in his usual stoic fashion he quickly got over it. It was the second time the song had not made it: he had also entered it in the 1992 contest. You would think that would be the end of that, but you would be wrong.

Brendan is a very determined man, and the following year he entered 'Rock 'n' Roll Kids' in the National Song Contest again. This time there was no fly in the ointment, because I was not on the jury. 'Rock 'n' Roll Kids' qualified for the 1994 National Song Contest Final. I think it was called Eurosong that year, but it would always be the National Song Contest to me.

A few hours after Brendan heard that 'Rock 'n' Roll Kids' had qualified for the final, he called me to tell me the good news. I was delighted for him. I asked if it was the version with just Paul on the piano; he said it was. I advised him to continue the journey with just Paul and his piano, and ignore the temptation to add in all the usual Eurovision bells and whistles: orchestra, dancers, etc. What he said next bowled me over.

'Yes … but I have a big favour to ask you,' said Brendan.

'Ask away.'

'I think there's just one element missing.'

'What's that?'

'You.'

'Shit, I wasn't expecting that,' I gasped.

'I know, but I think ye will have a great chance together.'

I was flabbergasted and caught completely off guard. He wanted me to join Paul with my acoustic guitar for the final. I said 'I don't know what to say, Brendan. That little song seems to have taken on a life of its own.'

'Well, think it over,' said Brendan, 'and come back to me in twenty-four hours with your decision.'

The Arigna Power Station, where I had been working, had closed down, and I was being transferred to the ESB's Cathleen's Falls hydro generating station in Ballyshannon. I was in the middle of buying a new house there, and was already commuting daily from Drumshanbo. It was not the ideal situation for me to be joining Paul Harrington at the National Song Contest final in Limerick. 'What if we won?' I thought.

Major discussions began with Goretti. I honestly didn't know whether I wanted to say yes or no. Goretti has always been my rock at times like this. We talked about all the pros and cons for hours, and eventually decided that I should give it a go. The biggest deciding factor for me was the song. I really loved the song and could clearly imagine how it would sound with the two of us. I had a feeling about it. I rang Brendan the next day and told him that I'd be delighted to join Paul for the final.

Mind you, I had been in the National Song Contest a couple of times down the years so I understood what was involved. In 1984 I reached the final with a cute little ditty called 'Bebop Delight', which I have already mentioned. It was a bit of nonsense that even I couldn't understand, and I had written it.

I also reached the 1987 final, with a song I had written about elitism, called 'Are You Shy?'; this time we used a backing track put together by Mudd Wallace. I was swayed by Mudd, who felt the song needed a 1980s arrangement. I have to say it wasn't one of my finer moments in music in that I had to sing the song in a way that I wouldn't have normally sung it. Still, it came third in the competition. I was pipped again by Johnny Logan, who represented Ireland that year with a great song called 'Hold Me Now'.

I really liked 'Are You Shy?' and felt it still had potential, so I recorded it again a few years ago for my album *The Man from 20*. This time I sang the song the way I originally wrote it, and I feel it's much better because of that. Have a listen and let me know what you think.

'Are You Shy?' (words and music by Charlie McGettigan)

You're cluttered up with secrets
You never show your hand
Very few arrangements in your band
I could talk all night about you
And not say a single word
You've got the shortest story ever heard

Are you shy?
Or are there some more reasons why?
You don't seem to laugh or to cry
Or is it simply that I can't see you?
Is it fair?
There has to be something to share
I wonder if you're really there
Or is it simply that I can't see you?
You keep a short selection
There's seldom someone new
You suffer their devotion to you
Stimulating conversation
Would seem where you are at
But mostly you're just talking through your hat

You get that look upon your face
The kind of look that you can't erase
I've got to face that you don't really want me

Soon preparations began for the final, to select Ireland's 1994 Eurovision entry. Brendan agreed with me that the 'bells and whistles' were out, and that it would be just the two of us, sink or swim. It was ironic that in my dreams prior to this of one day representing Ireland in the Eurovision Song Contest, Noel Kelehan always featured. There was always an orchestra, backing singers, etc., and you would hear those lovely words 'and conducting for Irlande, Mr Noel Kelehan!' That had been part of the thrill. Now here I was, and I wanted none of that. I think the song was telling me 'I'm just a simple song, don't complicate my charms.'

The last eight songs were being previewed, one each week, on Pat Kenny's Saturday night TV show *Kenny Live*. I still hadn't met Paul, so we arranged a meeting and a rehearsal on the Saturday afternoon at Lombard Studios. Paul came dressed in a black frock coat, with a head full of one-liners. His jokes lightened the atmosphere, and we got on really well from the start. We rehearsed for an hour and went straight to RTÉ for our camera rehearsal.

Kenny Live was a top-rated TV show, and all the usual preparations were going on in the studio. Up for rehearsal just before us was the Maynooth University Chamber Choir. I was mesmerised by the beautiful sounds they were making, and feeling a little embarrassed about our quiet little song. They were all sitting around in the audience seats as we commenced our first rehearsal of 'Rock 'n' Roll Kids'. When we finished there was a spontaneous round of applause from every member of the choir. I was astonished. They came over to talk to us and told us how much they enjoyed the song. I felt a small tingle at the back of my neck that was saying, 'There's a bit of magic here.'

Just recently the Minister for Tourism, Culture, Arts Gaeltacht, Sport and Media, Catherine Martin surprised me by telling me that she was a member of that very same Chamber Choir that night. She told me she loved the song as soon as she heared it. I met her in Drumshanbo when she lauched the 2022 Joe Mooney Summer School. What a pleasant surpirse that was.

Usually after appearing on a major TV show I would have expected some comments from friends or people I know. There were very few comments after our performance. It didn't worry me, but it did make me doubt a bit our decision to go 'unplugged' with the song. I hoped I hadn't messed it up, most of all for my friend Brendan Graham. Later in the week Shay Healy, who had written the Eurovision winner 'What's Another Year?', called and reassured me that our stripped-back arrangement was a good decision. I breathed a sigh of relief, as I valued Shay's opinion.

The National Song Contest final would take place at the NIHE Concert Hall in Limerick on 13th March. I knew two of the contestants, Fiona Kennedy and Darren Holden. The contest was televised, and the winner would be decided by juries from all around the country. I still believe that this is the best way to select the song that will represent Ireland in the Eurovision. There was no separate telephone voting, so the juries' decision was final.

When we sang 'Rock 'n' Roll Kids' that night there was a great reaction, but that would not necessarily sway the juries. Brendan was like our personal assistant, and was a very encouraging presence. He was happy with our performance, and that was good enough for me.

As the votes started coming in it was obvious that we would be in the reckoning, and as the final vote was registered we jumped for joy, having won the chance to represent Ireland in the 1994 Eurovision Song Contest. What a moment it was. We reprised the song and adjourned to the Castletroy Hotel to celebrate our win.

The next morning we stepped onto the publicity carousel, which kept spinning for a whole week as we appeared on TV programmes and radio stations to talk about the upcoming Eurovision Song Contest on 30th April. After the week we were old news, and quickly forgotten about from a public point of view. However, our plate was quite full doing a video of the song, and recording it for release to record shops and radio. It was all go, go, go.

We recorded the video in several locations, for example the newly opened Ballinamore to Ballyconnell canal and the Tyrone Guthrie Centre. We had great fun doing it, and Paul's beautiful hair getting blown in all directions as we cruised on the canal sticks out in my mind.

I was also getting to know Paul's family and ever-growing extended family. He lived in Killester in Dublin with his mum and dad. I found Paul's parents lovely down-to-earth people. Paul was the youngest in the family; he was indulged quite a lot by both his parents and his siblings. His brother Joe was a constant presence, but his other brother, Richard, was the real boss.

CHAPTER 45

The Eurovision Final

Paul and I had been involved in the music business for many years, and knew how to deal with a lot of the pressures that being Ireland's Eurovision entrants might entail. As 30th April approached, we began to be in constant demand again to appear at various events. We spent a lot of time at the RTÉ complex, where there was quite a big Eurovision delegation.

Anita Notaro, the head of the delegation, shepherded us hither and thither as the big night approached. Sometimes you felt like you were a little kid again, but Anita was one of the most professional people I had ever worked with. When you're on a rollercoaster like this, you just go with the flow and do what you're told.

We were accommodated at the Berkeley Court Hotel in Ballsbridge for the week leading up to the contest. I remember being highly impressed on our first morning at breakfast when I noticed that SDLP deputy leader MP Seamus Mallon was at the next table. He was having breakfast with Tom King MP, Secretary of State for Northern Ireland. The Troubles were still raging at this time, so obviously some sort of important discussions were being held.

Frances Ruffelle was representing Great Britain in the contest that year, and was also staying at the Berkeley Court. There was a heavy security presence for Frances: Paul and I would sit in the lobby trying to spot some of her security people, and looking to see how many of them had concealed weapons.

There were moments when you felt very comfortable with all that was happening around you, and other moments when you wondered what the hell you were doing there. I'll never forget when we walked into the Point Depot on the morning of our first rehearsal: the staging area seemed enormous, and my first thought was that we would be dwarfed by it. The overall theme was going to be the River Liffey and its surroundings: an obvious choice, as the venue was right on its banks.

There was a grand piano in the centre of the stage, and I could feel Paul's distaste for it. He immediately demanded a different piano, and I was shocked and surprised when one was provided. The man who tuned the new piano that was brought on stage was my old friend George Redmond. I had stayed in digs in George's house in the 1970s, and hadn't seen him since. He was the same lovely, affable man he always was, and we chatted about old times between rehearsals. It was great to see him again after all the years.

Each day for the rest of the week we would attend rehearsals for roughly an hour so that camera angles and sound tweaking etc. could be done. Brendan Graham was allowed to sit in the video mixing suite as we rehearsed. His suggestions were very much taken into account.

Following rehearsals, Brendan, Paul and I would discuss how everything was going. We were so lucky to have such a simple performance. We simply had to do what we normally do at a concert. Other acts had huge productions that involved singers, backing singers, dance routines and, of course, the full RTÉ Concert Orchestra. We knew some of the players in the orchestra, and they were all delighted to get a break while we rehearsed.

People often ask me if I was nervous at the Eurovision. In all honesty, I wasn't. I was really only doing what I normally do: singing and playing the guitar. As the week progressed the set became less and less intimidating, and we became quite blasé about the whole thing. After hearing some of the other songs and watching the rehearsals, I could have started worrying, but I kept remembering the first bit of advice I ever got about going on stage: 'Don't forget to enjoy it.'

The rest of our days were taken up with press, radio and television interviews. Not only had we to deal with the Irish media, but now we had media people from all over Europe to contend with. Basically this involved quite a lot of hanging around the hotel in case we were needed for anything. In the evenings all the other delegations had little parties that we were expected to attend. On the Thursday before the contest we had the Irish party, which was held at Kitty O'Shea's bar and restaurant.

Half of Drumshanbo attended, and we all had a mighty time mixing with the show business glitterati. People like Gerry Ryan, who was co-presenting the contest with Cynthia Ní Mhurchú, Pat Kenny and Johnny Logan were there. They were very easy-going about it all, and indulged our Drumshanbo guests with photos and autographs, which I still appreciate. The night ended up at three in the morning at the RTÉ Social Club in Donnybrook, where more drinks were quaffed.

Goretti's brother-in-law Dermie had taken a great shine to the Maltese delegation, and they to him. However, at one point all the pints got the better of Dermie and he fell over onto a table, scattering drinks, glasses, etc. all over the place. The Maltese delegation was very gracious and didn't make a fuss at all. I think they were all too drunk to even notice. It was one hell of a night!

The day of the contest arrived, and you might expect that we would be getting nervous, but there was nothing more we could do now, only do our best. There was a full dress rehearsal of the show in the afternoon, which was recorded and would run parallel to the live show later that evening. This meant that should any technical issues arise during the live show, they could switch seamlessly to the pre-recorded show. The rehearsal had a theatre audience as well, which made it really seem like the live show. Nothing was left to chance!

There was a tented village backstage at the Point; each delegation had a separate tent. There was also a huge communications tent where all the media and their equipment were accommodated. I'd say there were at least 200 media people there, all relaying their reports to their respective bases all over Europe. But … amid all this professionalism, there was a 'secret' that nobody seemed to know! All through the previous week we had been hearing about the interval act, but none of us had seen it. Indeed, none of us saw it at the dress rehearsal either. It was being kept carefully under wraps, and that alone piqued people's interest. Every reporter around the place was itching to get an exclusive.

After the dress rehearsal it was back to the hotel for a rest and dinner. We were both very happy with how our day was going. I should point out at this stage that we never, ever, sang the song exactly the same way twice. Paul and I had a kind of matching mindset, and if he played something different, I would just follow, and vice versa. We'd share a look or a comment, with one of us saying something like 'That was nice.'

It was all a bit surreal, because we were being treated like royalty all week, with our every need taken care of, and even some needs we didn't know we had. I was offered a massage, which I declined. I'm a culchie and we didn't do massages. We had our own hairdresser, make-up person and wardrobe person. Anita Notaro took care of everything.

Sometime during the weeks coming up to the show, she had taken us shopping for clothes, like little boys … not that we were complaining. They were paying! A navy double-breasted blazer, jeans, shirt and black boots were chosen for me, while Paul was in a suit with a frock coat and a string tie. For events I was given a green linen jacket, jeans and brown suede boots. Paul's hair was his usual shoulder length, and I sported a semi-mullet hairstyle.

Around 7pm we returned to the Point. Curiously, our bus driver throughout the week was the son of a man I had worked with in the ESB, which was kind of nice. For some reason, George Hamilton, the RTÉ sports commentator, was on the bus with us. Maybe he got the wrong bus, or did he think Eurovision was part of the sports department? Funny the things you remember.

We were in our little tent at the back of the Point and could hear some of the other contestants warming up with positively operatic vocal routines. We had no such exercises. An old friend, Maura O'Connell, when asked what vocal exercise she used before a concert, said 'I just cough and go "Ahem! Ahem!"'. Our exercise was something similar.

I always get a little paranoid about tuning my guitar before a concert, and I must have checked it a hundred times backstage that night. The guitar was very kindly gifted to me by Louden Guitars in Newtownards. Their instruments are played by many worldwide stars, like James Taylor and Ed Sheeran. It was a very good guitar.

We were third on the bill and were preceded by Finland's CatCat – two women dressed in what I can only describe as short satin pyjamas and dressing gowns – who had a quite energetic song called 'Bye Bye Baby', complete with two breakdancers. They had a big sound and I quietly thought 'We are going to seem very tame after them.'

Very soon we were standing backstage, ready to go on. I had the usual thought in my mind as we walked out on stage to a fantastic reception from the home audience: 'Don't forget to enjoy it.' Our performance had to be three of the most enjoyable minutes of our lives. We were on stage representing Ireland at the Eurovision Song Contest. The audience was just so warm from the time we were announced by Gerry Ryan until we left the stage. The fact that there were approximately 300 million people watching us all across Europe didn't actually occur to us.

Afterwards we adjourned to the 'green room': another big tent where the delegations from the different countries gathered after their performance. There were twenty-five countries in the contest that year, and yet the time seemed to fly by. When all the songs had been performed there was an interval, and the voting began.

Usually the delegations would be so wrapped up in their own thoughts that the interval act would be ignored. However, this interval act was being projected onto a huge screen in the green room, so it was impossible to ignore. The opening music commenced and utter silence descended on the room. People's jaws visibly dropped as Jean Butler and Michael Flatley tripped lightly across the huge stage of the Point Depot.

It was the very first performance of *Riverdance*, and what a moment it was. Everyone instinctively knew they were witnessing something special. Not just the audience at the Point, but also the entire group of delegations from other countries, erupted in a standing ovation for a historic moment of Irish music and dance history. I'll never forget that fantastic performance, which was to lead to what has become part of our Irish cultural heritage, and inspired millions of people across the globe to take up Irish dancing.

The voting started, and the tension in the room was huge. We were doing very well, and eventually it became obvious to everyone except Paul and me that we were looking like winners. There were still three countries to vote, but Anita Notaro kept telling me to get ready for the reprise. There was no way I was going near that guitar until the very last vote was in. I have never been great at winning things, but I was delighted when I heard Gerry Ryan say 'Ireland has won the Eurovision for the third time in a row.'

Doing the reprise as Eurovision winners was a proud moment for Paul and me. As we walked back out on stage I could see Mary Robinson, President of Ireland, on her feet giving us a standing ovation.

My first thought was to link up with Goretti and the family. After I found them, we were all put into limousines and taken on a whistle-stop tour of Dublin night spots. First was the Burlington Hotel, where Paul and I were invited on stage to sing 'Rock 'n' Roll Kids' with Paddy Cole and his band. This was a special moment for me, as I recalled getting Paddy's autograph back in the 1960s in Bundoran. Butch Moore had represented Ireland in the Eurovision in 1965, and that made him a huge star, even though he didn't win. Paddy Cole was the saxophone player in Butch's band, the Capital Showband, and was a musical hero of mine.

Goretti and the children were then taken to the Berkeley Court Hotel while Paul and I went to the National Concert Hall and after that to a nightclub called Lillie's Bordello. Twink, who was a huge TV star at the time, greeted us in Lillie's and in quite colourful language told us how happy she was about our win. Eventually, we joined Goretti and my family back at the hotel, where a suite had been booked on the very top floor. Paul's family and friends had assembled there too, and late-night drinks were available to all.

One could be forgiven for thinking that this quiet time was a bit of an anti-climax, but it was just great to get a break from all the hulla-baloo. The children were ferried off to a relation's house – at this stage it must have been about 4am on Sunday morning.

We stayed at the party for about an hour, but I wanted to be alone with Goretti just to savour the whole event with her as we have always done privately. We said our goodbyes and retired to our hotel room, where we quietly discussed all that had happened and eventually drifted off to sleep.

It had been a great occasion and I had enjoyed every minute, just as I had been advised to do all those years ago at the Ballisodare Folk Festival. Thus the day ended.

Rock 'n' Roll Kids
Brendan Graham (Acorn Music/IMRO/MCPS/Peer Music)

I remember sixty-two
I was sixteen and so were you
And we lived next door on the avenue

Jerry Lee was big and Elvis too
Blue jeans and blue suede shoes
And we never knew what life held in store
We just wanted to rock 'n' roll forever more

We were the rock 'n' roll kids
Rock 'n' roll was all we did
And listenin' to those songs on the radio
I was yours and you were mine
That was once upon a time
Now we never seem to rock 'n' roll anymore

Now Johnny's in love with the girl next door
And Mary's down at the record store
They don't wanna be around us no more
Golden oldies, but we hardly speak
Too busy running to a different beat
Hard to understand we were once like them
How I wish we could find those rock 'n' roll days again

We were the rock 'n' roll kids
Rock 'n' roll was all we did
And listenin' to those songs on the radio
I was yours and you were mine

That was once upon a time
Now we never seem to rock 'n' roll anymore

I was yours and you were mine
That was once upon a time
Now we never seem to rock 'n' roll
We just never seem to rock 'n' roll anymore

CHAPTER 46

Eurovision – The Next Day

B ack in Drumshanbo at Sunday mass, the St Patrick's Church Adult Choir sang 'Rock 'n' Roll Kids'. What an honour that was. We were still in Dublin when my parents rang and told me.

Although I'm not a particularly religious person, I have been a member of the choir for many years, as I mentioned previously: ever since I moved to live in Drumshanbo. I always found choral singing a very spiritual experience, and our church choir is a particularly good one. I still sing with them to this day, at mass most Sundays, and I always enjoy it. I like it even more during seasons like Christmas and Easter, which are really wonderful occasions. We have sung on radio and television, and our musical directors Orla Daly and Mairin O'Keeffe are brilliant, inspirational and patient people to work with.

When you are singing with the choir in the upstairs gallery, and looking down at the congregation, you discover a lot more about people you know than you were expecting. For example, people who you thought had great heads of hair are actually concealing bald patches under lavishly designed comb-overs. Some of the men are bald too...!

It happens when you are in the body of the church too. I remember sitting behind a fellow with a very obvious comb-over. He was praying feverishly, fingering his rosary beads with great deftness. Every now and then he'd scratch the right side of his head and then, a minute or two later, the left side. This was going on for about ten minutes. Eventually I tapped him on the shoulder and whispered in his ear. 'Get him

1994: Eurovision winners on stage at The Point Theatre; From left to right;
Programme presenter Cynthia Ní Mhurchú, Charlie McGettigan, presenter Gerry
Ryan, Niamh Kavanagh (the previous year's winner) and Paul Harrington.
(Courtesy RTE)

2012: Charlie in concert with Sandy Kelly at Millennium Theatre, Derry.
(Courtesy of Big Mountain Productions and TG4)

2017: Eleanor Shanley and Charlie McGettigan in concert in Germany.

Charlie with Paul Harrington in Boyle Church concert (Brendan McGee)

Paul Gurney and Charlie McGettigan (Shelly Corcoran Photographer)

2013: John Sheahan of Dubliners fame and Charlie McGettigan (Courtesy of Liam McGrath, Scratch Films Ltd.)

Charlie McGettigan and Eleanor Shanley with Miriam O'Callaghan on *Miriam on Sunday* RTE Radio 1.

Eurovision Winners on tour from left: Linda Martin, Paul Harrington, Niamh Kavanagh, Johnny Logan, Dana Rosemary Brown Scanlon, Charlie McGettigan. (Courtesy of Keith Arkin, Photographer)

out in the open and I'll hit him with my prayer book!' He gave me such a stern look that I knew he was not amused.

I know when we go to church we are usually in a solemn and prayerful mood, but I am sure God has a sense of humour as well. Sometimes things just happen and you can't stop laughing, even though you appear to everyone else at that moment as disrespectful and a bit of an idiot.

I was standing talking to a missionary priest one time as people were leaving the church after a very serious sermon. He told me that on the Saturday afternoon before, when his confession session was nearly over and he was getting ready to go home, he heard the church door open and footsteps coming towards the confessional box. He heard the door of the confessional open and a bit of a clatter as it closed again. He waited, but there was just a silence in the darkened room, which seemed eternal.

After a few minutes the priest knocked on the wall, but nothing happened. He knocked again, this time more vigorously. Suddenly he heard a voice: 'There's no point knocking, there's no toilet roll in here either.' We both started laughing, then got into a fit of the giggles as serious faces looked at us as they walked past. I was trying to ask him, 'Who … was … it?' It turned out that it was the town drunk. Every town has one, and this particular fellow was absolutely plastered that day.

The town graveyard is right beside the church in Drumshanbo. Often people spend some time after the Sunday service visiting the graves of their loved ones. One Sunday this very gaunt and stooped old man was wandering around the graveyard. The local 'wag' approached him and inquired 'Are you looking for something?'

'I'm looking for a grave' the old man replied.

'And what's wrong with the one you got out of?

Yes, you need to have a good sense of humour to live in Drumshanbo!

Back in Dublin, the European press had gathered in an outdoor area near the hotel, to take photos and ask questions when we emerged. This was all new to me … well, at this level anyway. The questions were flying from right, left and centre. Brendan Graham acted like a kind of chairperson, intervening whenever he felt we needed a little help. He was magnificent in this role.

One of the perks of winning the Eurovision was that Eircom gave us brand-new mobile phones: a relatively new phenomenon in 1994. Mine was about as big as a peat briquette; Paul's was a much neater affair. Somehow Paul's mum had got his number, and in the middle of the press reception she called him. Paul answered saying 'Ma! I told you not to be ringing me at work!' This got a great laugh from the assembled press. Paul has always had a very quick wit about him.

A few weeks earlier Frances Black, the well-known singer and recording artist, had asked me if I would come on as a guest at her concert in the Olympia Theatre the night after the Eurovision. I guess she figured that I would be in Dublin anyway, and I would not have much else to do! Frances had recorded a couple of my songs down the years, and I was absolutely delighted to agree to join her. I also knew my old buddy Brendan Emmett was playing in her band, so that was a bonus. I had no idea when we arranged it all that I would be turning up as 'Charlie McGettigan, the Eurovision winner'.

It was about a fifteen-minute walk from the hotel to the Olympia, and people were recognising me all along the way. Some came over to chat. This was great for my ego, although after a while it became a bit tedious. I was still only me, after all … but now everyone knew me, and to be honest it was a wee bit embarrassing as well.

It reminded me of when I first moved to Drumshanbo: I couldn't believe that it took only five minutes to walk from our house to the end of the town. I noticed I was getting funny stares from the people I met along the way, and realised that it must be my umbrella that was attracting the attention. A man carrying an umbrella was a rare sight in Drumshanbo back then, unlike in Dublin. I found out later that I earned my first nickname in the town in those early days: 'the Umbrella Man'.

When I got to the Olympia, Frances and all the crew congratulated me, except one of the musicians in the band who felt compelled to bring me down to earth. 'I spotted the mistake you made last night, boss,' he said, referring to our Eurovision performance. 'I put that into the song to test your powers of observation,' I lied. That's the strange thing about Ireland: there's always someone to bring you down a peg or two, even if you don't need it.

I then had a little sound check with Frances's band and a chat with my friend Brendan. When I came on stage later, there was a huge round of applause before I even started singing. The reaction after I finished singing 'Rock 'n' Roll Kids' was simply amazing. This little song had come a long way, and so had I. I was enjoying being a 'rock 'n' roll kid'.

CHAPTER 47

The Homecoming – Drumshanbo

Goretti and I decided that we would go home to Drumshanbo the following day, which was a Monday, and get some rest. We slowed down as we reached Rooskey when we noticed a cavalcade of cars assembled to accompany us the rest of the way to Drumshanbo. My good friend Enda McGloin was driving the lead car, accompanied by the cavalcade master of ceremonies, James McGuire.

James was a colourful character and a very successful estate agent. Every now and then he would announce that my arrival in Drumshanbo was imminent, trumpeting 'Come out! Come out and welcome home Charlie McGettigan, the winner of the Eurovision Song Contest!' 'Jesus,' I thought, 'I am not the Pope.'

James, not being used to using a microphone, didn't know he had to turn it off after he had made an announcement. This meant that everyone along the way could hear the conversation between him and Enda. 'Do you see that field there, Enda? I got twenty grand for that field last week' was one of his comments, which generated laughter from all in the vicinity.

As we neared Leitrim I began to notice that there were bonfires along the side of the road. These were lit to welcome us home. It was lovely to see loads of people waving flags and cheering. My win obviously meant a lot to the people of the area, and that made me very happy. Just outside Drumshanbo, we noticed that my mum and dad were ahead of us in a pony and cart. Goretti and I joined them as we travelled the last half mile into town.

There was a lot of speech-making, and despite the pouring rain people stayed to enjoy the moment. I was chatting and signing autographs for a few hours. Someone took a picture of me holding a baby that day which appeared a few years ago on my Facebook page. I shared the photo, and a few days later the woman who was the baby in the photograph contacted me. It was lovely to hear from her after all these years. She is now a doctor. Eventually we made it to our local pub, Conway's Corner House, for a few well-deserved pints. It was very late when we got to our own house.

As I reflected that night on all that had happened in Dublin, and the lovely reception we had received from the people of Drumshanbo, I looked at my diary to see what was next. The following morning, Tuesday, read 'Taoiseach's Reception'. This was to be an official acknowledgement by An Taoiseach (Prime Minister of Ireland), Albert Reynolds, of our Eurovision win, in the form of a breakfast at his office in the Dáil. However tired I must have been from the whole weekend, I found myself at Leinster House the next morning with Paul and Brendan as well as numerous other celebrities.

I remembered sometime over the weekend before asking Paul what the dress code would be for this occasion. 'Jacket and jeans' was his cheeky answer: 'We're rock stars now! We wear what we like.' I had always been very conscious of dress codes, so this seemed like a disrespectful way to present myself at Government Buildings. However, jacket and jeans it proved to be.

I always liked wearing jeans since the first time I ever saw them. It was in 1962, when a guy whose name I can't recall was home from England on holidays. He wore classic blue denims with the obligatory two-inch turn-up at the bottom, which was a lighter shade of blue than the rest. They also had the orange stitching on the leg seams, and pockets with copper studs on the joints. I can clearly recall that he wore them with a pair of black winkle-picker shoes and white socks. He also sported a Brylcreem quiff and a jet-black shirt with the collar turned up, and boy did he look cool. I wanted to be like him!

I pestered my parents to buy me a pair of jeans; eventually my mother gave in and came home one day with a brown paper parcel on approbation from Tom Culkin's shop. You cannot imagine my disappointment when she opened it: they were jeans all right, but black jeans! A cardboard tag stuck to one of the back pockets stated 'Wrangler work jeans'. She could see the excitement followed by disappointment on my face. 'They're all Tom has,' she said, adding 'and I've tried Slevin's and Stephens's as well.' They were still jeans, I decided, and it's the thought that counts, so I was happy to compromise.

They were a reasonable fit, if a bit wide and about two inches too long. My mother wanted to 'take them up', but of course I protested that I could turn them up myself on the outside, without cutting them. She couldn't understand this, but in the end she relented. I remember that there was green stitching instead of the orange stitching as on blue jeans, but I still thought they looked OK.

On my first day back at school I felt so cool parading around the playground in my new jeans, and the other guys in their Terylene grey trousers gazed on in envy. Then a harsh voice reached my ears: 'McGettigan, have you pretensions of being the new caretaker here?' It was Brother Robert, who wanted to know why I was wearing overalls to school. 'They're not overalls – they're jeans!' I pleaded. 'What, may I ask, are you talking about?' he retorted. Incredibly, in 1962 someone hadn't heard of jeans. I was sent home to put on proper trousers.

Still, I persisted with the black jeans out of school hours for that term. They were actually rather uncomfortable and became baggy at the knees after I wore them for a while, and certainly weren't leg-hugging like the ones I had seen that geezer wearing during the summer.

It was 1965 before I donned my first pair of blue jeans, which again were imitation denim and still not the real thing, but they were near enough. During the summers of my teenage years we would envy the holidaymakers from Derry and Belfast sporting their Levi's around the streets and coffee bars of Bundoran. They just couldn't be bought in our local outfitters. Some of my contemporaries made excursions to Sligo or even Dublin to buy Levi's in places like O'Connor's, which still sells jeans today. In the 1960s a trip to Dublin was a big event for a teenager living in Ballyshannon.

As the years went by, and I started to earn some money and moved to Dublin, I was able to buy any amount of jeans I wanted. I have watched them grow from being regarded as 'overalls' to becoming an essential fashion item for 99% of the world population. I still love to wear them because they are comfortable, durable and accepted virtually everywhere one goes. So when Paul said we would wear 'jacket and jeans' to the Taoiseach's office, which was fine by me. Little did I know that I would spend quite some time in the same jacket and jeans before I got a chance to change clothes again?

It was great to see Jean Butler and Michael Flatley at the reception. They had been kept away from everyone in the week running up to the contest, so it was lovely to meet these really charming people that morning. Little did we know that they would become stars worldwide about a year later, when the *Riverdance* show eventually hit the stage?

Sometime in the middle of the event Brendan Graham received a call from a Belgian television company who wanted us to appear that evening on a TV show. This was around noon, so you would think it was impossible to be in Belgium performing at 7pm the same evening. When Albert Reynolds got to hear about it, he said 'Nothing is impossible! First, let's get ye to the airport. Ye can take my car. My office will sort out everything else. Away with ye!'

In a flash we were in the Taoiseach's official car and driving through the streets of Dublin with sirens blaring. Our driver mounted footpaths and broke traffic lights, and in about twenty minutes we were checking in for a flight for Brussels. We had no baggage other than my guitar. The only clothes we had were the ones we were wearing, and, most importantly, we had neither tickets nor passports. Apparently, all official rules were being waived for us Eurovision winners.

Sitting on the flight I was thinking, 'What the hell am I at? This was not part of the plan for today!' But it was a bit late to be thinking like that. The television company had booked us into a hotel in the centre of Brussels. I have no memory of the interview or the show because we were so tired, but I presume we sang 'Rock 'n' Roll Kids'. Shortly after the show we found ourselves back at the hotel … a little bemused by the pace of it all!

Money was the one thing everyone forgot about, despite their great endeavours to make sure we had everything we needed. We literally only had about £20 (Irish punts) between the two of us. Paul liked to smoke cigars, so five of our twenty pounds went on a packet of his favourites. That left us with fifteen pounds for the evening. It was 1994, so neither of us had anything like a credit or debit card. I think we spent £10 on a few beers that night at the hotel, so that left us with £5 for the next day.

A call came through to our room from Brendan: we would be coming back via London, because Gloria Hunniford had requested that we appear on her BBC Radio 2 Show. Gloria Hunniford! Wow, we were impressed! We still had no passports or plane tickets, but everything was arranged for us, and again no one had considered that we might need some money.

We made it to Broadcasting House with a few hours to spare. At this stage we realised that a change of underwear might be appropriate. Radio studios can be small, confined spaces, and there was a likelihood that we were beginning to smell. We popped out to the nearest M&S store and spent our last £5 on two pairs of boxer shorts, although they could have cost more than we had. We couldn't believe that some of the shop assistants recognised us. They readily accepted our Irish currency when we told them the story of the previous day: they were Irish and only too willing to help us out. We changed in the toilet back at the BBC.

Eventually we entered Gloria's studio and she welcomed us with her winning smile. We sang 'Rock 'n' Roll Kids' and Randy Edelman's 'Uptown Up-Tempo Woman'. At that stage this was about the extent of our repertoire as a duo. Paul was delighted when Gloria told us that Randy Edelman had been a guest on her show a few days previously, and had sung his song playing the very same piano that Paul had just played it on. What a bit of magic!

We finished our slot with Gloria, said goodbye and thanked everyone. A couple of hours later I remembered that we had left a plastic bag with our old underpants in the corner of the studio. Nothing was ever said, but I'm sure someone found them!

We eventually arrived back in Dublin and got a taxi to our cars in the Dáil car park where we had left them on the previous Tuesday.

Pat Farrell, a very high-up official in the Fianna Fáil party, was there to meet us and pay the taxi fare. Pat was an old friend from Leitrim village.

I remember mooching around the Taoiseach's office trying to find my coat, which I had left behind earlier in the week. We were both totally exhausted. Paul set off to Killester and I headed for home in Drumshanbo.

I thought that would be the end of all this euphoria and rushing around, but it was only the start. Until then I had followed my music career in parallel with working for the ESB. This was my first ever chance to be a full-time musician. Joe Moran, chief executive of the ESB, very kindly gave me a year off work, for which I am forever grateful. It was such a thoughtful thing to do, and meant I did not have to make a choice between my work and my music.

We met Albert Reynolds again at a reception at a Dublin hotel for the Leitrim senior football team. and he ended up sitting at our table.

'I hope you're not going to rush me off to a foreign country again,' I said.

He laughed and said 'No, Charlie, I've just come from the Chamber of Horrors [meaning the Dáil] and I am too shattered to rush anyone anywhere, including myself.'

The events of that day would soon lead to a general election. Albert did look tired and worn out, but to my amazement he was soon on the rostrum, making a thirty-minute speech without any notes. He was witty and wise, a true professional politician, and whether or not you agreed with him, you had to admire his hard work and determination. He entertained us all, and I thought to myself, 'He didn't get where he is today without total devotion to his beliefs.'

CHAPTER 48

The Eurovision Carousel

In the following weeks we were more or less back on the roller-coaster, which kept moving for another nine months or so. Our days were always busy with recording or performing. For example, in the week following the Eurovision we appeared on *The Breakfast Show* with Zig and Zag for Channel 4, then boarded a train to Birmingham to appear on the BBC's *Pebble Mill at One,* and later that evening attended a function at the Mansion House hosted by the Mayor of Dublin, Tomás Mac Giolla.

I met an old friend at the function: Frances Grehan, of the Grehan sisters from Boyle, who was an old friend of the Mayor as well. I had played with her many times down the years, and it was a pleasure to see her again. That week we also appeared on RTÉ's *Live at Three* and did a record signing at HMV in Dublin as well as an interview with radio DJ Jimmy Greally.

The week after that, we attended a state reception on the Monday, and then we spent Tuesday and Wednesday in the Netherlands. On Thursday we attended a reception, hosted by Joe Moran, at ESB head-quarters. On Friday we went to Hamburg to appear on NDR TV and to meet executives from a very large German record label. On Sunday we did a record signing at Tower Records in Dublin. In the middle of all this we managed to fit in a few rehearsals, to develop our repertoire for live concerts.

I had noticed that some of the same people were turning up at our record signings. These turned out to be members of Paul's extended family, who would just show up to support us. Distant relations of my own whom I hadn't seen for years would come along as well: it was great to see them.

We would not have been able to continue as we did without someone looking after the management of our affairs. Brendan Graham more or less took up the challenge so that we could all capitalise on the win. We formed our own record label, RocKids Music, and Brendan negotiated several recording deals with record companies across Europe. I don't think anybody else could have done such a good job handling us. He is a very good businessman. He also engaged his daughter Niamh to handle the requests we were getting to play in Ireland and all over Europe.

One evening we were in Scotland, and booked into a place called the Busby Hotel. We were driving around for about an hour trying to find it. We spotted a policeman; Paul rolled down the window and, in his best Dublin accent, asked where the Busby Hotel might be. 'Ye bastard' came the reply. 'Pardon?' asked a stunned Paul. 'Ye bastard' the policeman repeated. 'Sorry?' said Paul.

The policeman, somewhat frustrated at this point, spoke each word firmly and slowly: 'I said … ye … passed it. It's just around the corner.' He was looking at us suspiciously as we thanked him and drove off. I think he was trying to work out whether we were really that dumb or were taking the mickey out of him. As soon as he was out of sight we got a fit of the giggles, and arrived at our destination still laughing.

The next day we were on a plane to Amsterdam to appear on a TV show, and went from there to Sweden for two days of more TV shows and radio interviews. This 'rock 'n' roll kid' stuff was really hard work. The next few months were more or less the same, with a series of plane journeys to places all over Europe.

We met lots of famous people on our travels, and had some funny chats with TV presenters. On one TV show in Germany the presenter asked, 'How is it that Ireland keeps winning the Eurovision Song Contest?'

'Well,' I lied, 'we are over here at the moment organising lessons in songwriting for all the other countries in Europe, to help them have more success in the contest.'

'Oh, this is wonderful!' said the presenter. 'Can you tell us when and where these lessons will be taking place?'

It was an awkward moment because he had not understood my joke. I didn't wish to make a fool of him, so I said, 'No, I'm only joking – I don't think even us Irish know the magic formula, but whatever we are doing, it seems to be working.'

'It certainly is,' he replied.

In a way all these experiences blend into one in my mind, but I know we did enjoy it.

Some funny moments at home in Ireland forestalled any danger that I would get 'notions' about myself. About a fortnight after we won the Eurovision, I was walking down the street in Galway City. Suddenly I was surrounded by a gang of women looking for autographs. I must have been there about fifteen minutes, and people were gathering to see what the fuss was about. 'Jesus,' I thought, 'I feel like Daniel O Donnell!' I ducked into a shop to get out of the fray but one little old lady followed me in with a Cadbury's chocolate bar wrapper in one hand and a pen in the other.

'Can I have your autograph?' she asked.

'Oh go on, then,' I said, doing my 'diva' bit.

While I was signing her piece of paper, she looked up at me quizzically. 'Who are you, anyway?' she asked.

That took the wind out of my sails, I can tell you.

I walked into Conway's pub in Drumshanbo, and who was sitting up at the bar only Peter Gilmartin, an elderly man who had worked with me in the power station a few years earlier. Peter was a very careful man but had a droll sense of humour. When he saw me coming he announced to the others at the bar, 'Here comes Charlie McGettigan. Sure the only time we see him now is on the television.'

'Ah yes, Peter, good to see you too. As a matter of fact, we're on the *Late Late Show* this Friday,' I said. Peter stroked his chin and considered for a moment.

'I *might* watch it.'

Another time, I was in a restaurant in Drogheda with a few friends. The waitress who was serving us had a lovely friendly demeanour and was making us all feel good. As she served the first course, she looked at me and said 'Do I know you from somewhere?' I said, 'I don't think so.'

When she appeared with the main course, she said, 'I'm sure I've met you before.' This time I didn't answer. Stars like me can't be bothered with this kind of chit-chat.

As she served the coffee, she said 'Ah come on now. I know I've seen you before somewhere. Who are you? Give me a clue!'

'OK,' I consented. 'Maybe the television?'

'Ah no,' she said. 'A fella up the road fixes our television.'

What can you say?

CHAPTER 49

What's Going On in That Room?

We took a week off in June to stay at the Tyrone Guthrie Centre, a lovely big house in the Monaghan countryside where artists, writers and other creative people from all over the world go to find peace and quiet, and an atmosphere that's conducive to creativity. We hoped to write some new songs for the album we were planning. I remember spotting a scale model of the stage set for Vincent Woods's great play *At the Black Pig's Dyke* in the lobby as we walked in. Vincent was from just up the road from me in Tarmon, Co. Leitrim. He was an old friend of mine.

The centre was run by Bernard Loughlin, a very serious man who didn't tolerate any frivolity from the residents. He insisted that everyone who was staying there had to have dinner together in the house every evening. As far as I am concerned, it was a good rule and easy to follow, because the food at the centre was fantastic.

Paul and I became very popular with all the other guests because we allowed them to make calls on our free mobile phones to anywhere in the world. We were like two big kids who had toys that the other kids wanted, so queues would develop outside our rooms every evening, and Bernard began to get suspicious.

It was a bit like that episode of *Fawlty Towers* where Basil suspects that one of his guests is using his hotel as a place to bring girls for sex. In this case Bernard was the Basil character. He wanted to know what exactly was going on, but he couldn't really ask straight out. When he discovered what all the queues were about, he was quite happy for the guests to use our phones, and I think we gained a few brownie points for this.

Mind you, I have to say we did very little creative work at the Tyrone Guthrie Centre. We got totally distracted by the World Cup: the Irish soccer team were competing, and it was on TV day and night in the bars of the nearby town. We followed it enthusiastically with a pint or two in our hands.

After that relatively quiet week, it was back on the carousel for a few days in Norway. Following one TV show we were brought to a restaurant for a meal. These social occasions could be tricky, as my knowledge of the Norwegian language was zero, and the conversation could be quite exhausting. To get a break and some fresh air, I went for a little walk. I wandered around for an hour or so but couldn't make head nor tail of the geography of Oslo.

I decided to go back to the hotel, but couldn't quite remember which direction I had been walking from. I realised that I didn't know the name of the restaurant or indeed the hotel where we were staying. Oslo was a snow-covered city that night, and at one point I thought I was going to end up sleeping rough on its streets. I was beginning to panic when I saw what looked like a police car, so I waved it down.

After many attempts to tell them I was lost, they gave up trying to understand what the hell I was saying and brought me back to the police station. A policeman who spoke English then took over, and called every hotel he could think of until eventually he found mine. I didn't ever wander away again in a strange city.

We appeared on a few TV shows and spent six hours doing interviews with the press and some of the 200-odd radio stations they have over there. After the first day I had begun to make up stories, as I became bored telling the same ones over and over. This has resulted in me finding it difficult to distinguish truth from fiction when I think about our adventures in Europe.

I still find it difficult to remember what actually happened, so most of what I'm writing now is basically true, but there may be a few fictional deviations.

CHAPTER 50

Get back to Drumshanbo, McGettigan

We soon got used to all the travelling and other stuff during 1994, but we did have some memorable moments that stand out. One such was when we were invited to play at a state reception at Dublin Castle for the Prime Minister of Pakistan, Benazir Bhutto, which would be attended by An Taoiseach, Albert Reynolds. It would be a very formal affair altogether. We were intensively briefed by civil servants on all the protocols that would have to be observed. At no point were we to engage in any kind of conversation with Prime Minister Bhutto, and, most importantly, we were not to shake hands or touch her in any way. We were fine with all that.

As the dinner finished, we were announced on stage. The audience was in evening dress and seemed to be very spiffy altogether. I was immediately struck by the radiance of the premier. She was a beautiful woman, with a genuine kindness in her eyes.

Paul and I did our usual few songs, which included 'Uptown Up-Tempo Woman'. As we finished our set, Albert Reynolds took the microphone: 'Come up here, lads, and meet the Prime Minister,' he boomed. 'What about all the protocols? We'll be shot!' I thought.

We made our way through the maze of tables to where the premier was sitting. She stood up and hugged both of us, saying how much she enjoyed our music, especially 'Uptown Up-Tempo Woman', her favourite song when she was at college in Oxford, she said. She then handed us a carved wooden trinket box each.

We did a short tour of Slovenia after that, where one of the TV shows was preceded by a bingo session in a really luxurious hotel with golden bath taps and every convenience you could want. The bingo was held to help finance the TV show. It was a most unusual TV appearance, where the floor manager shouted to the director rather than using an intercom. As we waited to go on the show, I was watching the bingo session thinking 'I could do better than that, and I have experience!' I remembered my time working in the bingo room in Bundoran back in 1964. I think the prizes on this TV show were a little better than 'a gold-coloured cup'!

The next day we went to Frankfurt, where we spent three days doing TV shows and playing at an event celebrating the 750th anniversary of the city. Upwards of 100,000 people attended. Strangely, we weren't a bit intimidated by the size of the audience. When we were about to finish, a voice from about the fourth row yelled out, 'Get back to Drumshanbo, McGettigan!' Anywhere you go, you can be sure you will find an Irishman: sometimes even one who knows you. I was delighted to hear that well-meant heckle among the crowd.

Back in Ireland we were guests on TV shows like *The Rose of Tralee* and *Gortnaclune*. Something really important happened that year when Leitrim won the Connacht senior Gaelic football final, beating Mayo in Dr Hyde Park in Roscommon. It was the first time in sixty-one years that Leitrim had won, and the celebrations were epic. My old pal Tony McGowan was on the county board that year, and I've rarely seen a happier fan. As Eurovision winners we were invited to a lot of their celebrations, and it was such a joy to be a part of it all.

I remember Paul and I flew in specially from Oslo to be at Croke Park when Leitrim faced Dublin in the All-Ireland semi-final. Tony had arranged seats for us in the Ard Chomhairle (VIP) section. One of the RTÉ cameramen called me over and asked where we would be sitting, so that he could get a good view of us both at some point during the game. Paul was from Dublin and I was from Leitrim, so this would make a great shot. I was dressed in my Leitrim jersey and Paul in the light blue of Dublin.

Dublin won the match, but Leitrim people were happy just to celebrate being in Croke Park. There were Leitrim parties all over Dublin that night.

I saw a recording of the match later, and at one point the cameraman was scanning the crowd, trying to find us. Just as he did, a man stood up wielding a magnum of champagne and spoiling the shot. Guess who? James McGuire, the auctioneer who led the Leitrim cavalcade on my return to Drumshanbo. He was always popping up somewhere!

Charlie broadcasting 'The Saturday Connection' on Shannonside Northern Sound.

At Shannonside Northern Sound: Broadcasting with my grandchildren;
Back left: Siofra. Front: Cathal, Show Producer Sinead Hughes and
Pádraig on violin and Charlie on guitar.

2019: Charlie with grandson Pádraig at Ray D'Arcy RTE 1 live broadcast from Acres Lake, Drumshambo, Co. Leitrim.

2020: A duet – Charlie with grandson Pádraig on stage singing 'Rock 'n' Roll Kid.

With friends – From left: Nollaig Casey, the late Arty McGlynn, Charlie McGettigan and Maura O'Connell.

2021: 'Two Auld Bucks' Charlie McGettigan and John Hannigan

The Diamond, Ballyshannon, Co. Donegal.
'No, this is the right way to play this chord Rory'

CHAPTER 51

Rock 'n' Roll Kids – the Album

In late August and early September 1994, Paul and I took some time to record our album in STS Recording Studio, over the Claddagh Records shop in the Temple Bar area of Dublin. As we were still working away in Europe we could only get into the studio for short periods of time, but eventually we completed *Rock 'n' Roll Kids – the Album*.

It was launched at the Harcourt Hotel on Tuesday, 8th of October: a very special night, attended not only by half of Leitrim but by some show-business legends such as Maureen Potter. Maureen had included a version of 'Rock 'n' Roll Kids' in her stage show, which was a great compliment. Donovan, Michael Flatley and Jean Butler were also there, and many more. At one point during the launch, Gibby (remember her?) spotted Michael Flatley and literally danced a highland fling across the bar to greet him: 'Take me, I'm yours!' she beamed. It was a special funny moment. Paul and I were very pleased with the album, and the launch was a big success.

A particular highlight for me was our appearance on the *Kelly* TV show in Belfast. One of the other guests was the legendary George Martin, who produced all the Beatles' records and whom I regarded as the fifth Beatle. I was a huge fan, of course, and I couldn't believe my luck.

We finished our slot and were sitting in the green room when I saw George Martin walking in my direction. 'I really enjoyed your song,' he said. I was absolutely gobsmacked and immediately tongue-tied! It was the kind of moment when you look behind you to check if he is talking to someone else!

Eventually I recovered and, after a bit of small talk, asked him about his earliest memories of the Beatles. It wasn't a very original question, but I wanted to hear if he had kept any mementos of the Beatles from that period. He told me that he just happened to be the producer in charge the day the Beatles first appeared to record their audition tape. He said he wasn't particularly impressed by their music, but he felt that they had something indefinable in their personalities. He had been in charge of comedy recordings for people like Peter Sellers, and he noticed the Beatles also had a kind of zany humour in their conversation. As they recorded more and more, he began to realise their true potential.

All in all, then, 1994 was a memorable year. Eurovision mania continued for a while into 1995, but bit by bit life returned to a semi-normal pace. I was happy that it did, and am even more so now that I am older and wiser. Hopefully, 'life after Eurovision' will form the basis of my next book, and I look forward to writing the chapters very soon.

I started this book with a quote from Olivia. Her brother Leo comes up with some memorable statements too. My daughter Ciara overheard Olivia and Leo talking about life in general one day: they didn't know she was listening at the door. Olivia said, 'You know, Leo, Mum and Dad are much older than us.'

'Yes,' agreed Leo.

'That means, Leo that Mum and Dad will die before us.'

'Yes,' said Leo, pausing before adding, 'And then we can do what we like!'

Out of the mouths of babes!

I hope you enjoyed reading my memories, reflections on the social history of the twentieth century, and my songs. Thank you from Charlie McGettigan, and I am:

FOREVER A ROCK 'N' ROLL KID

For more music and craic from Charlie McGettigan go directly to his website by scanning the QRcode.

Also you will find Charlie in Facebook, YouTube, Twitter and Instagram.